Outdoor Life
COMPLETE TURKEY HUNTING

Lovett Williams photo

Outdoor Life
COMPLETE
TURKEY
HUNTING

by John E. Phillips

Photos by the author unless otherwise credited

OUTDOOR LIFE BOOKS, New York

Distributed to the trade by Stackpole Books, Harrisburg, Pennsylvania

Photo credits for mezzotint reproductions in book part titles:

Pages 33, 123, 249: Dave Kenyon, Michigan Department of Natural Resources
Page 91: Len Rue Jr. (Leonard Rue Enterprises)
Page 185: Irene Vandermolen (Leonard Rue Enterprises)
Pages 213, 293: Leonard Lee Rue III
Page 225: Ken Carlson painting, courtesy National Wild Turkey Federation
Page 273: Lovett Williams, Florida Game and Freshwater Fish Commission

Library of Congress Cataloging-in-Publication Data

Phillips, John E.
    Outdoor Life complete turkey hunting / by John E. Phillips.
    p.   cm.
    Includes index.
    ISBN 1-556-54028-0
    1. Turkey hunting.   I. Outdoor Life Books (Firm)   II. Title.
III. Title: Turkey hunting.
SK325. T8P48 1988
799.2'48619—dc 19   87–26945
                                                                              CIP

Manufactured in the United States of America

*A*lthough life isn't easy, it can be joyous when there's someone to encourage, cheer, push, and pull you along. Writing this book has demanded much of my time as well as that of my wife Denise. As I dedicated the turkey to Denise in the photo below, I now dedicate this book to her for her time, effort, energy, and unwavering encouragement.

Contents

Preface   **10**

Turkey Hunting Terms   **13**

PART 1: GETTING STARTED
North American Turkeys *by John E. Phillips*   **35**

The Master Turkey Hunter *by Harold Knight*   **43**

Developing Your Hunting Skills *with Lovett Williams*   **45**

Basics from a Master Teacher *with Ben Rodgers Lee*   **51**

Mistakes Hunters Make *with Harold Knight and Terry Rohm*   **57**

Where Does Patience Begin and End *by Charles Elliott*   **61**

I Don't Believe in Secrets *with Aaron Pass*   **67**

Teaching a Beginner *with J. Wayne Fears*   **73**

Guns and Ammunition *with J. Wayne Fears*   **77**

How to Dress *by John E. Phillips*   **85**

PART 2: CALLING TURKEYS
Talking Turkey Does Not Equal Taking Turkey *by John E. Phillips*   **93**

Henning and Gobbling *with J. Wayne Fears*   **99**

Mastering Turkey Talk *with Wilbur Primos*   **105**

Gobble Your Way to a Tom *with Walter Parrott*   **113**

Firing Them Up *with Bill Harper*   **117**

Owl-Hooting the High Country *with Ray Eye*   **121**

PART 3: TACTICS AND TECHNIQUES
Hunting the Strut Zones *with Bill Harper*   **125**

Mapping Your Way to Gobblers *with Terry Rohm*   **133**

Finding Gobblers from the Road *with Paul Butski*   **135**

High-Noon Turkeys *with Harold Knight*   **137**

Following Spring Turkeys *with Tom Kelley*   **141**

How to Hunt Jack-Frost Turkeys *by John E. Phillips*   **145**

Hunting Them Hard *by John E. Phillips*   **149**

Double-Circle Technique *with Brent Harrell*   **153**

Cool 'em Down to Kill 'em *with Gary Stilwell*   **157**

How to Outcompete Competition *with Glenn Terry*   **161**

Call-less Turkey Hunting *with David Hale*   **163**

If Too Many Turkeys and Too Many Hunters *with Lewis Stowe*   **167**

Moving in Front of Walking Birds *with Ben Rodgers Lee*   **169**

Napping for Gobblers *with Rob Keck*   **173**

The Big Seed Turkeys *with Jay Brown*   **177**

Playing the Game Fairly *by John E. Phillips*   **180**

PART 4: **SPECIAL SITUATIONS**

Fred Darty: Trophy Hunter *by John E. Phillips*   **187**

Pasture and Field Gobblers *with Seab Hicks*   **191**

Bad-Weather Birds *by John E. Phillips*   **193**

How to Take Swamp Turkeys *with Nathan Connell*   **199**

Hunting the Rio Grande Turkey *with Dave Harbour*   **203**

Hunting the Merriam Turkey *with Jim Zumbo*   **207**

Merriams Could Be the Easiest *with Doug Harbour*   **209**

PART 5: **BOWHUNTING**

Should You Bowhunt Turkeys? *with Charles Farmer*   **215**

Bow Tactics for Turkeys *by Hugh Blackburn*   **219**

Turkey Decoys: The Bowhunter's Best Bet *by Kelly Cooper*   **223**

PART 6: **SHARING THE SPORT**

Staying Friends Even Though It's Turkey Season *with Billy Maccoy*   **227**

The Day Patience Nearly Died *by John E. Phillips*   **231**

Teaming-Up for Turkeys *by John E. Phillips*   **237**

A Boy's First Hunt *with John E. Phillips Jr.*   **241**

The Disabled Can Hunt Turkeys *by John E. Phillips*   **247**

PART 7: **TURKEY TALES**

Uncle Roy Talks Turkey *by John E. Phillips*   **251**

Luck May Intervene When Skill Fails *by John E. Phillips*   **257**

Jim Beam's Unforgettable Gobblers *by John E. Phillips*   **259**

Turkeys in the Rain *by John E. Phillips*   **263**

The Origin of the Mouth Yelper *with Jim Radcliff, Jr.*   **269**

The Greatest Turkey Fighter of Them All *by John E. Phillips*   **271**

PART 8: **AFTER YOU SCORE**

Preparing and Cooking Wild Turkey *with Sylvia Bashline*   **275**

Denise Phillips' Turkey Cookery *by John E. Phillips*   **281**

Turkey Taxidermy *by John E. Phillips*   **285**

PART 9: **TURKEY MANAGEMENT**

How to Have More Turkeys *with Dr. Dan Speake*   **295**

The Flock That Baffled Biologists *by John E. Phillips*   **301**

THE MASTERS: BIOGRAPHICAL DESCRIPTIONS   **307**

INDEX   **314**

Preface _____

Over the years, I have hunted in all weather and terrain with many of the best—and even legendary—turkey hunters. On these hunts and in interviews, the master hunters have shared their unique insights and tactics. But asking a master hunter for his secrets sometimes forces him to make a difficult decision. Should he reveal the secrets that have made him one of the most successful hunters in his region? Reveal secrets to eager challengers? Fortunately, for you and me, these masters were generous.

Although I've carefully recorded all the secrets of the masters and studied every turkey hunting book I could find, I still don't pretend to understand everything about turkey hunting. For no matter how much you learn, you can never know it all. Yet it is my hope that this book covers the fundamentals, fine points, and trade secrets both thoroughly and entertainingly—and increases your enjoyment of the unique madness we call turkey hunting.

The preparation of this book has been an odyssey with pitfalls, misadventures, and discouragements. But the outdoors men and women I've met along the way have been as eager to see this book in print as I have. So as you read, please know that this is the work of many and not just one.

Besides the master hunters featured in each chapter, I must thank first and foremost my wife Denise, who had a baby, underwent two major surgeries, and spent countless hours in the hospital with our youngest son, Hunter, while I was writing. From her hospital bed and my son's hospital room, Denise typed, edited, encouraged, chastised, suggested, and generally pushed this book toward completion.

Another faithful and supportive friend has been my mother-in-law, Marjolyn McLellan. None of the mother-in-law jokes apply to Mrs. Mc-

Lellan. She has worked long and hard—sometimes so tired that she could barely see the keys on the word processor.

Success is often slow in coming to writers who do not find a mentor to help, direct, and sometimes prod them early in their careers. I was lucky to meet a man who taught me about the craft of outdoor writing by grabbing me by the scruff of the neck, dragging me through swamps, throwing me into poison oak, forcing me to write and take pictures when I didn't want to, snatching me up every time I fell down, and doing everything he could to encourage and push me. He was my mentor, as well as my teacher and friend. Thank you, J. Wayne Fears, for being there when I needed you.

I am also grateful to Game and Fish Publications, *Outdoor Life* magazine, *Turkey Call* magazine, Harris Publications, Winchester Press, Aquafield Publications, and *Turkey* magazine for allowing me to reuse my material from their magazines. I especially want to thank magazine editors, who are often taken for granted by the reading public and rarely given the recognition they deserve. Thanks to those editors who have jumped on my case when I needed it, and who have encouraged me when I was ready to quit writing.

I'd also like to thank my editors on this book. Thanks to Parker Bauer who handled the basic copyediting and to Neil Soderstrom, who helped develop the initial proposal and then produced the book for Outdoor Life Books. Neil has demonstrated patience, wisdom, genuine concern, and friendship over the years this book was in the works.

I pray that when of all the contributors to this book reach that big roost tree in the sky they will have good limbs to stand on, shade to protect them, and a gentle breeze to cool them.

John E. Phillips

Even though this hunter is well camouflaged, has positioned himself well, has called well on his box call and has a proper three-inch magnum shotgun, a gobbler still manages to slip behind him.

Turkey _____
Hunting _____
Terms _____

Affliction, or turkey affliction: A disease that temporarily cripples many turkey hunters by making them unable to keep their minds on their work or their families. When the affliction befalls a certain type of hunter, he becomes a turkey-hunting bum the entire turkey season. Once the season is over, the hunter usually regains himself and rarely remembers the effects of the affliction. He'll swear that he'll never catch it again. But, sure enough, the next turkey season, he'll come down with it.

Beard: A hairlike growth that protrudes from a turkey's chest. Both male and female turkeys can have beards, but the beard is the primary sexual characteristic of the male. Beards generally grow at a rate of four to five inches a year, growth beginning when turkeys are about five months old.

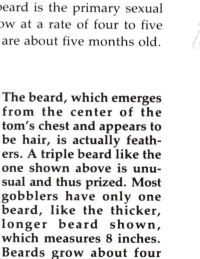

The beard, which emerges from the center of the tom's chest and appears to be hair, is actually feathers. A triple beard like the one shown above is unusual and thus prized. Most gobblers have only one beard, like the thicker, longer beard shown, which measures 8 inches. Beards grow about four inches each year.

As shown at right, the feathers called greater upper secondary coverts are more prominent in adults than in juveniles. (From *Wildlife Techniques Manual* with permission of the Wildlife Society)

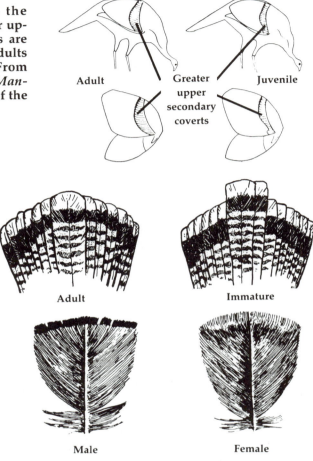

At left are comparsions of primary feathers (making up wing tips) of immature and adult Eastern wild turkeys. Note that the tip of the adult primary is broadly rounded and barred, with white almost to the extreme tip. The primary of the immature bird is pointed and plain gray and lacks definite barring. *Top row* compares the uniformly rounded spread of the adult and the irregular spread of the immature bird. *Above,* the breast feather of the male is flattened and black-tipped, but the female's is rounded and buff-tipped. (Drawings and captions from *Wildlife Techniques Manual*, permission of Wildlife Society)

Box caller: A thin-walled wooden box with a wooden paddle lid attached to one end. With this box—really a musical instrument—nearly all turkey calls can be imitated. To create the friction-based sounds, the lid and two sides of the box are usually chalked.

Lynch's World Champion box call.

Cackling: An excited call given by the hen turkey and made up of a series of fast yelps.

Calling: Sounds made by the hunter to lure a gobbler into gun range. Calling is not limited to the use of hen or gobbler voice imitations. To mimic other sounds made by turkeys, many hunters scratch in the leaves, beat a turkey wing against tree limbs and bushes, or slap the sides of their legs with their gloved hands. **Sweet calling:** Any turkey voice imitation performed with a smooth, clear, crisp tone. A sweet call may be compared to a love ballad. **Raspy calling:** Any turkey voice imitation performed with a coarse tone. Think of a raspy call as one made by a hen with a sore throat or the beginnings of laryngitis. To understand the difference between a sweet call and a raspy call, imagine the same love ballad being sung by Barbra Streisand (sweet) and Willie Nelson (raspy). Just as some people prefer Streisand while others like Nelson better, so there are some turkeys that will come to sweet calling and others that will be pulled in by raspy calling. And some turkeys will come to both types of calling. Others, however, will not come to any kind of calling at all.

Call-less hunting: Attempting to bag a turkey without calling to him. To be a productive call-less hunter, you must know where and when you can meet a tom in the woods during his daily routine. This type of hunting requires much more knowledge of the turkeys, their movement patterns, and their likes and dislikes than does hunting with a call.

Call-shy: A term describing a turkey that won't come to conventional calling. Often, this bird has been called to by hunters and perhaps shot at and spooked. A call-shy gobbler may not come to a hen but will gobble and wait for her to come to him, as she's naturally supposed to. If he gobbles and she doesn't come, some hunters think he'll walk off because he assumes the calling is coming from a hunter.

Cedar box with striker: A cedar box caller, similar to the box and paddle box caller which most hunters are familiar with. However, instead of a paddle for the lid of the box caller, the hunter has some type of striker that he holds in his hand and freely passes across the lid to produce the calls of a wild gobbler.

Cedar box with striker.

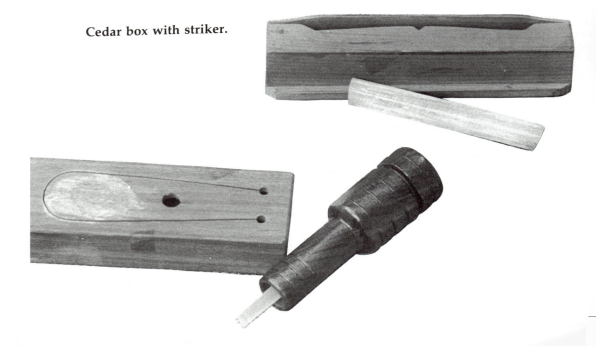

Chufa: A grass that has nutlike roots that turkeys like to eat.

Chufa is sometimes called nutgrass. (Photo by Neil Soderstrom)

Cluck: A hen turkey's sound that's much like a woman talking to herself. **Contented cluck:** The sound a hen turkey makes while walking through the woods when everything is great in the world: there's plenty to eat, the sun is shining, and she's anticipating a good day. **Excited cluck:** A hen turkey's sound that can mean "I think there's something over there we'd better look at. I'm not sure what it is, but I know we'd better check. Hang on, honey, I'm on the way."

Controlled burning: The act of setting fire to the woods to burn away the litter on the ground. The fire releases nutrients into the soil and causes a new growth of young plants without damaging or destroying the timber. Controlled burning is a key management tool.

Crow call: The sounds that crows make when they notify one another of their positions. The crow call is used by turkey hunters to cause a tom to gobble instinctively. Many times when a turkey hears a high-pitched noise like a crow call, he reacts as you do when someone jumps out of a dark closet and shouts, ''Boo!'' You may scream, because that's the first vocalization that you give to the emotion you feel when you're frightened unexpectedly.

Cutting: Very fast, loud stutter yelps and clucks much like the beginning of a cackle, but not going all the way through a cackle. Cutting often means ''If you're looking for a date, I'm the lady who can satisfy.''

Decoy: An artificial reproduction of a hen turkey. Many hunters use a mounted hen or a plastic replica as a decoy. Some tough gobblers will come in to a hunter only if they see as well as hear what they perceive to be a sweetheart.

Diaphragm caller: A caller made of tape, lead, and latex rubber that is inserted into the roof of the hunter's mouth. When air passes over the rubber diaphragm, the hunter can make many of the calls of the hen turkey and the gobbler.

Ben Lee places a diaphragm call in the roof of his mouth. Lee then blows the air over his tongue and the latex part of the call. As the sound is emitted, Lee will then use his lips and his cupped hand to muffle the sound, imitating a hen turkey. *Below middle:* **The Triple Reed Mouth Caller is a diaphragm call made of three overlapping pieces of latex rubber in the center. The Triple Reed requires more forced air than a single reed to make the latex vibrate. Usually the Triple Reed emits a much more raspy sound than a single or double reed.** *Below right:* **The Triple Reed Split Mouth Call has a split piece of latex rubber that causes a very raspy sound.**

The decoy at right helped bring this gobbler in. (Michigan Department of Natural Resources photo)

Displaying: The strutting of a gobbler.

Displaying—the strutting of a gobbler. When the male turkey wants to impress the female, he spreads his tail feathers, drops his wing feathers, and forces all of his body feathers up and out. When a gobbler displays, he acts much like a muscle man showing off at the beach.

Dominant gobbler: The gobbler whose strength, size, age, and intelligence put him at the top of the pecking order in a flock. Sometimes called a boss gobbler. Many times a dominant gobbler will keep subdominant toms from gobbling. He claims the right to breed the hens because of his superiority.

Dominant hen: The female boss of a flock. Often the dominant hen determines which way a flock will travel, and she's generally the one that calls a scattered flock back together.

Double calling: Calling done by two hunters at the same time, to imitate a number of turkeys in the same area.

Droppings: Turkey excretion in a stool form. A **gobbler dropping** has

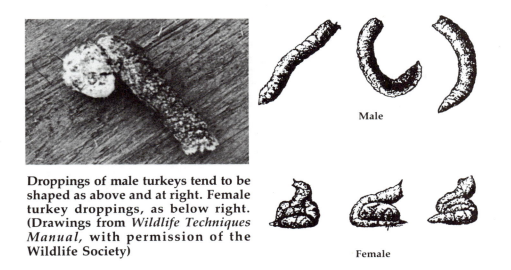

Droppings of male turkeys tend to be shaped as above and at right. Female turkey droppings, as below right. (Drawings from *Wildlife Techniques Manual,* **with permission of the Wildlife Society)**

Male

Female

the shape of a fishhook or question mark. A **hen dropping** stool is round and resembles a small cow dropping.

Drumming:
The sound a tom turkey makes when he struts. This sounds much like the shifting of gears of an 18-wheel tractor-trailer truck—*Vutt-V-roooom.*

Earl:
A term for a turkey gobbler that denotes his majesty.

Fly-up/fly-down cackle:
An excited call that the hen turkey makes when she jumps off a limb in the morning and flies down to the ground to greet a new day, or when she jumps off the ground to fly into a tree to welcome a night's rest. The cackle usually begins with a series of excited clucks, followed by a series of fast yelps.

Free-ranging dogs:
Wild dogs with no permanent home, or dogs allowed to run free by their owners. Free-ranging dogs often prey on turkeys.

Friction call: Any type of call consisting of two objects rubbed together to produce the sounds that turkeys make. A slate and peg, a box call, or a Twin Hen (a call made of aluminum and wood with a peg striker) are all examples of friction callers.

These friction calls are about 4 inches in diameter and can be operated by rubbing them with the pegs shown. The friction caller, near right, employs a Plexiglas striking surface encased in a hollow plastic shell. The call on the far right has a slate striking surface with a plastic shell under the slate.

The Twin Hen friction call has a slate striking peg held by corncob handle. The peg is then drawn down the aluminum strip in the plate. With this device, a skilled caller can closely imitate all calls made by a hen turkey.

Gobble: The sound made by a tom that gives away his location, calls hens to mate, and notifies other turkeys that he's in the area.

Gobbler: A male turkey.

Hawk call: The sound that a hawk makes as it flies overhead. This is the same call that turkey hunters use to cause turkeys to shock-gobble.

Hen: A female turkey.

Hung-up: Said of a turkey that stops just out of gun range and refuses to come closer to the hunter.

Infection, or turkey infection: A disease similar to turkey affliction. A turkey infection starts gradually when the hunter first goes to a calling contest, picks up a mouth yelper, or begins to play with a diaphragm caller. Then he begins to listen to veteran turkey hunters talk about their experiences, and will usually accompany a hunter on a turkey hunt. Once he hears that first wild turkey gobble, the vector starts to incubate and infection spreads. Then, when seeing his first wild turkey gobble and strut in front of him—just out of killing distance—the hunter feels the hair on his neck stand up, his face becomes flushed, his breathing becomes heavy, and his whole body begins to tremble with uncontrollable muscle spasms. He knows he's infected with turkey fever—both body and mind. One of the surest symptoms of turkey infection is a hunter's uncontrollable babbling about turkeys, turkey hunting, and turkey calling.

Intergrade: A turkey produced by the interbreeding of two different turkey subspecies. Intergrades of the eastern turkey and the Florida turkey are common in a narrow zone across the South.

Jake: A one-year-old gobbler.

Kee-kee run: A young gobbler's squeal and call. This is the call most often given by young gobblers before they learn how to gobble and the call that turkey hunters imitate mostly in the fall, though sometimes in the spring. In the fall the jakes (one-year-old gobblers) haven't matured enough to be able to gobble. So their sound resembles, "*Peep, peep, peep, yelp, yelp, yelp,*" which is the kee-kee run. The jakes are usually what is hunted in the fall, because they are the easiest to call and bag. Older gobblers rarely come to calling in the fall, since spring was mating time. Besides, longbeards do not like to be around the juvenile birds, which prefer to flock with the hens in fall. Often jakes come to this kee-kee run thinking there's another young gobbler instead of a hunter in the area. In the spring, the kee-kee run is used mainly to fool an old gobbler into thinking that a young jake is attempting to mate with one of his harem.

Longbeard: A dominant or boss gobbler, usually more than two years old.

Lost call: A call given by hunters to pull a turkey flock together or to locate a gobbler. Another name for the lost call is the assembly call.

Mouth yelper: A diaphragm caller.

Noble whistle: Brand name of an English whistle used by policemen, basketball referees, and dog trainers. After removing the ball from this whistle, many hunters have found the whistle useful for making the kee-kee run sound.

Owl hooter: A caller that reproduces the voice of the barred owl. The owl hooter is used to locate turkeys, which will shock-gobble in response.

By blowing in the round hole of the owl hooter (far right), a hunter can imitate the sound of the barred owl. This causes turkeys to shock gobble. The cadence of the blowing should follow like, "Who cooks? Who cooks? Who cooks for you all?"

Owling: Hunter calls that imitate the sound of an owl.

Pattern board: A sheet of plywood or metal that catches the shot from a discharged shotgun shell. On the pattern board, the hunter can see the density and size of the pattern of shot expended from his shell. Shooting at a pattern board tells him how effective his shotgun will be at various ranges with different loads.

Mounting an image of a turkey's head on a pattern board for test shooting.

Pecking order: The social hierarchy of the turkey flock; the order of dominance of the individual turkeys within a flock.

Peg: A wooden stick or a round piece of plastic that is stroked across a slate box, a piece of slate, or an aluminum-covered box to imitate the sound of a turkey. The peg is a part of a friction call.

Poult: A baby turkey.

Young turkey poults like this nine-day-old bird are susceptible to predators. Therefore knee-high grass is important for brood range because the poults can hide in the grass, while the hen watches for predators. (Leonard Lee Rue III photo)

Predator: An animal that feeds on other animals. Some of the predators of turkeys include wild dogs, bobcats, foxes, raccoons, eagles, coyotes, wolves, crows, skunks, and snakes.

Purr: A contented sound made by a hen, much like a woman's humming.

Push-button call: A simple friction call that requires the hunter only to push a peg with his finger to produce hen calls.

Push-button call is a simple friction call. You simply push the peg with your finger to produce hen calls. This is the easiest call for beginners to use.

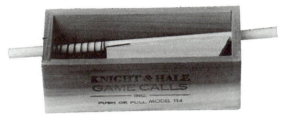

Putt: An alarm sound given by a turkey.

Roost: A particular tree where a turkey perches during the night for sleeping.

Unless disturbed, turkeys will usually roost in the same tree for several weeks. Even in strong winds the turkeys will sleep in a roost tree. (Marilyn Maring/Leonard Lee Rue photo)

Scouting: Taking inventory of the area you plan to hunt. Looking for turkey sign, listening for turkey sounds, and becoming aware of the terrain and habitat can help in determining a hunt plan.

Set-up: An area where you determine a turkey should come, and where you'll take a stand to call and wait. A good set-up will generally be in clean woods with no natural barriers that the turkey would have to cross to get to you.

Shock gobble: The instinctive reaction of a turkey in response to some type of loud sound. A tom may shock-gobble when he hears a car door slamming, a train whistle, a clap of thunder, a crow call, or any other loud, high-pitched noise.

Slate call: A caller consisting of a peg and a piece of slate. The peg is stroked across the slate to produce the sound of the turkey. The slate is sometimes enclosed in plastic, wood, or any substance like a turtle shell.

Snood or snoot: A bump on the forehead of a turkey that changes size according to how excited the turkey is.

Snood or snoot: See accompanying definition. (Dave Kenyon, Michigan Dept. of Natural Resources, photo)

Snuff box: A caller made from a snuff can. The bottom and half of the top are cut away, and latex rubber is stretched over part of the open half of the top. To operate the snuff box caller, the hunter rests his bottom lip against the rubber and blows air across it. The sound made from the air rushing across the rubber is amplified within the snuff can. The snuff box was the forerunner of what is commonly known today as the tube caller.

This snuff can caller is about 3 inches long and an inch in diameter.

Spur: A horny growth on a male turkey's leg, which sometimes also occurs on a hen's leg. At two years of age, most gobblers have one one-inch spur on each leg. However, some gobblers have no spurs, and some have multiple spurs.

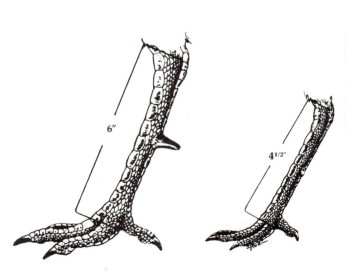

The length of the spur usually denotes the age of a gobbler. The longer the spur, the more prized the trophy. (Drawings from *Wildlife Techniques Manual*, with permission of the Wildlife Society)

Striker box: Either a slate-covered or an aluminum-covered wooden box used by rubbing a wooden peg across it to imitate the call of a wild turkey. This type of caller is also known as a friction call.

Strutting: The action seen when a turkey coils his neck, causes his feathers to stand up, spreads his tail, and drops his wings to impress a hen. A strutting turkey is much like a man on the beach who flexes all his muscles to draw attention to himself and impress any ladies who may see him.

Strut zone, displaying gobbler, and hen. (Leonard Lee Rue III photo)

Strut zone: An area where a turkey goes on a regular basis to strut and meet a hen for breeding.

Subdominant gobblers and hens: Turkeys subservient to the dominant birds in a flock. A subdominant turkey may become dominant if the dominant turkey is removed from the flock.

Tight pattern: A shot pattern in which the pellets are close together at the point on the target where the hunter is aiming. A tight pattern is much more effective for turkey hunting than a loose pattern.

Traveling turkey: A gobbler that will answer a call but moves farther away from the call each time he hears it.

Treading note: A call known today as a cackle. (This term is used in my chapter on Uncle Roy Moorer, a grand elder who hunted into his nineties.)

Tree call or tree yelp: A very soft series of yelps given by a hen before she flies down from her roost. The tree yelp may be best described as a quiet yawn.

Trophy scoring: Based on a system devised by outdoor writer Dave Harbour to establish records on the most outstanding turkeys taken throughout the United States. With divisions for each of the wild turkey species, the World Gobbler Records are now kept by the National Wild Turkey Federation in Edgefield, South Carolina. Trophy scoring for each species also has several subsections including the following:

1. Best Overall Typical (not more than one beard or two spurs) Gobbler with a score based on the tom's beard and spur lengths and weight. To figure the best overall score, use the sum of the weight score and the length of the beard multiplied by 2 and the length of the spur multiplied by 10.

2. Best Overall Non-Typical (more than two spurs or multiple beards) Gobblers

3. Gobblers with Longest Typical Beards

4. Gobblers with Best Non-Typical Beards

5. Gobblers with Longest Typical Spurs

6. Gobblers with Best Non-Typical Spurs

7. Heaviest Gobbler (Typical and Non-Typical)

Tube caller: A caller made of plastic and resembling a miniature megaphone. The tube caller has a piece of latex rubber over its end that the hunter blows against to make the sounds of the turkey. The tube caller is the modern descendant of the snuff-box caller.

Tube caller: Ben Lee, a master turkey hunter, uses many different calls. With the tube call, Lee has the capabilities he would have with a loud box call as well as the soft tones of a diaphragm call.

Turkey dog: Any dog used in hunting turkeys. Turkey dogs are illegal in most states today, and are almost extinct. In the old days, a turkey dog was used to trail and flush turkeys in the fall. The dog would return to the hunter and sit by his side until he called the turkey in. When the turkey was shot, the dog would run, grab him, and hold on until the hunter came.

Turkey management: The manipulation of habitat, predators, turkeys, and hunters to produce the optimum number of turkeys on a given piece of land.

Turkey sign: Anything left on the ground that indicates that a turkey is in the area. Sign includes droppings, feathers, scratches, dusting areas, and tracks.

Wattles: The fatty tissue around a turkey's neck.

Wattles are made up of fatty, lumpy tissue around a gobbler's neck. Wattles are generally most prominent where the neck skin joins the breast feathers. They swell, recede, and change colors in response to a gobbler's mood. (Leonard Lee Rue III photo)

Wing-bone caller: A caller made from a turkey's wing bone. The hunter sucks air through the bone to make the sound of a wild turkey. There are also artificial wing-bone callers that resemble pipes.

Handmade from a turkey's wing bone, this call emits sound when you suck air through the bone. Wingbone callers are 6 to 7 inches in length and about ¼-inch in diameter.

Yelp: A call that varies in rhythm from turkey to turkey. **Contented yelp:** A call a hen gives when she's walking through the woods with nothing in particular on her mind. **Excited yelp:** A call a hen gives when she's either frightened, looking forward to meeting her gobbler, or excited for some other reason. **Prospecting yelp:** A call that says, "I'm over here. Is there anyone out there to talk to?"

Part 1

GETTING
STARTED

The Eastern wild turkey *(Meleagris gallopavo silvestris)* is the largest of the North American wild turkeys. Biologists predict that these Eastern gobblers will eventually evolve to 30 pounds. (Len Rue Jr., Leonard Rue Enterprises, photo)

North American Turkeys

by John E. Phillips

*I*t is said that when Noah made his voyage in Biblical times, two of the birds on board were wild turkeys. After the big rain, Noah sent one of his sons down to the lower level of the ark to bring up the tom turkey, a fine bearded fellow. They threw the tom out into the air, and he flew away. After about an hour, he returned to the ark and flopped over, exhausted.

Seeing this with his son, Noah asked, "Son, now what does that mean?"

"Well, Dad, there must be no land out there for that turkey to light on."

They watched the turkey carefully as he recovered his strength. Then they carried him down into the hold. A couple of weeks went by, and Noah called his son again.

"Go fetch me that tom turkey," he instructed.

Straightaway the son brought the gobbler up.

"Now fling him over the side again," Noah ordered.

Noah's son chucked the bird over the water again and watched as he flew away. After an hour, there was no sight of the turkey. After two hours and finally three hours, Noah looked at his son and asked, "What does the bird's not coming back to the ark mean, Son?"

Scratching his head, the son pondered the question for some time and then smiled as he replied, "Well, Father Noah, we must be over the U.S., and today must be the first day of turkey season."

Although some may question whether turkey hunting had become popular enough to merit official seasons during Noah's time, outdoorsmen have been hunting the turkey, *Meleagris gallopavo*, the largest and most intelligent upland gamebird in North America, for quite a spell.

NAME AND SUBSPECIES

It's not certain how turkeys received their common name. Some people think the Indian name for the bird, which was "furkee" or "firkee," may have been changed in pronunciation to "turkey." Others point to the turkey's scientific names, *Meleagris*, which means guineafowl, and *gallopavo*, which is derived from "gallus" (cock) and "pavo" (peafowl), to back a theory that the turkey was confused with the guineafowl *(Nunida meleagris)* at one time. The guineafowl was thought to have originated in Turkey, so the turkey came to be called a turkey.

Fossil evidence shows that turkeys were present in the western hemisphere thousands of years before Columbus arrived. And the highly civilized Aztec Indians of Mexico farmed and raised turkeys, as did the Indians of Virginia and North Carolina, although not to the extent of the Aztecs.

Authorities believe that Cortez probably took the Mexican turkey *(Meleagris gallopavo gallopavo)* back to Spain after he explored Mexico. This Mexican subspecies was domesticated and spread across Europe, and was most likely the turkey the early colonists brought to our shores.

Today, there are six living subspecies of the North American wild turkey. They differ mainly in coloration.

The Eastern wild turkey *(Meleagris gallopavo silvestris)* is one of the largest turkeys, and biologists predict that eventually these birds will evolve to reach about 30 pounds. Their original range extended from Florida to southern Maine and Ontario, and from Texas to South Dakota. Today the Eastern wild turkey has been stocked successfully across much of the U.S.

The Merriam turkey *(Meleagris gallopavo merriami)* has whitish tail tips like other western turkeys and is distinguished by a white patch on its backend. (Colorado Div. of Wildlife photo)

Left: The Rio Grande turkey (*Meleagris gallopavo intermedia*) is a large turkey that sports white tail tips and is light-colored near the white tips. *Right:* The Florida turkey (*Meleagris gallopavo osceola*). (Left photo by Jim Zumbo; right by Au Coin Associates)

The Merriam turkey (*Meleagris gallopavo merriami*), which has whitish tail tips like other western turkeys, is distinguished by a white patch on the rump. The original range was mainly in Colorado, New Mexico, and eastern Arizona. Today, the biggest Merriams come mostly from California, Washington, Colorado, Minnesota, New Mexico, Nebraska, and Wyoming.

The Rio Grande turkey (*Meleagris gallopavo intermedia*) sports white tail tips and a light-colored upper tail. It was found originally in Texas and northeastern Mexico, and in parts of Oklahoma and Kansas. Today, most trophy Rio Grande turkeys are bagged in Texas, Oklahoma, and California. Darker than the eastern turkey, the Florida turkey (*Meleagris gallopavo osceola*) has always occurred only in Florida. However, crossbreeds between the Florida and eastern turkeys exist along a line from southern Louisiana to the extreme southeastern part of South Carolina. These crossbreeds are intermediate in coloration.

The Mexican turkey, mentioned earlier, is found only in Mexico and is the ancestor of the domestic turkey. This wild turkey originally occurred in the central part of Mexico.

The Gould turkey (*Meleagris gallopavo mexicana*) is another subspecies found only in Mexico. It grows very large. In the 1500s, the Gould turkey was found mainly in northwestern Mexico, including the Baja peninsula.

HISTORICAL RECORD

The population of the North American wild turkey in pre-Columbian days has been estimated at over 10 million. The native peoples utilized the wild turkey in many ways. Although we think of Indians feasting on turkeys, many tribes did not like to eat them, including the Apaches in the Southwest. And some of the eastern Indians preferred fish to turkey.

But parts of the turkey were used in many ways—particularly the wing feathers for fletching arrows, and the spurs as arrow points. Cherokee children played games by making disguises from turkey skins. And according to Captain John Smith, some Indian tribes made ceremonial capes from the turkey's vibrantly colored feathers.

Of course the first American settlers ate many turkeys and often wrote about the abundance of turkeys. According to early observations by colonists, there were sometimes as many as 5,000 turkeys in a single flock. Thomas Morton wrote that the Pilgrims learned to keep a "gunne . . . in redinesse, [which] salutes them with such a courtesie, as makes them take a turne in the cooke roome."

The colonists utilized the turkey's fat for cooking, the wings for fans, the meat and eggs for food, and the entrails for catfish bait. So, of necessity, these settlers employed deadly tactics for taking turkeys, including shooting them from stands and over bait, double-circling them, flushing and running them with dogs and horses, shooting them on their roosts, and trapping them in trenches by baiting. Ben Franklin considered the wild turkey of such importance to the colonists that he proposed designating it the national bird.

In later frontier times, hunters killed dozens of turkeys in a day to sell as food. John James Audubon noted in his writings that outdoorsmen hunted the wild turkey by imitating the hoot of the barred owl and the *whoo-whoo-oohoo* of the horned owl, which turkeys will answer.

In the early 1800s, however, wild turkeys began disappearing from the East, and by the late 1800s they were nearly gone from the Midwest. By 1920, 18 of the original home-range states had no wild turkeys. This resulted in part because most of the virgin forests had been cut for timber. And wild turkeys prefer mature or nearly mature forest without undergrowth, which makes them feel too vulnerable to their enemies. Yet the loss of forests was not the major problem for the turkey population. Many biologists think that the turkey was simply overhunted.

Although some private hunting clubs and state game departments made attempts to help turkey populations, they almost always failed. Their pen-raised turkeys were unable to survive in the wild—even when they had been raised from wild eggs.

Then, in the early 1940s, trap-and-transfer tactics were applied to aid the growth of the wild turkey population. State game departments captured wild turkeys with cannon nets and relocated them in suitable habitat where there were no turkeys.

**Key to
Wild Turkey Map**

Eastern

Florida

Rio Grande

Merriam

Gould

This shows the original range of the five wild turkey subspecies.

**Key to
Wild Turkey Map**

Eastern

Florida

Rio Grande

Merriam

Gould

Hybrid

Here is the present range of the five wild turkey subspecies and hybrids.

At first, restoring wild turkeys was mainly an eastern concern, but in the 1950s and '60s western states began making efforts to help the Rio Grande and Merriam turkeys. By 1975, only 12 states had no open season on wild turkeys. In 1986, with the national turkey population estimated at 2 million, only three states—Nevada, Delaware, and Alaska—had no open season. And some states, such as Alabama, Missouri, North Dakota, Wyoming, Arizona, and New Mexico, had almost all of their suitable range occupied by turkeys.

HUNTING SEASONS

Generally, turkeys are hunted in two seasons each year—fall and spring. Many states have only a spring season, while some states have both spring and fall seasons. And the tactics and reasons for hunting turkeys during these two times of the year are vastly different.

The most traditional turkey hunting occurs during the spring gobbling season, which is the time of the year when the male bird is most vulnerable. Driven by the urge to breed, he gobbles to let the hens know where he is. In so doing, he reveals his location to the hunter.

In nature, the hen goes to the gobbler to be bred. But turkey hunters try to reverse nature by bringing the gobblers to them. The best technique for spring hunting is to wait where a tom wants to travel anyway. Then by making hen calls, the hunter notifies the gobbler of the supposed hen's position.

The gobbler thinks, "Well, since I'm moving in that direction, I may as well stop off to meet this hen. Then I'll go about my business." In springtime, this decision often proves fatal for the gobbler.

Spring hunters are relying on the turkey's natural urge to breed and his machismo. But fall hunters need other techniques.

During the fall, an older gobbler doesn't have sex on his mind. For the most part, he doesn't even like girls and stays away from the flocks of hens and juvenile birds. This is the reason that very few longbeard gobblers are taken in fall by calling. The senior bronze barons harvested in the fall are often taken by other means.

However the fall is a good time to bag young gobblers, commonly called *jakes*. In fall, hens and juvenile birds have a need to flock together for company and protection. The juvenile birds learn from hens how to exist and escape from danger.

And any time a flock of turkeys is scattered, the young birds will try to regroup with the dominant hen as soon as possible, which is why using calls like the assembly call (usually given by the dominant hen) is the most effective in the fall for jakes. When a jake comes in to the hunter, he will be looking for the old hen that has status as mother and teacher.

Flocks of older gobblers may travel together in the fall. After scattering a flock of senior toms, it is often very difficult to call these older birds into gun range. It is not nearly as productive a tactic as calling a jake back, as if to its mixed flock of hens and jakes.

There are three reasons that some states have spring and/or fall turkey seasons. These are (1) tradition, (2) the ability of that state's department of conservation to educate hunters, and (3) the size of the turkey flock within that state. In some states, turkeys have been hunted only in the spring. In those states, hunters may believe that fall hunting is a mortal sin. In other parts of the country, where fall turkey hunting has been practiced for many years, hunters associate the color change in tree leaves with turkey hunting.

States that have an abundance of turkeys can often have both a spring and fall season, without reducing the numbers of turkeys available each year. By the same reasoning, states that have a large number of turkeys often have an either-sex turkey season so that the surplus hen turkeys can be called and turkey population can be better controlled.

ESSENTIALS

Today hunters know many intriguing facts about turkeys:
- They eat fruit, nuts, weeds, grasses, cultivated grains, and insects, but they favor acorns.
- When frightened, turkeys take a couple of fast running steps, hop several times, and then fly, to get out of gunshot range quickly.
- They can fly up to 55 miles per hour for short distances but tire easily.
- They must have water on their range.
- The greatest predators of the wild turkey are the horned owl, golden eagle, bald eagle, fox, bobcat, coyote, wolf, dog, raccoon, crow, skunk, and snake.
- Turkeys cover two to four miles in an average day but may cover 15 to 18 miles.
- Gobblers three years of age may have beards 8 or more inches long, but beards are not reliable indicators of age since they can wear down and some turkeys may have four or five successive beards.

HEAD COLORS

One of the perennial controversies between hunters and taxidermists is over the color of a turkey's head. When the bird is mounted, the head must be painted to restore color. So it's important that hunter and taxidermist agree on color before mounting.

Many hunters believe that a turkey's head is ivory with violet coloration around the eyes and along the back and the sides of the neck—and that the throat and wattles are always red. Other hunters believe that a tom's head is red and that there may or may not be a shade of white or ivory on top of the head but certainly no violet or blue at all. Still other hunters will swear that a turkey's head is blue with no white whatsoever and that the wattles are either red or white. And some hunters will make a case for a tri-colored head of red, white, and blue.

One hunter who came into my taxidermy shop continually aggravated me by advising me, "John, you still haven't learned how to paint a turkey's head correctly." I simmered.

Finally one day, this self-proclaimed head-color expert and I pitted our skills against a *Meleagris gallopavo* in a patch of woods east of my home. Sitting side by side against a large water oak, we flipped a coin to see who would call and who would shoot. Since my friend had won, he would call and I would shoot.

When a turkey first appeared, I whispered, "What color is that turkey's head?"

"White, just like I told you," my friend answered.

As my hunting companion gave some cutting calls, we watched the turkey's head turn traffic light red.

"Psst," I whispered. "What color is the turkey's head now?"

"Okay, it's red," he admitted.

And as the turkey cooled off and started to walk in even closer to us, his head colors again changed—white crown, red and white head with violet mottling around the eyes, and pink—not red—wattles.

I then squeezed the trigger, and the gobbler tumbled. We both raced toward it.

"Watch," I told my friend.

As we watched, the turkey's head made three color changes before finally turning deep blue. It remained blue until we got home.

Thus, a turkey's head is much like a chameleon's body. It can be different colors, owing to blood flow or lack of it near the surface. The head can be almost any color from purple, blue, white, and/or red, depending on the gobbler's mood and possibly the time of year and the location.

So now when a hunter brings me a turkey to mount and says, "Be certain you paint the head right," I make sure he explains what his idea of "right" is.

The Master
Turkey Hunter

by Harold Knight

What does it take to be a master turkey hunter? Harold Knight of Cadiz, Kentucky, has taken a world-record turkey and won many calling contests around the country. Here's what he says about mastery:

1. A master can kill a turkey without calling to him. One of the best examples I know is David Hale from my hometown of Cadiz. David has been hunting turkeys since the early 1970s. The first six years he hunted, he didn't have a caller—but he still killed turkeys.

David told me that not having a caller was the best thing that ever happened to him, because he had to get to know the turkeys well before he tried to take them. He had to learn where they were going, and what they were going to do when they got there. Once he knew that, he knew where he needed to be to kill them.

Then, after David got a call, he was a much more effective hunter. A hunter who's willing to learn the ways of the wild turkey and how to kill him without calling is well on the way to becoming a master.

2. A master can hunt and kill a turkey at any time of day. Almost any hunter can take turkeys when they fly down off the roost. And many hunters can bag them just before they fly back up. But the hunter who can locate and take them all through the day has to understand turkeys and their habits. This hunter must be a master outdoorsman.

3. A master can hunt turkeys no matter what weather conditions he faces. Weather affects turkeys a great deal. But a master will know what they do in snow, rain, wind, and hail. He'll know how and where they hole up. Then, when they move, he'll know where they're going.

When a master wakes up and looks out the window, no matter what the weather is, he knows what he must do to kill a turkey that day. And he's thinking, *Today is a good day to chase a gobbler*. The truth is, you can't take a gobbler if you don't go hunting.

4. A master can hunt effectively when the woods are full of people. I know plenty of good turkey hunters who haven't learned to adapt to hunt-

Harold Knight, who bagged the world-record eastern turkey shown on page 138, takes gobblers with call or without because he has studied turkeys, their behaviors, and their preferred habitats.

ing pressure. If they're hunting a good gobbler and someone walks in and flushes him, they'll quit and go home—but not the master. He'll go and look for another bird, or continue to hunt that spooked turkey knowing that getting him into range is going to be more difficult. The hunt may have been changed by the pressure, but it hasn't been ruined.

5. The master is the hunter that other hunters call when a gobbler has whipped them. Often an old gobbler will get so smart that he's not any fun for the average hunter to go after. That turkey may be so smart that he's embarrassing hunters, and he may have a reputation of being impossible to kill.

This is when the master is called. He's much like the hired guns of the Old West. He's brought in to bring back peace and do away with the bad guy. In this case, the bad guy is a super-smart turkey. The master picks up his gun and accepts the challenge, putting his reputation on the line. Win or lose, he takes pride in pitting his woods wisdom against the best woods wizards. Whether he actually takes the turkey or not, he learns something from each tough tom he hunts.

6. Last, the master turkey hunter shares his sport with others. After all, how many turkeys do you have to kill to prove to yourself and others that you're a master? A true master will take more pleasure from developing other good turkey hunters than from collecting boxes and drawers full of beards and spurs.

Developing Your Hunting Skills

with Lovett Williams

*M*ost people who try to become master turkey hunters go about it all wrong. They learn techniques for dealing with gobblers that hang up. They look for ways of calling an old gobbler away from his hens. They try any new method they hear about from anybody who has ever hunted turkeys, and they rely heavily on luck. But these approaches are the worst ones to take.

Turkey hunting is unlike any other hunting. You can't rely on decoys to lure in a turkey. You can't depend on a dog's nose to find him, or on another hunter to drive him to you. To become a master turkey hunter, you must have confidence in your own skill. Turkey hunting is a discipline that requires lots of practice.

KNOWING TURKEYS

The most important thing to know about is the turkey itself. Without knowing the game you hunt, the hunting becomes far more difficult and luck is the only card you can hope to win with.

Read books and magazines on turkey hunting, listen to lectures, and go to turkey-hunting seminars and calling contests. Learn the places where turkeys like to roost, the movement patterns they most often follow and the times of day when they engage in various activities. For instance, find out what time turkeys fly up in the afternoon, what time they fly down in the morning, where they like to go when they fly down, where they spend the midday hours, and where they prefer to be just before they come back to the roost. Learn to identify the sounds they make and what the different sounds mean. You will discover, for instance, that the turkey hen yelps so other turkeys can locate her. The yelp has an acoustical quality that allows it to travel great distances.

One important thing you'll learn from books, seminars, and so on is

When a gobbler struts, you can hear his wings dragging, flexing, and snapping back. The sound resembles the simultaneous crushing of cellophane and the thumping of a pencil.

that no matter how much you know, there's still much more to learn. However, a basic knowledge of turkeys will help you start taking them, and help you understand what you're doing right. When you know why turkeys do what they do, you'll develop a great deal of confidence in your hunting ability.

Another way to learn about turkeys is to find yourself a mentor. By that I mean locate a successful, experienced turkey hunter who will take you under his wing. Such a person can greatly increase your knowledge and awareness of turkeys.

The next source of knowledge is the turkeys themselves. Spend time in the woods listening to turkeys and looking at them. A master turkey hunter will observe turkeys before, during, and after the turkey season. You should try to correlate what you've read and what you've heard from other hunters with what you see in the woods. When you see a turkey strut, drum, or fly up to roost, you should be able to say to yourself, I know why that turkey is doing that—I read about this habit or heard someone mention it.

Beware of misinformation about the turkey's ability to think and reason. A turkey is a bundle of instincts, innate reactions, habits, and nerves. He doesn't have a big brain and isn't able to figure anything out as a human would. If you hunt turkeys believing they can reason like a human, you'll never be able to understand them. If you watch turkeys, you'll soon learn they're as predictable as programmed robots. From your observations and reading, you'll learn not to believe the turkey is smarter than he actually is.

To gain knowledge about the turkey, you'll have to rely much more on your ears than you do with most other game. I'm convinced most hunters don't know how to listen for turkeys. I would rank the hunter's ability to hear the turkey much higher than his ability to see it.

You should be able not only to hear a turkey gobble, but also to hear him drag his wings when he's strutting. You should understand what a putt is. You should be able to hear a turkey walking. You should know all the sounds the hens make and what they mean. You should be able to judge your distance from a turkey by sound alone.

What you hear in the woods should be combined with what you observe, what you read, and what you hear from other hunters. With all this information, you can get to know the turkey very well.

LEARNING TO READ SIGN

After you've learned what a turkey likes to do and where he likes to do it, the next step is to read and interpret the sign he leaves in the woods.

Often hunters see turkeys in a particular area and then assume that's where they should hunt. However, this is a big mistake. When you see turkeys, they have already spotted you and are retreating from where they were or where they wanted to go. So there's a very good chance they may not be in the area you plan to hunt.

Finding turkey sign is a much more reliable method of choosing a place to hunt than actually seeing the turkeys. Turkey sign has a degree of permanence. Most tracks and droppings will last until the next rain, and feathers will generally last until the next year. So what you have in the woods, once you learn to see and identify it, is a record of what the turkeys have been doing. There's a tremendous amount of evidence for the hunter who can read the sign. I prefer to hunt the areas where the sign indicate where the turkeys should be, not the areas where I've actually seen a turkey.

The quickest way to learn to read sign is to go into the woods with an experienced turkey hunter. Let him show you the difference between turkey scratchings and places where squirrels have dug in the leaves for nuts. He can point out turkey tracks and probably give you reasons why a turkey was walking in that particular area. He can spot turkey droppings and teach you the difference between hen and gobbler droppings. He can show you how to tell an old scratching from a new one.

Hen droppings are shown at left, gobbler droppings at right.

A fresh scratching will have loose dirt around it. Often turkey tracks will be present in or near the scratching, and the ground will be relatively clear where the turkeys have been working. Also the toenail markings will be clear and easily defined. And if the turkeys are scratching in the leaves, the leaves will be piled up. Often—if the turkeys have been scratching there that day—the bottoms of the leaves will still be wet.

An old scratching will not have any fresh dirt around it. The actual scratches may not be well defined, and there may be leaves or pine straw in the scratched-out dirt. In an old scratching, the leaves will be relatively compacted.

The main thing you're trying to learn when you look for turkey sign is whether there are turkeys in the area you plan to hunt. If you know you're hunting where there are turkeys, you have more confidence in your calling and hunting. Your confidence will be much greater if you find a roost tree, get in the vicinity of that tree before daylight, and begin to call knowing there's a turkey that should answer.

If you find a fresh track, you know the turkey shouldn't be more than a mile away. And the odds are he'll be much closer than that. If the weather has been dry for several days and you discover a soft dropping, you know the turkey is so close he's liable to be looking at you.

Once you start to read and understand sign, you can really sharpen your turkey-hunting skills and knowledge. The main thing that sign tells you is where the turkeys are. Then you can determine where to set up a blind to call them.

LEARNING TO CALL

Many turkey hunters find one skill at which they are really good. Some are endowed with especially sensitive ears, and rely on their hearing more than any other sense when they hunt. Others are master woodsmen—able to read and understand sign quickly, and to predict where a turkey will show up without ever hearing or calling him.

Hunters who are musically inclined may admire a turkey caller and imitate him the way some musicians admire and imitate concert soloists. Good turkey callers have an ear for music and a knack for playing an instrument, even though that instrument may be a diaphragm caller, a cedar box, or a slate and peg. But once they perfect their skill with it, they depend more heavily on their calling ability than on any other skill.

Many master turkey hunters say that calling is only 10 or 20 percent of what is required to take a turkey. That may be true some of the time. However, I've found that often my ability to call is 100 percent of the reason I take a turkey. This is especially true when I hunt a strange area and don't have time to study the sign or turkeys there. Then I depend 100 percent on my calling ability. On the other hand, a hunter who scouts more, reads sign better, or knows what turkeys do in that area needs to depend on his calling as little as 10 to 15 percent.

To become an effective caller, listen to cassette tapes of actual turkey calls or of expert callers. Next, visit with some experts and let them show you the finer points of calling. Go to turkey-calling contests and listen to the calls the contestants make. Once you have learned to make the basic calls, the next stage is to develop confidence in your calling. To do that, you have to go out in the woods and begin to call.

Remember that a turkey doesn't walk around thinking, "Is that a man or a turkey making that call?" Turkeys just don't reason that way. If they hear a noise that sounds like another turkey, they may go to it. So there's no reason not to go into the woods and try your calling as soon as you have the chance. You're not going to scare the turkey. Turkeys are not paranoid about calls. And as soon as you see a turkey come to your call, even if the call isn't just right, you'll work more and more on your calling and develop more confidence in your ability.

LEARNING TO SHOOT

Learning how and when to shoot is the last skill that a turkey hunter needs to develop. The other skills I've discussed should be developed first.

A common mistake is not having a good gun to hunt with. When a person spends as much time, money, and effort as most turkey hunters do in learning the sport, not spending the extra money to buy the kind of gun he needs is foolish.

The right gun may not be the same for every person. The gun you use should be one you have confidence in. There's no point in using a gun that throws a 65-percent pattern at 40 yards, when you can buy one that throws an 85-percent pattern. A good gun may cost several hundred dollars. If you miss three turkeys, however, turning those three bad experiences into good ones would have been worth many hundreds of dollars more.

Another mistake is to use shot of improper size. In my opinion, there's some terrible misinformation about the shot sizes best for killing turkeys. Most turkey hunters use shot that's too large. Don't use shot any larger than no. 6. No. 7½s in a high-velocity shell are effective, but no. 8s are best.

All that's required to kill a turkey is a single no. 8 shot in the brain. When you use bigger shot, you reduce the number of shot that can kill the bird. With the smaller size, you have more shot directed at the turkey's head. And since the smaller shot can kill just as effectively, I'd choose a denser shot pattern instead of the larger shot.

It's also important to know the capabilities of your gun at various ranges, so you won't try to shoot farther than it can carry a tight pattern. I hunt with a gun that has both a shotgun barrel and a rifle barrel in states that permit hunting with this type of weapon. If a turkey is in close, I can blast him with the shotgun barrel. But if he's hung up out there at 50 yards, I can take him with the rifle barrel. The rifle barrel I want under my 12 gauge is a .222.

In my opinion, the .222 cartridge as it comes from the factory is too fast to kill effectively. If you hunt with a .222, shoot hand-loaded cartridges that are loaded down so that the bullets won't travel so fast. Use soft-nose bullets, and load your shells so the bullets will travel at about 2400 feet per second.

Before you squeeze the trigger on either the rifle or the shotgun, you've got to know if you're close enough to the turkey to make a kill. I recommend getting a turkey silhouette or decoy, placing it in the woods, walking away from it, and trying to judge the distance. Check your accuracy with either a range finder or a tape measure.

Finally, practice shooting from awkward positions on the ground. As master turkey hunters know, a turkey often will walk up so you have to shoot from a strange position, off balance or screwed around so you can barely hold your shotgun, let alone shoot. If you practice in unorthodox positions, you'll be better prepared for whatever shot a turkey presents.

The more you practice all the skills of the sport, the more consistently you'll take turkeys. If you're a beginner, the best advice I can give you is to start hunting. Sure, you'll make some mistakes, but you'll also learn from them. A turkey has no magic powers. If you hunt him, you can take him. If you don't get out into the woods enough, you'll never become a successful turkey hunter.

Basics from a Master Teacher

with Ben Rodgers Lee

*T*o hunt turkeys with me, a hunter has to have certain equipment. He'll need a good camouflage suit—pants and a jacket or shirt that will pretty much match the terrain we plan to hunt. The suit should be big enough so the hunter can move around without being restricted in any way. Also required will be a camouflage mask or head net and a good turkey gun—either a 12-gauge or 10-gauge shotgun. He'll need to shoot that gun at a board 30 to 35 yards away before the hunt and make sure he has a good, tight pattern that will kill a turkey.

The guns I recommend are the Remington 1100, the Browning automatic, and the Ithaca 10 gauge. I shoot Federal premium shotgun shells, or Winchester XX or Remington shells. Since each gun will shoot every type of shell differently, a hunter must know which shell will pattern best in the gun he's selected. All three brands are excellent for taking turkeys. I shoot no. 4 shot and use 3-inch magnum shells, which are far better for turkey hunting than 2¾-inch shells.

The next pieces of important equipment are a turkey caller and an instruction tape. The instruction tape enables the hunter to practice his calls and compare them with the calls on the tape.

FALL HUNTING

For fall hunting you should be able to make two different calls—the basic yelp and the kee-kee run. Most of the time you'll need only the yelp, but you'll be better prepared if you also know the kee-kee run.

Next you need to locate an area with some turkeys to hunt. If you're a novice, I recommend that you find an experienced turkey hunter to hunt with. Then you have someone to teach you how to hunt and how to read sign. If you don't know another turkey hunter, the next-best person to talk to is a bowhunter out for deer. These hunters sit in tree stands for long periods and hear turkeys fly down. They see turkeys walking and find all kinds of turkey sign—if there are any turkeys around.

Once in Pennsylvania I drove through some woods I had never hunted before. I went down a road and ran into five different groups of bowhunters. Each group had seen turkeys. And each told me where the turkeys were located and what they were feeding on.

The key to finding turkeys is to determine their primary food source, especially during the fall. At this time of year there are not many grasses or insects to feed on, so turkeys will eat beech mast, wild grapes, dogwood berries, and acorns. Knowing what turkeys are eating enables you to find them faster.

When you locate an area with turkeys and have a good idea of what they're eating, look around mud holes for tracks. Also check for droppings. Once you find droppings, you need to know whether they're gobbler's or hen's. The gobbler's dropping is shaped like a question mark, the hen's like a little curlicue. Also turkeys molt a great deal, so look also for wing, tail, or breast feathers.

Turkey tracks are most easily found after a rain in soft ground such as in washes, gullies, or fields, or around waterholes.

During the fall, it is not uncommon to see gobblers flocked together like this. But calling up a mature gobbler in fall may be a difficult task.

Another good place to look for sign, especially in national forests, is around watering holes. During dry spells in the fall, these holes are an excellent source of fresh water for turkeys. Many times a whole flock will come to a watering hole early in the morning, to get that first drink after coming off the roost.

When you've found sign, go into your hunting area late in the afternoon and listen for turkeys flying up to roost. The best places to listen are ridges. Be alert for the sound of wings beating the air. Often you'll hear an old hen cackling as she flies up, a few hens yelping to each other, or young gobblers doing the kee-kee run.

Once you know where those turkeys are roosting, wait until dark and try to slip in under them. Then snatch a vine that goes up a tree, scream and holler, throw sticks, and do everything you can to drive the turkeys off their roosts. The next morning before daylight, slip back into the roost area and sit back against a big tree. Many times you don't even have to call the dispersed turkeys. They naturally return to that roost area at day-break to try to get back together. But if you want to call them, start yelping or do a kee-kee run.

One of the easiest callers to use is a Noble whistle, which is made in England and is primarily utilized in dog training. It has a cork ball inside that should be removed. Then you just blow through it while saying, "Boy, boy, boy." This series of calls perfectly imitates a kee-kee run. So all you have to do, once you've scattered the turkeys the night before, is sit down, do a little calling—either yelping or kee-kee runs—and the turkeys will come to you.

Having turkeys in front of you, however, doesn't guarantee turkey on the table. You've got to know when to put your gun up, how to aim, and when to shoot. If a turkey answers your call or you hear him walking in leaves, get your gun up and be prepared to shoot. If you can actually see the turkey, wait until he steps behind a tree or bush before bringing the gun to your shoulder. That way he won't be able to see your movement.

Don't aim for the head. Aim for the spot where the neck joins the body. Then your shot pattern will cover the entire head and neck, which is the best area to hit.

Hold your shot until the turkey is about 25 yards away. A slightly longer shot is okay if he starts acting nervous. When he gets within 30 or 35 yards and then sticks his head straight up and starts looking, you'd better shoot, because he's getting ready to fly or run.

These tactics should ensure your taking a fall turkey.

SPRING HUNTING

To score during the spring, you must learn several calls. In addition to the kee-kee run, you need to know the yelp and the cluck. You can learn these easiest on a box caller or on my Super Hen, which has a peg and an aluminum striker box.

After you learn the yelp and cluck, you're ready to go scouting. Ride the woods roads at daylight before the season begins, and listen for crows. Take a crow caller along, and as soon as you hear them cawing blow that caller about four times, good and loud. If there's a turkey in the area, he'll gobble at your call. If you get no response, take your box caller out before you leave the area, and yelp just as loud as you can. Go through this same process in the mornings and the afternoons, trying to locate three or four turkeys prior to the season. Then if you pull up on opening morning and there's a vehicle parked near the spot you planned to hunt, you'll still have other spots you can go to.

On opening morning, take a stand about 100 yards from the place you think a turkey is roosting. If the roost is on a slope, try to find a stand on the high side of it. Ninety-nine times out of a hundred the turkey will fly to the high side of the slope, since the distance to the ground is shorter there. By positioning yourself on that side, you're already in a place he wants to come to.

After you find turkey sign, visit the area in late afternoon to listen for the sounds of turkeys flying up into roost trees. The best places to listen are on ridges between hollows. (Tennessee Valley Authority photo)

Once you sit down, give the turkey two or three soft clucks. If he gobbles at them, you'll know he doesn't need much more encouragement. Give him just a few more clucks. The closer the turkey gets to you, the less you need to call. If he doesn't gobble at your clucks, however, then start clucking more often. Once he starts coming in, put your box down, pick your gun up, and get ready to shoot.

IN SHORT

Those are the basics of fall and spring turkey hunting. In a way, hunting turkeys is like going to college. You can take a test to get in, but there's a lot more learning to go through before you graduate.

Other than actual scouting and hunting, there are several ways you can increase your knowledge. The easiest method is to read all you can about turkeys and turkey hunting. You don't need to hunt a hundred turkeys to know how it's done, if you'll study the many books and articles written by highly experienced hunters.

An important source of information on your own area is your state fish and game department. Almost every state has a specialist who knows where to find turkeys and how to hunt them. In many states the departments hold seminars where you can get plenty of free tips on hunting your area.

The National Wild Turkey Federation, in South Carolina, can put you in touch with chapters and turkey hunters in your area. And sporting-goods stores, especially in large cities, will often sponsor seminars on turkey hunting or calling where local turkey hunters will come in and tell you where and how to hunt.

I advise any beginner to tap these information sources.

You need nerves of steel and great patience to sit still long enough for a turkey to walk in this close. But getting a tom in close is what is required.

Mistakes

Hunters Make

with Harold Knight and Terry Rohm

"The two of us have probably made every mistake in turkey hunting at least two or three times," Harold Knight says. "So we feel we're pretty much experts on mistakes. One of the biggest mistakes is trying to get a turkey to do something he doesn't want to do, or something that's unnatural for him.

"The most critical factor in killing a turkey is setting up in the right place to call him. No matter how well you can call, you're not going to kill a turkey if you set up in the wrong place. Here are some general rules:

"Don't try calling a turkey across water. Turkeys don't like to cross water, and the chances of calling one across it are extremely slim.

"Don't attempt to call a turkey through a thicket. Turkeys don't like thickets, because they sense danger there. Most of the time they won't come through a thicket even to date a romantic hen.

"Don't try to call a turkey down a hill. Walking up a hill is usually easier for a turkey than walking down. Get above him if you're going to call.

"Don't take a stand in a treetop or thicket. A turkey will not come to a place unless he can see well in all directions."

Terry Rohm believes many people try calling from too great a distance: "I've seen hunters attempt to call turkeys from 300 or 400 yards away. You *can* call one in from that kind of distance, but the chances are great that a hen, another hunter, or water or some other natural barrier will come between you and the turkey. So you need to get as close as you can without spooking him. If the terrain permits, move within 100 yards of him before starting to call.

"And some people just don't know where to sit down in the woods," Rohm continues. "I know hunters who take stands in treetops where the only way they can shoot is straight in front of them. If a turkey walks to either side of them or comes up behind them, they can't shoot him. I also know hunters who lie on their stomachs and look up at the hills watching for turkeys. If a turkey isn't right in front of them, they can't shoot him.

"The best way to sit when turkey hunting is with your back to a tree and your knees pulled up. When you hear a turkey coming, put your gun to your shoulder and rest your elbows on your knees. Then you can shoot to both sides and to the front. If a turkey walks up behind you, the tree provides a blind. And if another hunter attempts to shoot a turkey from behind you, then the tree offers you protection."

"I wouldn't sit down next to the biggest tree in the forest," Knight cautions. "I know that when I'm walking through the woods, if I see an unusually big tree that's the first thing I look at. And I believe a turkey may do the same thing. The tree where you sit should be wider than your shoulders, but not the biggest tree in the area."

"Another mistake that hunters make is the camouflage they forget to wear," Rohm says. "Some hunters wear camouflage suits and camouflage head nets or paint, but many times the white of their T-shirts and the white soles of their boots stick out like a sore thumb. You have to be totally camouflaged and match your surroundings if you're going to take a turkey."

"I'd be careful not to wear blue, red, or white," Knight says. "Those are the colors of a turkey's head. If you're out in the woods making noises like a turkey, and another hunter sees something colored like a turkey's head move, you could get shot. Like Terry, I believe in total camouflage. Make sure the soles of your boots are dark colored, or hide them under the leaves so they can't be seen. If the soles are light colored, they'll run off every turkey you try to call up."

Rohm says many hunters are afraid to call enough: "Lots of tales lead

Having the proper camouflage for the area you're planning to hunt; sitting down beside a tree that's wider than your shoulders; and using camo tape on your gun barrel, forend, and stock are usually essential.

hunters to believe that the less they call, the better their chances of killing turkeys. But I disagree. When I go into the woods in the springtime to hunt turkeys, I want to hear them gobble. I want to hear them gobble as loud and as much as they'll gobble. So I do a lot of calling.

"Calling a great deal, especially when a turkey is coming in, enables you to keep track of him much better. If you know where he is, you're encouraged to stay on your stand. If you don't know, you may get discouraged and leave.

"One reason most people are afraid to call is that they think they'll make a mistake in their calling. What they fail to realize is that hen turkeys aren't perfect either. Hens make mistakes when they're talking. Some of them stutter, and some of them squeal. If you make a mistake on a caller, you haven't committed the unpardonable sin."

"A turkey sounds more like a person walking in the woods than anything else I know," Knight observes. "Often I've thought someone was walking near me and would ruin my hunt. I'd get mad and ready to jump on his case, only to turn around and be eyeball to eyeball with a big turkey. In other instances I've heard people calling at the same time and in the same location I was calling. I'd hear them get out a gobble box, shake it, and make the most awful sound you ever heard. I'd decide the best thing to do was to get up and leave—because with those folks in the woods, I probably wasn't going to kill a turkey. Then when I got up, I'd see the racket I'd heard was a group of hens and some gobblers who couldn't talk any better than some hunters call. Many times a hunter won't get his turkey because he assumes what he's hearing is another hunter. I don't believe most hen turkeys could win a calling contest, because they call so poorly they'd be eliminated."

"On the other hand," Rohm notes, "some hunters get so keyed up they imagine everything they hear is a turkey. They're afraid to move but also scared not to move. They're so nervous they just can't hunt. A good turkey hunter is like the gunslingers in the Wild West. He stays relaxed until the time comes to shoot. Then he's deliberate and decisive in his actions.

"When I first started turkey hunting, I was afraid of turkeys. Finally my Dad assured me that if I slowed down, relaxed, enjoyed hunting, and didn't worry about killing a turkey, I'd be more successful. Sure enough, I killed many more turkeys. During turkey season I've seen people run up and down hills, go without food, and scream at their wives and kids. That mood is not conducive to good turkey hunting. It's a form of insanity. To be a good turkey hunter, you have to learn to relax and enjoy the sport and the time you have in the woods. With that calm attitude, you'll be far more successful.

"Many people fail because they're not patient enough to wait for the turkeys to come to them. Often a hunter calls to a turkey and gets an answer, but never hears anything from him after that. Discouraged, the hunter gets up to leave. As he stands, he flushes the turkey he'd hoped to call into range.

"Sometimes a gobbler will walk to a hen and not make any sounds. Other times, all you hear is a faint drumming. Most hunters run out of patience and walk off leaving turkeys they could have killed if they'd stayed a little longer. If a turkey is within 100 yards and has answered, an hour and a half is not too long to wait."

Knight says the number-one rule of thumb, especially helpful to beginners, is to "stay as long as you think you should, and then wait 30 minutes longer."

Another mistake, according to Knight, is to shoot too soon: "Hunters often think a turkey is closer than he really is, and shoot when he's too far away for a kill. Before I sit down and start calling, I pick out four or five trees, a bush, and a stick or something else that I determine to be about 30 yards out. I decide I won't shoot until a turkey comes closer than those marks. That way I don't have to worry about judging distance when I'm trying to watch him.

"Also, hunting aggressively will get you more turkeys than hunting timidly. If you think you should be closer to a turkey, get up and move. If you think you should circle him and call from another direction, then make that move. Aggressive turkey hunting is a relatively new tactic. In past years, the whole sport of turkey hunting was to wait for the turkey to come to you. But today most of the better hunters try to move in closer, so the turkey doesn't have to walk so far and will be easier to take.

"If you go after a turkey and do whatever it takes to get close enough to kill him, you'll go home with more turkeys for the table. Being aggressive and patient, and knowing when to be which, will result in more successful turkey hunting."

Where Does Patience Begin and End

by Charles Elliott

One common trait of people today is impatience—the urge to force every issue, to get the goal behind us so we can rush to something else. Impatience may serve well enough when we strive toward a modest goal such as winning a governorship or becoming the president of General Motors. But when our goal is something really important, such as bagging a big old tom, impatience heads the list of countless things that can spoil our chances.

Turkey-hunting guide Doug Camp tells why impatience doesn't work: ''No matter how interested an old gobbler may seem, there's no way to rush him. A jake is more likely to go along with you, but most turkeys, especially the cagey old gobblers, just won't come in till they're good and ready. Like most guides, I'm anxious to have my hunter succeed, and I'm guilty of trying to hurry the turkey. I lose many old gobblers by not waiting them out.''

In turkey hunting, patience is vital. Of course it's not the only thing you need in your bag of tricks. You must also have a sharp eye and ear, know how to hide yourself in the woods, and be able to call well enough so a turkey won't peg you as a jaybird with a sore throat. But none of these means anything unless you also have the mental stamina to anchor yourself and wait, when all conditions are right.

True, patience can be carried too far. You don't want to imitate the diligent bird dog in an old story, who disappeared one day on a hunting trip. Not until two years later did the dog's owner find his skeleton still on point, with the skeletons of 10 quail just beyond his nose.

Knowing where patience begins and ends is a matter of common sense. You won't sit in a blind all night, for instance, when you know that turkeys fly up to roost a little before dark. And you won't hunt in the middle of a logging operation, with saws, tractors, and shouting all around you. On the other hand, I've sat for half a day in a severe thunderstorm, because I knew an old gobbler was in the vicinity. I'd talked with him earlier. And

"I was about to move but then heard footsteps in the leaves. The cadence was that of a man, stalking cautiously. I was watching intently for a man when the gobbler appeared, walking slowly. And he looked half as tall as a man." (Dave Kenyon, Michigan Dept. Natural Resources, photo)

perseverance paid off. When I brought my prize in, he was almost as drenched and bedraggled as I was.

In my opinion patience comes in many sizes, from the ten-minute variety to the infinite. I've been in the woods with fellows who were nervous and fidgety almost from the moment they sat down. They squirmed and wiggled as though we'd plopped ourselves on an ant hill. They wanted to smoke. They wanted to talk. If we'd remained immobile and silent as long as we should have, I would have needed strait jackets to get them out of the woods.

I admit that parking your carcass for long periods is not easy, even though you heard gobbling at dawn, found abundant food and fresh scratchings, and all other conditions are right. You sit and sit, and don't hear or see anything except the normal life of the forest, which can get mighty boring. But you know the turkeys are there. The turkey conversation you are carrying on may be a monologue only, but many times a gobbler or hen in the vicinity will investigate out of sheer curiosity. Suddenly you look up and see a turkey standing there.

I know several hunters who build permanent blinds in stretches of woods that turkeys frequent. These hunters park themselves comfortably in their blinds before daylight, then remain there all day, calling at intervals. They get up and move only to go to a gobble. This is not my idea of the most exciting way to hunt, but it often pays off in roast turkey on the table.

An acquaintance only a few years into gobbler chasing confided that he'd killed half his turkeys by getting himself situated in a blind, calling every 10 or 15 minutes for an hour or so, and then going to sleep. When he woke up, a gobbler would be standing there, looking him over.

"You've bagged half of your gobblers by doing that?" I asked. "How many have you killed since you've been hunting?"

"Two," he admitted.

I'm sure that's a pretty good average for this method. Still, there's more than a grain of effectiveness in it, thanks to the survival instincts that we've inherited from the cave man. When I know I'm in good territory and have no special reason to change locations, I often lean back against a tree and go to sleep. Though most of me may hang on the border of the netherworld, remnants of the cave man's brain still function. I'm conscious of every sound in the forest around me. A pine cone falling, the snap of a stick, footsteps—any of these noises will bring me alert. The inquiring cluck or putt of a turkey will blast into my awareness.

Those same survival instincts keep me from moving until I identify the sound that woke me. I've killed several gobblers in just this way. Had I been awake, straining every sense or feeling restless, chances are I never would have remained so long in one spot. Sleeping is a great way to keep patient.

Stick-to-it-iveness may come in bigger packages that last for weeks or months, even years. I've known hunters who kept after one special gobbler, passing up all others, from one season to the next. Normally, I'm proud of myself when I hang with one turkey for six hours, more or less. But the prize gobbler of my turkey-hunting career, two-thirds of a century, outsmarted and outmaneuvered me for three years. I've bagged every species of big-game animal and most of the birds, but my trophy of a lifetime—if I had to select only one—was that special gobbler.

He was with two jakes the first time I saw him. The jakes were fully grown, but he dwarfed them by a good head and shoulders—if the butts of his wings can be called shoulders. He was the largest mountain gobbler I'd ever laid eyes on. By the time I could have shot at him he was running and was already at the limit of the shot pattern. So I passed him up. But he set me on fire. I went back the next day and the next, all the rest of that season.

For the following two years I confined most of my turkey hunting to the ridges and coves where he lived. I saw him any number of times and would have known him if I'd met him walking down Peachtree Street in Atlanta. I was convinced I could even identify him by his gobble. Several times while I was trying to work him, other gobblers came to me. I simply passed them up. At that time the limit for the season was one. I don't believe I pulled many boo-boos, but not a trick I knew would get that old boy close enough for a sure shot. And I tried them all.

My patience was inspired by an obsession to bag that feathered Goliath. This was the kind of patience that comes in big packages. But the smaller kind of patience saved me on the day when that big turkey's luck finally ran out.

I'd heard no gobbling that morning and worked in a circle to where my car was parked on a logging road. I leaned against the door, smoked a pipeful of tobacco, and was about to slide under the wheel for the drive back to camp when the hunch hit me that I should make at least one last-ditch call. I stepped to the side of the road, yelped my box, paused a minute, and rattled the box to simulate gobbling. Then, loud and clear, that special gobble I'd heard so many times blasted back at me from the top of the next ridge, a couple of hundred yards away. I stood, straining every sense, until he gobbled again to tell me that he was coming along the ridge, paralleling the ridge I was on.

I sprinted away from the road and made a big circle, to get in front of him on the ridge he was traveling. I sat down in a natural blind. When I yelped, he gobbled again and continued toward me until he reached a narrow ridge that branched off. He hesitated there for a long two or three minutes. When he gobbled again, he was on his way back to the management area where he lived. Meanwhile, another gobbler behind me had answered my yelps and was coming toward me. I left him and went after the granddaddy that had kept my blood percolating for three years. When he seemed to hang up near the top of the ridge, I built a quick blind and sat down to try to call him back, without much hope of seeing him again that day.

I didn't look at my watch and have no idea how long the hunt took, but it seemed like the rest of the morning. I'm sure the turkey remained in one spot for an hour. He gobbled occasionally, then clammed up. I couldn't get another note out of him. In my experience, when a turkey hangs up, gobbles, and then quits, he either has lost interest and gone about his business, or is on his way to investigate. So I settled down to wait, no matter how long, determined not to muff this opportunity as I had a few others.

After an interminable time in which absolutely nothing happened, the rocks, roots, and sticks beneath me changed from dead, inanimate objects into live ones, and began probing a tender part of my anatomy. At long, long last I ran out of patience. There's just no other way to put it. I could visualize the gobbler wandering off with a hen somewhere, or scratching placidly for grubs and shoots, while I sat there suffering. I thought, *To hell with it*, and put my hand down to help shift my weight and stand up. At that same instant a stick cracked somewhere in front of me. I froze, straining my eyes for the sight of a deer. After at least 15 minutes without seeing a movement or hearing another sound, I was about to move but then heard footsteps in the leaves. The cadence was that of a man, stalking cautiously. I was watching intently for a man when the gobbler appeared, walking slowly. And he looked half as tall as a man. I was so startled I almost forgot to put my gun to my shoulder when his head went behind a tree. Then when he stood magnificent in a shaft of sunlight, I almost forgot to shoot.

I knew by his size and appearance that this was the gobbler I'd been after for three years. And surely I would have missed him again, if circumstances hadn't forced me to stay patient. It makes a fellow wonder how many gobblers he's missed over the years because his patience ran out.

Two more times I had similar experiences, both while hunting with Roscoe Reams in the Blue Ridge Mountains of Georgia. At neither time were turkeys gobbling, but the signs were there and we knew the turkeys were too.

Before daylight, Roscoe left me on a narrow bench and went on up the ridge to a place where he'd seen turkeys fly off the roost. For almost two hours I remained where Roscoe had left me. I clucked, yelped, and gobbled on each of the four callers I'd packed along, but got nary a peep in reply. The morning was growing old. I knew if I expected to hear a gobble, I'd better try a few more locations before the turkeys throttled down for the day. I left my blind and moved down the ridge, away from Roscoe. I stopped and called a few times before I reached a gap and climbed to follow another ridge.

Half an hour later, Roscoe, not having heard a gobble, headed for the bench where he'd left me, to suggest that we explore other territory. He was brought up short about 70 yards from the blind I'd deserted. An old gobbler was stomping around it, clucking and *pop-pop-popping* as a turkey does when trying to find a hen he knows should be there. Since I didn't shoot, Roscoe realized I was no longer around. He yelped with his caller, but the gobbler had a fix on the first call he'd heard and came on toward the gap, looking for me.

Exactly the same thing happened the next season, on the same acre of ground. Both times I went off and left a gobbler looking for me. Both times I flunked out, because I had fallen short on patience.

Once, in the Ocoee National Forest of Tennessee, I picked up a fellow who was walking to his car, a couple of miles away. He was with three other hunters, he told me. Every season for the past 12 years they had come down together from Michigan to hunt turkeys.

"Have you got your gobbler this year?" I asked.

"We've never killed a turkey," he replied. "None of us. But one of these days we will."

Many times I've been asked, Can you acquire patience or do you have to be born with it? The answer is simple. Patience grows when you practice—and life will give you plenty of opportunities to do so.

Sometime soon you may find yourself lined up at a grocery check-out counter, and there at the check-out a shopper will wait stolidly until the cartload of purchases is rung up, then decide for some reason to check them all again, then fumble for a check, neatly write it out, then fumble once again for an ID or two, and fail to find them. Or possibly you'll be stuck in an endless line of traffic, creeping along at 5 miles per hour, when you're already late for an important meeting. (One of my hunting partners uses time in traffic jams to practice notes on his diaphragm caller. And I've often thought that I should have a caller with me at check-out counters too.)

But if you can make yourself relax at times like these, staying calm and collected instead of fretting, you'll gain practice in showing real patience—the patience you'll need to collect that old longbeard.

Leonard Lee Rue III photo

I Don't

Believe

in Secrets

with Aaron Pass

I've been chasing gobblers for more than 15 springs, and all I am certain of is that I've gotten more of them than they have of me. That doesn't make me a master; it doesn't even mean I'm a particularly good turkey hunter. It just means I'm stubborn.

So having disclaimed the title of master turkey hunter, I'll go further. I don't believe in secrets—not in this age of turkey hunting. There aren't any secrets left.

Today, with the wild turkey successfully restored to healthy, huntable populations across the nation, would-be turkey hunters are clamoring for information on turkey hunting. And calls manufacturers, outdoor writers, and other turkey-hunting experts are more than happy to try to satisfy this demand. Books, magazine articles, audio tapes, and even video tapes are available, chock-full of the latest tricks of the trade for effective turkey hunting. By and large the information is timely and useful.

Also, today's marketplace boasts a wide variety of specialized turkey-hunting gear, and an even greater variety of really good turkey calls. This puts the modern novice in a far better position than those of us who were trying to learn the what's what of this turkey-hunting game 15 or 20 years ago. Back then good calls were scarce, and helpful information was even scarcer.

At the same time, this explosion of equipment and knowledge has knocked the bottom out of the turkey-hunting-secrets business. Once turkey hunting had secrets galore; in fact, almost everything about turkey hunting was a secret. By the early 1900s, the North American wild turkey had been extirpated from more than 70 percent of its native range. And the few surviving flocks were little more than pitiful remnants, hanging on in some tract of woods that was too steep, too wet, or too worthless to be farmed, mined, or logged.

In the first half of this century, wild turkeys, if not gone entirely from a region, were simply too scarce to interest more than a handful of hunters.

Also, one generation gave way to another, and the supply of old-time turkey hunters dwindled like the bird they had hunted. In going, these veterans left not very much in the way of written records or advice, and what was left was soon out of print.

However, when the good work of state game departments began to restore and protect wild turkeys in the 1950s and 1960s, hunters once again got interested in turkey hunting, and the remaining old-timer hunters were sought out for advice.

This period was the heyday of turkey-hunting secrets. Dutifully, the veteran would take the aspiring novice out to a grove of chinaberry trees by the hog lot, look all around for eavesdroppers, and then whisper the secrets of successful turkey hunting. And some of these were wonderful secrets.

Much of the advice had to do with calling, which, the veteran admonished, had to be perfect. One false note, and the gobbler would be gone.

The love call of the hen and the wildcat call of the gobbler were pretty standard revelations. The wise-old-veteran tactics leaned heavily to utmost caution and a degree of patience that made Job seem fidgety.

The standard lesson went something like this: "When the tom gobbles, call three times real low and then put the call down. He's heard you, and he knows where you are. Don't call again for nearly an hour and always call softly." The hunter was advised to stay put until the gobbler showed up or until the next Tuesday—whichever occurred first.

Today, with all our raucous contest-calling styles, and with our penchant for dashing about in the woods to locate an active gobbler, cut off a traveling gobbler, and unhang a hung-up gobbler, the foregoing advice seems timid, antiquated, and, well, quaint. We know that aggressive calling and changing our position will work. So we wonder if the veterans were pulling our legs.

Perhaps sometimes they were, but many of their admonitions were the best advice they could give, based on their experiences. Remember, our granddaddies were dealing with what was possibly a very different turkey-hunting situation. Since wild turkeys were scarce in the old days, once our granddaddies located a gobbler they stayed in there with him. They didn't casually saunter off, confident they would find a more responsive gobbler in the next hollow. Also, those old-time turkeys, scarce as they were, got hunted hard. Seasons were long, and the local human populations usually didn't take much notice when they were closed. A wild turkey seen was usually a wild turkey shot at, and the ones that survived put real meaning in the term "wild turkey." So probably our granddaddies learned their turkey hunting from some tough turkeys.

Today it's fashionable to scoff at the three-soft-yelps-and-sit-still-until-moss-grows-on-your-north-side school of turkey hunting. However, when you read your brand-new, high-tech, state-of-the-art turkey-hunting book and turn to the chapter entitled "Hunting the Call-shy Gobbler," what does the modern-day expert recommend? Likely he'll tell you to call sparingly and softly, not to move around much in your hunting area, and to be patient because wary gobblers generally don't rush right to you. All of these subtle tactics are not much different from what the ancient veterans advised out by the log in the 1950s.

On the other hand, we're not hunting the birds of a half century ago, and under today's conditions and with today's equipment, we've discovered new tactics that also work to our advantage against a spring gobbler. Each of these was once someone's secret—as, I'm sure, were almost all of our now-standard turkey-hunting tactics.

For instance, someone had to be the first to identify and imitate what we now describe as the tree call. Some brave soul also had to discover that imitating a gobbler (probably with a box call) would not only stimulate a dominant gobbler to answer, but also might bring that old sultan raging to the scene, his head red and his caution dulled by jealousy.

As turkey hunting became more popular, calling contests sprang up. These challenged the callers not only to improve their calling, but also to be more dynamic so as to outshine the competition. And as the legend goes, a janitor from Alabama showed up at a northern contest and stunned both the audience and the judges with a wild cacophony of clucks and yelps. He got a zero on the score sheet. This loser was the world-famous turkey caller Ben Rodgers Lee, and the call was the cackle—now standard in most contests and a highly useful hunting call.

More recently, cutting has become the new thing to do—both in contests and in the woods. Cutting, which consists of clucks, whines, and short yelps in no particular order, is almost but not quite a cackle. It too is a highly effective hunting call. It imitates an excited hen and is used to stir up a gobbler that seems less than enthusiastic about your standard yelps and clucks.

Of course much of this innovative calling is the result of the steady advancement in turkey calls, particularly the diaphragm. This call has now evolved from one layer to four layers of latex. Still newer is the cut call in which the top layer is cut at an angle. This cut call produces the very raspy yelps so much in demand by today's turkey hunters. I've often suspected the old-timers favored the three-yelp series for a simple reason: If they managed to get three good yelps in a row on some of those old homemade calls, they quit while they were ahead.

I remember the time when going away from a hung-up gobbler was the hot secret tactic that avid hunters were muttering about. I tried it once, and it worked. But I must admit I utilized it by accident, having given up on a recalcitrant gobbler that I couldn't get to cross a creek. I was just calling out of frustration as I moved away. Not only did he cross the creek; he cut me off before I crossed the first ridge.

No, I didn't get him, but I did enjoy a very interesting two minutes

This is no blunt-toothed Dracula. Rather it's author John Phillips readying a diaphragm call. These calls are now available with from one to four layers of latex. In some diaphragm calls, the top layer is cut at an angle (a split reed call) to produce the raspy yelps so much in demand by today's turkey hunters. (Sara Bright photo)

that included: (1) a misfire, (2) a hangfire that went off straight up, (3) lots of falling pine bark and needles, (4) another gobbler that showed up, (5) missing that second gobbler by 40 feet, (6) two flying gobblers, and (7) a real understanding of how much can happen in a short time while turkey hunting. However, I still find walking away from any gobbling turkey—even when he's obviously hung up—very difficult.

The gobbler with hens is also a common problem, particularly these days with our turkey populations growing denser. Every year there seem to more hens, and they stay with the gobblers longer and later. One tactic for this situation is to try to call in the hens, which you can do (sometimes) by doing what they're doing about as often as they're doing it. The big disadvantage of this tactic is that if the hens do come, they invariably come ahead of the gobbler. Then you have to hope he'll get in range before the hens see you and spook.

This tactic doesn't work all of the time. It doesn't even work most of the time. ''Occasionally'' is about the best odds I can put on it. But if I kill a gobbler occasionally, I think I'm having a hell of a good time.

However, all of these hunting and calling tactics are no longer secrets. I doubt they ever were. They were discovered by hunters who couldn't resist sharing them with their hunting buddies after, of course, swearing them to silence—a silence those buddies invariably broke as soon as they ran into someone they wanted to impress. Such is the nature of hunters.

More and more, I'm coming to believe that the most effective secret tactic in modern turkey hunting is no secret but is so obvious it's overlooked. The real secret is not to rely on a secret tactic.

Too much attention to the tactics of turkey hunting causes the hunter to forget who the boss of the hunt really is. Of course the gobbler is the one that calls the shots. If he chooses, he does the initial gobbling that leads you to him, and if and when he feels like coming to your call, he'll come. The turkey hunter's role is essentially reactionary—he must react to the gobbler's initiative. And to dwell on a preformulated list of tactics is to unconsciously develop an agenda for the hunt that may or may not coincide with the gobbler's idea of what should be happening. And you know whose agenda will take precedence in the woods!

What's needed by the hunter is a basic strategy—an overall plan based on: (1) a good knowledge of turkey behavior, (2) a fair amount of woodscraft and (3) reasonable competence with a turkey call. This strategy may incorporate certain tactical expedients—cackling or cutting to warm up a gobbler that seems less than hot, or moving on one that just won't budge. But the key is to play the ball as it lies and have the basic knowledge to react appropriately to the situation presented by each individual gobbler and hunting situation.

In terms of specific tactics, be assured of one of the few certainties of turkey hunting—there's almost nothing that won't work with turkeys sometimes, but certainly nothing that will work all of the time. Another certainty is that a gobbler can always stand behind a tree 40 yards away longer than you can hold up a 9-pound shotgun.

But I do have one tactic that I rely on above all others. I think persistence may be the one real secret of successful turkey hunting. You can't kill a gobbler if you don't go. And you won't kill one while you're sacked out in camp or lounging around the coffee shop. But as long as you're in the woods, hunting diligently and to the best of your capabilities, whatever they are, you've got a chance to take a gobbler.

Although I may not be a master, I'm stubborn. After thinking about this "master turkey hunter" label, I'm not too sure that anyone who's still an active turkey hunter really ought to play too loose with that title. A wild turkey gobbler can bring real meaning to the Biblical saying "Pride goeth before destruction, and a haughty spirit before a fall" (Proverbs 16:18).

A hot gobbler, without hens, who's desperately trying to remedy that situation, can make an expert out of a novice with his first scratch on a turkey call. But even the woods-wise veteran turkey hunter who encounters a woods-wiser veteran gobbler will receive a thorough refresher course in turkey hunting—and usually find out who's really a master in this turkey-hunting business.

J. Wayne Fears likes to position a novice hunter between his legs so that he can announce the approach of a turkey and whisper instructions. Normally Fears would require that his client wear camouflage gloves as well.

Teaching
a Beginner

with J. Wayne Fears

The first thing I do with a beginner is take him to a pattern board and let him pattern his shotgun. Most beginners just grab whatever shotgun they've got lying around the house, without having any idea how it will pattern at various distances. So the first thing to do is to show him what his gun will do at different distances, how his pattern will lie relative to the turkey's head.

Next I want to see how accurately the beginner can shoot. In other types of shotgun hunting, you can usually kill your game by shooting close to it and hitting it only with an edge of your pattern. But in turkey hunting you have to shoot your shotgun like a rifle, aiming exactly at what you want to hit.

The beginner sees a big bird out in front of him, and thinks there's no way he can miss. He fails to realize that most pellets won't penetrate to the vital organs if the turkey is shot in the body. The beginner has to be shown that the head-and-neck area is the only target to shoot at for a sure kill.

Then I have him put on his hunting clothes as if he were going hunting. I want to know he has a head net, gloves, camouflage pants and jacket, and dark-soled boots. Sometimes I've gone into the woods with a beginning hunter and asked him to put on his head-net, and he's looked at me blankly and said he didn't know he needed one. When that happens, we've wasted a morning.

When I take a beginner into the woods, I want to locate a turkey but get no closer than 100 yards. When I hunt by myself, I like to move as close as 50 or 75 yards. But two people make more noise than one, and most beginners don't realize how sensitive to noise the turkey is. They tend to step on sticks, stumble, fall, talk too loud, swat mosquitos, cough, and scratch.

Once I have my hunter 100 yards from the turkey, I get him to sit right between my legs. That way I'm able to control the situation. I can see that

73

Vital areas

Ideal center
of pattern

By firing at a turkey head silhouette on a pattern board, the hunter can see where his pellets will hit. At varying distances, a shotgun will pattern different shells either tighter or looser.

he's wearing his head net and gloves, and that he's not swatting mosquitos. Also, I can view things from the same angle he does, and can keep my mouth close to his ear to whisper instructions, preventing a lot of mistakes.

While the turkey is still out of sight, gobbling, I try to anticipate which direction he'll come from. I line my hunter up in that direction, then have him raise his left knee (or his right knee, if he shoots left-handed) and rest his gun on it. Getting set early keeps movement to a minimum once the turkey comes into range.

Once we're set, I start calling. I do all the calling myself. When I spot the turkey I whisper where to look, since most beginners won't spot one on their own until he's right in front of them. I also whisper when to raise the gun and when to shoot. Beginners usually misjudge distances and want to shoot when the turkey is too far away.

If the shot connects, the hunter should switch his gun on "SAFETY" and move as fast as safely possible and stand on the turkey's head. Many

Life-size turkey silhouettes give vital practice at estimating distances. Often, beginners are surprised to learn how far away the silhouettes are.

beginners think that when they roll a turkey over with that single shot the hunt is finished. They don't realize that often a turkey can shake himself off, jump up, and run away. I tell all my hunters, "Be on that turkey's head before I get there, and we'll take him home to dinner."

The best way a beginner can learn is by going out with a seasoned hunter. To become a staunch hunter himself, the beginner needs to hear a turkey gobble and see him coming through the woods. He needs to see a turkey strut. If possible, he should actually bag one.

Once he has that first gobbler, he'll go back, more often than not, and learn everything necessary to call and bag one on his own.

Camo tape on barrel, forend, and stock will help to disguise the gun.

Guns and Ammunition

with J. Wayne Fears

*T*he most revolutionary gun in years for hunting turkeys is Remington's Model 1100 Special Purpose Turkey Gun. It sports a 26-inch full-choke barrel, and has a parkerized finish (a dull finish on the metal) and a sling with swivels for easy carrying in the woods. It shoots 12-gauge 3-inch magnum shells, and patterns as well as most guns with 32-inch barrels. This may be the best turkey gun on the market today.

My second-choice turkey gun is the Ithaca Mag 10 with a 32-inch barrel. This 10-gauge, 3 ½-inch magnum also has a parkerized finish and swivels for the sling. I've used this Ithaca for six years and have found it can take turkeys 60 yards away. I don't advocate shooting them that far, but the gun does have the power.

The old standby Remington 1100 with a 30- or 32-inch full-choke barrel, chambered for 12-gauge 3-inch magnum shells, is my third choice. You need to put camo tape on this gun, because the barrel has a blue satin finish and the wood has a slick finish. I like the 3-inch magnum since a turkey is so hard to kill. And I prefer the bigger gauges not to gain more distance but to have a denser pattern and more knockdown power than the smaller gauges will give me.

The Browning automatic is deadly on turkeys at 30 or 40 yards, holding a very tight pattern. It also has a slick finish and requires camo tape. For this gun I recommend only no. 4 or 6 copper-plated shot. If the terrain you are hunting favors close shots, I recommend no. 4. And by "close," I mean from 15 to 30 yards. If you expect to shoot at distances of more than 30 yards, I suggest the no. 6 shot. Then you have more shot going toward the turkey's head.

I prefer copper-plated shot because it doesn't deform while traveling through the barrel or when hitting light brush. Thus it flies straighter and gives a denser, more even pattern than lead shot. I've examined copper-plated shot that penetrated the breast of a turkey and lodged beneath the skin of the back, and it was still relatively round.

The Remington Model 1100 SP autoloading shotgun with a 26-inch barrel may be the best turkey gun on the market today, according to Fears.

Fears' second choice for a turkey gun is the Ithaca Mag 10, which is capable of taking a turkey 60 yards away.

The Remington 1100 shotgun is Fears' third selection, especially in the bigger gauges. This shotgun comes in 12, 16, 20, 28 gauges and .410.

The best muzzleloader for turkey hunting is a 12 or 10 gauge with no. 4 or 5 shot. You need to shoot equal volumes of shot and powder—the volumes varying with different guns. At present, all muzzleloader barrels are unchoked. They limit the range to a maximum of 30 yards, so a muzzleloading turkey hunter must be able to call a turkey in closer than a hunter using modern weaponry. Navy Arms, however, is developing a full-choke muzzleloader especially for hunting turkeys.

CHOOSING THE WEAPON

I know some hunters who bag their gobblers every year with a 20 gauge or a .410. The reason they use these guns is that the game they're playing is different from the one most turkey hunters play. Their ultimate goal is not merely to kill a turkey, but to call one within 20 yards of where

The Remington Model 11-87 SP Magnum auto shotgun with interchangeable "Rem" chokes handles all 2¾-inch and 3-inch Magnum shells.

The Browning automatic is deadly on turkeys at 30 or 40 yards and holds a very tight pattern. However since the Browning automatic is a slick-finish gun, Fears uses camo tape to hide it from turkeys. It is available in the 5-shot "Sweet Sixteen," as well as 12 gauge for turkey hunting.

Black-powder turkey hunters shoot the traditional muzzleloaders like this Connecticut Valley Arms (CVA). But with such a gun, the bird usually must come within 30 yards for a kill.

they're sitting. Then he'll be within the effective range of these small shotguns. However, you need to check the hunting regulations in your state before you use any gauge smaller than 12 to hunt turkeys. In many states hunting turkeys with these smaller gauges is forbidden.

THE SHORT-BARREL SHOTGUN

In the last few years more and more hunters have gone to short-barrel shotguns for turkeys. They're beginning to learn what gun experts have been telling them for a long time—that full-choke barrels longer than 18 inches add nothing to accuracy. Although the sight radius is greater with a longer barrel, turkey hunters shoot their shotguns like rifles and have learned that the shorter full-choke barrels, 24 inches long, are just as capable of killing a turkey. The short-barrel guns are easier to handle in the woods and easier to shoot.

USING THE GUN YOU HAVE

I believe that a person who spends a lot of time hunting turkeys should have a special shotgun for turkey hunting. However, many gobblers fall each year to the standard 2¾-inch 12 gauge. If your only choice is to hunt with the gun you use for other game, consider these suggestions:
- Use the heaviest load your gun will handle.
- Pattern your gun and make sure you know what its limitations are.
- Use camo tape to cover a gun with a shiny finish so it won't spook the turkey.
- Be sure you can see the bead sight on the muzzle in low light.

RIFLES

In the East turkey hunting is primarily a shotgun sport, but in many areas of the West rifle hunting for turkeys is permitted. The rifles I recommend are the .222, .223, .22/250, and, at the maximum end of the scale, the .243.

Since any of these rifles can blow a turkey apart if the body is hit, the hunter should shoot for the head-and-neck region. The trick is to place the shot where the neck joins the body. The turkey's head is rarely still and is an extremely difficult target for a rifle. But where the neck joins the body, there's not as much movement. A bullet placed here will kill the turkey and not damage much meat.

The Steyr/Mannlicher Model SL-L Varmint Rifle in.222, .223, .243, .22/250 is a good choice for hunting for turkeys with a rifle in the West. (Photo by Gun South, Inc.)

The Steyr/Mannlicher Model L with half stock comes in .22/250 and .243 calibers for rifle turkey hunting. (Photo by Gun South, Inc.)

HANDGUNS

Handgunning for turkeys has become popular in recent years. The Thompson/Center Contender can be bought in many calibers, so many rifle hunters have switched to this type of handgun for hunting turkeys. Again, the target is not the body or head but the area where the neck joins the body.

In choosing a handgun, be sure to get one you can shoot accurately up to 50 yards. In the states that permit the use of handguns for turkeys (check your state regulations), I advocate using a scope, because it has good light-gathering capabilities for early morning shooting. I also prefer

Because you can change the barrels, the calibers, and even mount a scope on this Thompson Center Contender, this handgun makes an excellent turkey gun, with many options.

a jacketed hollow-point bullet. Some hunters advocate a solid-nose bullet, but I've seen turkeys hit with solid-nose bullets run a mile before they dropped dead. I prefer the jacketed hollow-point bullet because it will do much tissue damage and will shock the bird so he won't run off.

PATTERNING YOUR SHOTGUN

If you plan to hunt turkeys with a shotgun, you should know how it patterns at various ranges. Shoot several rounds at a turkey head-and-neck silhouette on a pattern board, from distances of 20, 30, 40, and even 50 yards.

From this exercise you can learn two things. First, you discover how far out your gun will deliver a killing pattern. When you know the limitations of your gun, you understand how close you must call a turkey before shooting. Second, you discover how well you can shoot from a sitting position. Don your head net, cap, gloves, and complete camo suit, sit down next to a tree or stump, and simulate the shot you would make if the silhouette were an actual turkey. Most beginners don't realize how difficult it is to shoot from a sitting position while wearing headgear and gloves.

JUDGING DISTANCE

No less important than the capabilities of your gun is your ability to judge distance.

According to studies done by the Army Artillery School at Ft. Sill, Oklahoma, no one has the inborn ability to estimate distance accurately. Even after intensive training, artillery spotters and forward observers are only about 30 percent accurate. So distance judging is something you must work at very hard.

Judging distances is even more complicated when you're sitting. I recommend that you and a friend take turns setting out turkey silhouettes for each other. When you set them out, measure the distances so you know exactly how far they are from the tree where your friend is sitting. He should then try to judge these distances. By playing this game, you can soon learn to judge distances in the woods much more accurately.

One of the biggest mistakes turkey hunters make is to shoot when the turkey is out of range. In the woods a big gobbler can seem much closer than he actually is. Unless the hunter has a better-than-average idea of how far he is from the turkey, he will shoot when the gun has no chance of killing.

A Ranging range finder is a valuable aid in judging distance. When

A Ranging Rangefinder helps hunters learn to judge distances to their birds. Look at a tree or bush in front of where you are and guess the distance. Then look through the Rangefinder and find out how close to the correct distance you judged. The ability to judge distance correctly from where the hunter is sitting to the tom often is the difference between bagging and not bagging a bird. Most hunters underestimate distance and shoot at gobblers that are outside the killing range of their shotguns.

you set up on a turkey, you can look through the range finder and determine the distance of various trees in the area. Once you know which trees the turkey has to pass to be in range, you can determine when to shoot.

Distance judging is something you should practice year round. While walking down the street, try judging the distance to a power pole, parking meter, fireplug, or garbage can. Then pace off the distance to determine how accurate you were.

When you see a gobbler in full strut, you're under a lot of pressure and may misjudge the distance, especially in unfamiliar surroundings. Even though you have the right gun and shells, and know how your gun patterns, misjudging the distance usually means missing the turkey.

SLINGS

Slings for a shotgun are important to some hunters but not to others. If you must travel a long way in the woods, a sling can be a real advantage. I don't use a sling myself until I kill a gobbler. When you kill an 18-pounder with inch-long spurs way back in the woods, you have a job getting him out. I use the sling to carry my gun so I can switch my load back and forth.

THE BEAD ON THE SHOTGUN

Most turkey hunting is done in poor light. A bead sight that can be easily seen in such light is vital. If your bead is difficult to see, paint it a bright, luminous color.

Sitting for a long time and leaning back against the rough bark of a tree can cause a hunter to fidget, which may spook a turkey. Ben Lee is using a comfortable backrest here. His camo hat and headnet make his face seem to vanish. A headnet and gloves also help ward off insects.

How to Dress

by John E. Phillips

I've seen people hunt turkeys in everything from brogans and overalls to tennis shoes and short-sleeved shirts. As soon as you start explaining to a turkey hunter how he should dress, he'll begin to tell you why that particular type of clothing won't work. What hunters wear into the woods is about as personal as whether they prefer jockey shorts or boxer shorts. However, I think the majority would agree that something special should be worn to hunt *Meleagris gallopavo*.

To start with, buy underwear shorts that fit. If you've put on an extra 10 to 20 pounds since you last bought underwear, the waistband on that underwear—whether jockey or boxer shorts—will make you extremely uncomfortable when you sit scrunched up for a long time while hunting. The same advice applies to women turkey hunters.

And don't wear your usual white T-shirt. Get a green one, similar to Marine Corps issue and available at Army-Navy stores, or a camo T-shirt of the kind that dove hunters wear. If you're turkey hunting in cold country where long underwear is required, wear it next to your chest and put the camo T-shirt over it. I recommend Duofold or Thermax long underwear, which keeps you warm while wicking away perspiration. This characteristic is especially important on cold mornings when you make long walks or when you run to get in front of a turkey. Such activity will cause you to perspire. Then when you sit down and are still, you'll become extremely cold unless that perspiration is wicked away from your body.

Be sure you have comfortable socks. The early-morning dew can be very cold, and socks that will keep your feet warm cannot be overrated. The same system that mountain climbers use to keep their feet in condition will work for turkey hunters in colder areas. Climbers put polypropylene socks on first, to wick away moisture. Over these they wear cotton or wool socks, for warmth. When hunting in the South, you may wish to wear only one pair, either polypropylene, cotton, or wool.

Next you must consider outer garments. If you're hunting in snow country, I recommend 10-X's down-filled camo coveralls or something of

85

Left: **Mixing camo to match the woods you plan to hunt makes for better concealment. Fred Darty, pictured here, wears face camo paint. Darty's tiger-striped shirt matches the tree that he has been leaning against. The leaf pattern on his gloves and pants blend in well with leaves.** *Middle:* **The woodland pattern of Fred Darty's clothes resembles the trees and leaves in the background.** *Right:* **Here the camo pattern does not blend in with the background. Even though the pants of this suit may fairly closely resemble the fallen leaves, where Darty is sitting, the jacket would contrast with tree bark. Thus a tree-bark-patterned jacket would have served better here.**

equal quality. Remember that you'll be sitting absolutely still, totally exposed, maybe for hours at a time. You need some type of outer garment that can break the wind and keep you warm.

If you're hunting spring gobblers, lightweight camo pants and a camo shirt or coverall suit are appropriate. Most veteran turkey hunters carry two or three different colors of camo so they can match the environment where they're hunting. If there's a lot of spring green-up, then a green camo suit may work best. For hunting in a pine forest with very little greenery on the ground, either Trebark or brown camo will be better. For hunting in snow country, white camo is a must.

Most experienced turkey hunters often mix their camo. For instance, they wear Trebark or brown camo pants to resemble the forest floor, and a green jacket or shirt to blend with the foliage. The basic thing to remember in choosing camo is to match it to the terrain that you'll be hunting.

Most turkey hunters deck themselves out in camo but forget one of the most important parts—their boots or shoes. I like the 10-X camo leather boots because they're lightweight, warm, water repellent, and comfortable, and they have a brown sole. The color of your soles is critical. If they're yellow or white and you sit with your feet propped up until you spot the turkey, often the turkey will see them and be spooked. Another recommended kind of boots, suitable for warm weather, is American Footwear's uninsulated, leather and Gore-Tex camo boot, which is very lightweight.

Also, camo tennis shoes ideal for some types of turkey hunting are now available. They're comfortable and quiet. They provide little or no snakebite protection, however, and most of them do not repel water.

Your hands must also be camouflaged. Otherwise they resemble white flags being waved. To camouflage your hands, you can paint them or wear camo gloves. I prefer thin, lightweight, knit gloves to any other type, for a couple of reasons. They permit my hands to breathe, and also prevent them from being attacked by mosquitos.

Your head is another exposed region. And there are several schools

Left: In woodsy areas, Realtree camo blends-in better, especially after leaves have fallen. As shown, veteran hunter David Hale may call a while and listen for a turkey to answer before donning his headnet. *Right:* Although this hunter blends in with the hillside on either side, he stands out from the dark tree trunk. A darker shirt would have served better.

of thought about hunters' heads. One school advocates covering your face with camo paint, which allows you to hear and see without interference. And since you need all the advantages you can muster to bag a woods wizard, this idea has great merit. Another school advocates a camo face net that leaves your neck, ears, eyes, and forehead exposed, but does give some protection from mosquitos. The third school of thought is a mixture of these two. You wear a camo head mask that covers your face, neck, and ears, and a camo hat that you pull down just above your eyes, which may have black and green paint around them. Your ears and eyes are unobstructed.

My own preference, however, is a full camo head net that covers the entire head and neck and has eyeholes. In most of the areas where I hunt, mosquitos are abundant. Even though I use an effective repellent, I don't like the little critters thinking they have a chance to gnaw on my hide. And I don't enjoy them buzzing close to my ears. With the net I am not nearly as tempted to swat a mosquito as I am without it. For me the head net is a security blanket.

The last part of your body to camouflage, and the most difficult, is the whites of your eyes. Many a keen-eyed gobbler has spotted a hunter's eyeball moving from side to side, sounded the alarm putt, and run off.

Tucked in against the base of this large tree, these two hunters in camo are almost invisible.

A camo blind like the one pictured allows the hunter to move without being seen. With a few holes cut in the blind, the hunter has the option of shooting through it or over it.

The successful hunters I know, when they're hunting a mature gobbler, will squint to keep the whites of their eyes from shining.

Yet another piece of gear often overlooked but critical for many hunters is eyeglasses. I've known hunters who buy all types of clothing and equipment but then leave their glasses at home, so no one will know they're not Old Eagle Eye. However, hunters who can't see well are at a disadvantage in turkey hunting. If you're serious about bagging a turkey and suspect you have a problem with your vision, have an eye exam before you ever buy the rest of your gear. If you need glasses, wear them.

Also, if you can't hear well, you're probably wasting your time and the turkey's time when you're in the woods hunting. Hearing aids are not necessary for some hunters, but are an asset for others. Don't hesitate to get a hearing aid if you need one. I know hunters with perfect hearing who have purchased hearing aids to amplify the sounds in the woods. Wearing the aids enables them to hear turkeys in the distance that other hunters can't.

Insect repellent is another essential item of equipment. Any of the brands that advertise 100 percent DEET will usually repel mosquitos, redbugs, and ticks if you spray your ankles, waist, armpits, hands, and your entire head. Allow the repellent to dry before you pick up your gun. A repellent with that much DEET can damage the finish.

Author John Phillips carries these items in his camo fanny pack: (left to right) an Olympus XA camera, which is a lightweight automatic 35mm; a Mag Lite, a small lightweight flashlight; a film canister containing matches and a striking board; a Noble police whistle to give the kee-kee run in the fall (with ball removed) or to use with ball in if he is lost or injured; a space blanket in case he must spend the night in the woods, two tubes of camo makeup, a compass, a Coleman Roughcut knife, some rope, a bottle of Chigger-Rid for the bad bugs in the spring woods, and a binocular. (Sara Bright photo)

OPTIONAL EQUIPMENT

Although most hunters consider the following equipment optional, I think most of it is a necessity.

● A lightweight fanny pack. Easily carried, this provides a place to put additional gear.

● A compass. This should be a part of any turkey hunter's gear. Always take a compass reading before you enter the woods. When you're attempting to catch up with an old gobbler, becoming disoriented is easy. I know several hunters who had to spend a night in the woods because they went in without a compass.

● A couple of candy bars, a length of rope, additional camo paint and insect repellent, a space blanket, matches, a flashlight, something to carry the turkey in, a knife, and a lightweight binocular such as the green, armor-coated Simmons.

● Extra calls. The serious turkey hunter usually carries three or four extra calls in addition to his main call, for use when needed to bring an old gobbler into gun range.

In turkey hunting you must often move quickly and quietly through the woods, and cover great distances. But all the above equipment is lightweight and compact, so it won't overburden you or impede your progress.

Part **2**

CALLING
TURKEYS

As this caller gives the lost call, you can almost hear the pleading emotion he puts into his calling.

Talking Turkey Does Not Equal Taking Turkey

by John E. Phillips

Sitting in the back of the gymnasium where a turkey-calling contest was being held, I listened to two spectators in front of me.

One of the men was clad in faded overalls and had a toothpick behind his right ear. From the lump in his left cheek and the frequency with which he spat into a Coca-Cola bottle, I assumed his tobacco was getting quite a workout. The man sitting next to him wore a well-tailored suit and had nicely groomed hair. The exactness with which he spoke hinted that he might be a salesman. The two men were contrasts in vocation and education, yet both were turkey enthusiasts.

Speaking of a teenage caller, the tobacco chewer said, ''Now that last caller gets my vote as the best in the contest. They'd better lock the back door of the gym, or else all the turkeys that heard him calling will rush in here and jump on that young boy.''

The businessman agreed and they both laughed.

The next caller in the contest, an old hunter, was a shy fellow. Timidly he gave the required calls on an old slate box. Then he used a cedar box that looked worn-out.

''That guy never will make it as a caller,'' the businessman observed. ''He'll scare off more turkeys than he'll call up.''

The man in the overalls chuckled. Although by most contest standards the last caller had not performed very well, the two spectators in front of me did not know everything.

The teenage caller they admired was a master musician all right. For the past three years he had bought tapes, listened to veteran turkey-calling professionals, and then practiced and trained to be a competition caller. Four afternoons a week after school, he had taken his mouth yelper out of the little tin he carried it in, and practiced. Each sequence of calls had to be perfect. Every note had to be clear and distinctive. He had gone to his school gym to practice so he would know how much volume was required. The calls had to be loud enough for the judges to hear, but not too

Big trophies are now being awarded for contest calling. As MC I've awarded some handsome prize money too. A caller can earn $1000 for a win, besides prestige and a possible contract with a call company.

loud. Yet although he was a master musician, he had bagged only three turkeys in the last two years.

The contestant whom the businessman and the man in overalls had criticized, spent very little time with his calls. A week before the season began he took his calls out of the closet and began to test them. Instead of practicing calling, he spent most of his time scouting and hunting turkeys. Each year he found several different gobblers to hunt during the opening week. He knew the turkeys personally. He knew where they would go and why. Years of experience in the woods had enabled him not only to fill his limit of five gobblers a year but also to call turkeys into range for friends and relatives. Many hunters said that the old woodsman "knew more about turkeys than a turkey does."

This old woodsman had been encouraged and persuaded by friends to enter the calling contest. "So many folks asked me to take part in it that I felt obligated," he explained.

When the contest was over, the teenager had won a trophy. But the old hunter was not even called back for the final elimination round.

The fact that a hunter can warble like a sexy hen does not mean he can cause an old gobbler to lose his head. The hunter who bags his limits of bronze barons each season may finish in last place in a turkey-calling contest.

"Turkey hunting and turkey calling are two different sports," says Harold Knight of Cadiz, Kentucky. "A good hunter may be able to take his gobbler 30 percent of the time by not calling. He knows where and when a gobbler is likely to show up on a given morning in the spring. By simply being at the same place at the same time as the turkey he can bag him without calling."

Left: **By cupping his hands over his mouth, Hunter Burns can throw the sound of a mouth yelper from behind a screen on stage to the judges who are usually seated on the floor away from the stage. When Burns gives the fly-down cackle, he uses his cupped hands to turn the call away from the judges, imitating the sound of a hen flying from her roost.** *Right:* **Standing behind a screen so that he can't be seen by the judges, Kenneth McLeod uses a diaphragm mouth call to give the kee-kee run. McLeod uses his hand to throw the call, much the way a ventriloquist throws his voice. The lanyard around McLeod's neck holds a snuff can (tube) call. Often competition callers will utilize several different calls.**

Let's take a look at the two kinds of people who pursue these separate sports.

First, the turkey hunter. His number-one ambition is to find and take a turkey. To achieve this goal consistently, he must learn volumes about the birds he plans to hunt. He has to know the intimate sex life of an old gobbler during the spring, and understand the flocking habits of turkeys in the fall. He must discover where a gobbler roosts, feeds, meets his mate, struts, and travels. He must learn how to lure an old gobbler away from his harem, how to bag one that's hunter-wise and call-shy, and how to circle a gobbler and arrive at a place in the woods where the gobbler naturally wants to go.

Then—and only then—the hunter must be able to give calls that will cause a turkey to come into gun range. He has to decide how many calls to give and when to be quiet and wait. If his game plan works, the prize is a fat gobbler standing within range.

The contest caller, on the other hand, never has to enter the woods. Although most good callers are also superb hunters, hunting skills are not needed to win turkey-calling contests. Mastery of one or more calls is the contest caller's key to success. Practicing for hours, listening to tapes, and talking to judges and other contestants all help to produce proficiency in calling.

Even though the sport is named turkey calling, the contest actually is "judge calling." The contestant who the judges think sounds most like a hen turkey will be declared the winner and receive a trophy. But who knows what a hen turkey really sounds like?

Some of the worst calling I've ever heard has come from hen turkeys. Several tendencies of live hens would eliminate them from today's calling

Kenneth McLeod uses a tube call to cutt. Often the contestants stand in front of the audience and the judges will be seated behind a screen. In other contests, the contestants will call from behind a screen, and the judges will be seated in the audience.

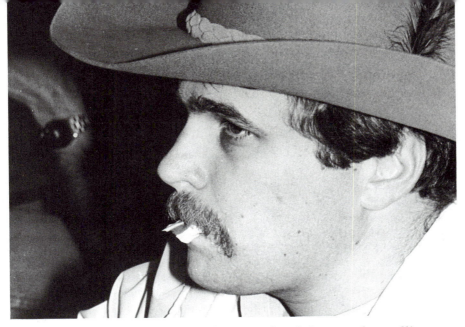

Winner of the Dixie National and International Open turkey calling contests, Bob Dixon may keep his diaphragm call in his mouth an hour or two before the contest. A contest caller wants his diaphragm call to be as comfortable in his mouth as a good pair of false teeth.

contests. Many times their rhythm is not smooth, their voices may be very coarse-sounding, and often they call too much.

I've also heard renowned turkey takers in contests. These super hunters often fail to make the final rounds. Yet judging from the beards and spurs hanging from their barns doors, they have shown they can call wild turkeys.

Judges at turkey-calling contests are much like historians. Sometimes history is a fable agreed on by a few and taught as fact to many. And so it is with the mating call of the hen turkey. Several men known as judges will find in one contestant certain characteristics of a call they prefer. The majority of the judges will agree that this contestant's style sounds the most like a hen turkey. But whether the calls actually do sound the most like a wild turkey hen is debatable. On a different day, the same set of judges hearing the same group of callers might award the prizes differently.

A good parallel to turkey hunting versus turkey calling is cowboying versus rodeoing. Real cowboys may ride horses and sometimes rope steers. They have broken horses and may have ridden a bull or tried to bulldog a steer—but usually just for fun, to break the monotony of their work. Their main job is to take care of the cattle. But the rodeo cowboy rides, ropes, and performs for the judges in much the same way the turkey-calling contestant performs his calls. The turkey hunter's main job, however, is to outsmart the turkey and bag his bird. Calling is only one of the tools he employs.

Though the sports of turkey calling and turkey hunting do overlap somewhat, expertise in one is not mandatory for success in the other. Nor is one sport better or more glamorous than the other. No successful hunter should feel less of a sportsman because he never wins a turkey-calling contest. Nor should a champion caller feel inadequate for not filling his limit of birds each season.

Personally, I advocate both sports. I enjoy pitting my skills against the old woods wizards each spring. Through my mistakes, the turkeys teach me new techniques of hunting every time I face them in open competition. The turkey wins most of the time—but every now and then I win.

I also enjoy paying an admission fee and listening to some of the best turkey talkers in the country sing those lovely melodies that make the hair on the back of my neck stand up. I'd rather hear good turkey calling than any concert performed by professional singers. Also, I like to try to pick the winners.

I think there are several reasons why turkey-calling contests have gained so much popularity:

• You can call turkeys even when you can't hunt them. Most hunters like to fool around with turkeys. They like to hear turkeys answer a call, walk into range, and strut even if these callers don't have a gun. And contests are another place where you can practice calling turkeys—even if the season isn't open.

• A contest caller can enter an event and test his calling skills in a competition with other hunters from his area and around the nation. He can hear how his calling compares to that of some of the best callers in the country.

• Contests provide an opportunity for enthusiasts to get together and trade information on new calling and hunting techniques. The classic example is a new call—cutting—that was introduced in competition a few years back. Cutting is an exciting call similar to the beginning of the fly-down cackle, but continuing much longer than the cackle. This call not only excites judges and wins trophies, but also turns on the gobblers and brings them running to the guns in many instances.

• A hunter can find understanding of his turkey insanity at a calling contest. Most spouses can't understand why a hunter can easily awaken at 3:00 A.M. during turkey season when waking him up at 7:00 A.M. the rest of the year ordinarily takes 30 minutes. Bosses can't understand why a turkey hunter will be late to work and feel no shame because a cantankerous gobbler took an extra 30 minutes to work within range. But at a calling contest there is a mutual bond among these hunters.

We are doubly blessed because the turkey has given us two sports, hunting and calling, both of which are deeply rooted in our country's history. So the next time you go to a turkey-calling competition and hear a caller who sounds as if he doesn't have a chance of winning, don't be too critical. That particular caller may be the one of the best turkey hunters in the contest.

Henning and
Gobbling

with J. Wayne Fears

*I*n a state like Alabama, where I do most of my hunting, there are plenty of turkeys. So roosting one in the afternoon is not nearly as critical to success as it is in many other states.

MORNING HUNTING

To find a gobbler in the morning, I generally use a Lohman's crow call. I know a turkey gobbles not necessarily because he's looking for a hen, but because he has a hormone called testerone in his body that brings on the mating urge in the spring. All night while he holds onto a limb, the hormone is flowing through him. By the next morning, he has so much energy stored that any high-pitched noise will cause him to release it in the form of a gobble. A .22 rifle going off, a train passing by, a car door being slammed, even a radio in the distance—any of these will make him gobble.

Over the years, I've learned that blowing a Lohman crow call four times very loudly will cause a turkey to gobble more than any other call will, including owl and hawk calls. The pitch is the key. The fact that you're using a crow call really has nothing to do with the turkey's gobbling, because he's just reacting to the pitch. You're not actually trying to imitate anything. You're merely trying to hit the pitch that will cause the turkey to release his energy with a gobble.

Adjust the reed in the crow call so you get the highest pitch it can make. The best way is to move the reed so far it will make no sound at all, then back it up to the point where it makes a very high-pitched *caw-caw*.

Once you've located a turkey, any of several calling techniques will work. One of the hardest turkeys to call is a boss gobbler that may have

A crow call helps locate a gobbler in the morning. J. Wayne Fears suggests adjusting the reed in the crow caller so that he can produce as high a pitch as possible. (Sara Bright photo)

as many as 20 hens with him. This old boy has all the hens he can take care of, and the hunter who tries to call him using traditional tactics will fail most of the time. A boss gobbler may gobble at your calling, but then he'll just walk off with the hens he's collected. Why should he walk across the street to check out a new hen when he has 20 beauties all around him? The only way you can kill this turkey is to challenge his manhood.

To perform this feat two hunters are needed. Your hunting buddy needs to be able to gobble—either on a gobbling box or with a tube he can shake. The best method is to go into the woods before daylight. Once the boss begins to gobble, have your hunting companion get on one side of him with the box or tube, and place yourself on the other side and plan to utilize hen calls. When that gobbler pitches out of the tree, he'll usually land around the hens he can already see. As you begin to yelp and cluck, he'll probably gobble at you, but more than likely he won't leave his harem.

Once the turkey is on the ground gobbling, your buddy should start to gobble. The turkey will become annoyed as he hears that other turkey (your buddy) gobbling and hears you yelping. Generally, he'll start moving toward the gobbling. When this happens, you need to start yelping loudly. I usually do a series of loud yelps followed by a cackle. The old gobbler will probably decide not to fight the gobbler he's heard, but instead will head toward what he thinks is a hen ready to be serviced.

Your hunting companion should wait three or four minutes after he hears your loud yelps. Then he should give another gobbling call. When that happens, the old gobbler will gobble, turn, and head where he believes there's another gobbler. At that point, you should give several cackles followed by several yelps. When you do all that cackling, the old gobbler gets so frustrated and worked up he'll often break to run toward you. Nine times out of ten, he'll come to the hunter who makes the hen calls. But every now and then, he'll head toward the hunter who does the gobbling.

This tactic puts a lot of pressure on an old gobbler because it gives him two things to worry about. His manhood is challenged by another gobbler that may be moving in to take over his harem, and a hen is just out of sight waiting to be serviced. So the old boy gets terribly, terribly frustrated and often has to make a hasty decision. He knows he has to go one of two ways. What he usually decides to do is service the hen first and possibly fight the gobbler later. But if he thinks he can run the gobbler off quicker and easier than he can service the hen, the hunter who's doing the gobbling may get the shot.

This is the best technique I know for taking a hard-to-kill boss gobbler. You must confuse him. The hunter doing the gobbling has to be certain he's well-protected by a big tree, so there's no chance another hunter will mistake him for the gobbler he's trying to call.

Nathan Connell and I used this tactic on a turkey we named Big Ben Tom, a gobbler with 1¼-inch spurs and a 12-inch beard. I'd tried for over two weeks to kill that gobbler and never could because he had more than 20 hens. Finally, Connell took the gobble box and went on one side of the turkey, and I waded a slough and got on the other side. When we took Big Ben Tom, he weighed only 16 pounds and had very few feathers on his underparts. I believe he'd just about mated all the hens he could mate. What made him come in was the thought that one more hen was ready for him and that another gobbler might get to her first.

If you don't have a buddy, there's a different method you can use on a boss gobbler with hens. First, try to determine the direction he pitches off his roost and the direction he usually moves early in the morning. Then move in close to the roost, locate him with a light tree call, and wait for daylight. You can give a few more yelps to make sure you've got him gobbling and ensure he knows where you are. Next, try to determine when the hens with him are likely to fly out of the tree. Then give a loud flydown cackle. With your gloved hand, pat the side of your leg to imitate the sound of a hen flying out. (The best way to learn how to make these calls is to listen to tapes and to practice imitating the calls.)

The gobbler sitting up there on a limb thinks this is the first hen that's

If you can find a gobbler displaying on the field in the afternoon, chances are good that you can call him to the gun if you know how.

flown down that morning. He thinks she's ready to be mated and she's in the direction he wants to travel. Usually he'll pitch out of the tree and come to you without hesitation. As a matter of fact, when you give that fly-down cackle and pat your leg, you'd better have your gun up and be ready to shoot. That gobbler may just pitch right into your lap.

AFTERNOON HUNTING

In the states that permit afternoon turkey hunting, I've discovered a tactic that's almost sure to work. Turkeys like to get out in fields to feed, strut, and eat bugs in the afternoons. If possible, position yourself on a rise where you can see many fields, clear-cuts, or pastures where turkeys may be. Then use a spotting scope to locate turkeys and watch what they do.

What you usually see, if you find a flock, is gobblers and hens feeding together. What you should look for, however, is a gobbler strutting. He'll usually be off to the side of the other turkeys and doing a lot of displaying. This gobbler is a subdominant male and probably hasn't mated that morning. He's trying to impress some of the hens, so they'll leave the gobblers they've been mating with and permit him to breed them.

Once you spot a gobbler like that at a great distance, put on all your camouflage gear, circle him, and try to sneak within calling distance. Set up in the edge of some woods looking out into the field, and begin your calling with a series of yelps. Pause 10 to 15 minutes between yelps, so you give the impression of being a hen that doesn't belong to the flock and has just walked near it. Usually you'll get the attention of the gobbler that's been displaying. He'll look for you, but he won't come to your calling.

Once you're comfortable in a good shooting position, give a really commanding cackle as though you're ready to be bred, and follow this with a series of yelps. After you cackle and yelp one to three times, that subdominant gobbler will usually break from the flock and come to you on a dead run. Remember he's looking for a hen that doesn't belong to the flock and hasn't been serviced that morning. Since he's the subdominant gobbler, he's going to try mating with that hen before one of the boss gobblers decides to mate with her or before she's sucked into the flock.

This technique works really well in the afternoons or in the late mornings. If you can find a gobbler that continues to strut, and if you can get close enough to call him without going out into the field, he'll usually be an easy turkey to take. But every gobbler is different, and each situation calls for a different tactic. That's the reason I like to hunt turkeys.

Wilbur Primos has found that the most reliable call for early mornings is a turkey's wing flapped so it hits a few bushes and some of the leaves on the ground. Primos says that this trick gets a response 80 percent of the time. (Sara Bright photo)

Mastering Turkey Talk

with Wilbur Primos

Most turkey hunters understand the basic language of the turkey, but not the subtleties of that language. Often the subtle variations in the volume, rhythm, and pitch of a turkey's call mean just as much as the kind of call it is. In some cases, they may mean even more. The most skillful turkey hunters—the masters of the sport—know how to add these subtleties to their calling.

THE TREE CALL

Although some hunters name this call the tree yelp, I believe it's as much a cluck as a yelp. When I try to describe it to somebody, I say it's a muffled yelp made in a monotone. The tree call is a hen's way of yawning when she wakes up in the morning.

This call is usually the first sound a gobbler hears from a hen each day. The gobbler has been in that tree all night long thinking about sex. When he hears that yawn and knows his sweetheart is waking for the day, he really gets charged up. If you hear a tree call in the morning when you've slipped into the woods, you realize you'll have competition from a hen for that gobbler. Just join in with a tree call yourself, and try to be a part of the flock.

Many hunters give a tree call the first thing in the morning, when the woods are still dark. But this really lessens their chances, especially if they're hunting a river bottom or flat ground fairly close to the gobbler. When a gobbler sitting half-asleep in his tree hears a tree call on the ground, he'll often be spooked. I believe he wonders what a hen could be doing on the ground when there's not enough light to see. A gobbler will be very cautious of any hen like that.

Never give a tree call until the woods brighten up. Remember also that if no hens are calling, there probably aren't any close to the gobbler. If you give a tree call, he'll wonder what's going on, because he didn't hear a hen fly up close to him before dark. He's had no contact with a hen—then all of a sudden one calls before daylight. An experienced old gobbler may be spooked off if you try a tree call before daylight.

THE HEN-TURKEY–WING CALL

The most reliable way to get a gobbler's attention in the early morning is to call him with a hen turkey wing. I use a hen wing because a gobbler wing is too stiff and large to produce the right sound. I flap that wing so it hits a few bushes and some leaves on the ground. This sounds like a hen that's just flown or walked into the area and begun to flap her wings, in the same way you stretch your arms in the morning.

Eight out of ten times, this flapping call will get a response from the gobbler. He'll either gobble or fly down. Then I use a series of soft yelps. Once you begin to think like turkeys, you can begin to understand their calls, and you're better able to communicate with them.

THE LOST CALL

Another call is the lost call—which is different from yelps, because this one has yearning in it. The lost call means "I want you to come to me, or I want to come to you. I don't want to be here alone." I use the lost call primarily in the fall, after I've scattered a flock of turkeys. I rarely use it in the spring.

The difference between a lost call and a long series of yelps is the slight tonal changes you make when giving the lost call. If a lost call doesn't sound pleading, it's not a good one. What separates the master callers from the hunters who merely call is that the masters put life and emotion into their calls. The slightest difference in inflection can completely change the meaning. When you hear the lost call in the woods during the fall, you know there are turkeys out there searching for one another. If you give the lost call, you can reel them in as though they were on a string.

THE YELP

In meaning, the yelp is probably the most complicated call. It can be a coy, contented call that a hen gives when she walks around feeding on

When the dominant hen gives the lost call, she calls the flock back together again, which means that the young gobblers will return where she is. Therefore if a hunter can scatter a flock of turkeys in the fall and then give the lost call like a dominant hen, he can bring the jakes within gun range. (Don Domenick, Colorado Game, Fish and Parks Dept. photo)

grass, bugs, or acorns. A hen giving this contented yelp is like a woman saying, "I know you're over there, and I know you think you're hot stuff. But you don't flip my switch at all." The yelp can also be an excited invitation to a gobbler to come and make love. This excited yelp is like the response a woman may give when she's waited for an hour and then the telephone finally rings. She'll grab it and say, "Where have you been? I've been waiting for you!"

Both these types of yelps will call a gobbler into gun range. Sometimes only one type or the other will work on a particular gobbler, but a lot of the time either will work. The contented yelp may bring a gobbler in just as quick as the excited yelp—often even quicker.

Many old gobblers are like certain men. When a female is coy, they just have to come running to show off their stuff. They assume that, if she could actually see what she was missing, she'd be much more excited. So they really fall for that coy, contented yelp.

Yet another type is what I call the prospecting yelp. This is the one a hen gives when she's just trying to locate a gobbler. You can use it a few times while walking down a logging road or over a ridge, just to let a gobbler know that you're in his area and that you're available. This signals to him in much the same way as a woman walking down the street in a short red dress signals to men. When a gobbler answers your prospecting yelp, then you can decide whether to call him in with the coy, contented yelp, or the excited, come-on-over-big-boy kind of yelp.

THE CLUCK

Turkeys cluck for various reasons. There's a contented cluck the hen gives when she's out in a field chasing grasshoppers or other insects. Then there's the cluck that means real excitement, which the hen gives in a series when a tom gobbles.

This excited cluck can get hunters into trouble. If a hunter doesn't know how to give it properly, or if a turkey misinterprets it, it can sound like a putt. Actually, the putt is a variation of the cluck, but the putt means "Danger! Get out of here." To prove this point, I once played a turkey-calling tape to a yard full of turkey poults. Every one of them took off and hid, because for some reason they interpreted the cluck as a putt.

To tell the difference between the two, notice the pitch and sharpness of the call. If it's high pitched and very sharp, it's a putt. If it's not so high pitched and has a flatter sound, then it's a cluck. There's a fine line between the cluck and the putt.

For that reason, I never use a cluck to call a gobbler unless I follow it with a series of yelps. Then there can be no mistaking the call, because no hen is going to putt and then yelp. If I want to use only a couple of really excited clucks, I always throw in one or two yelps at the end. That way I won't frighten the gobbler off.

THE PUTT

The putt is the alarm call and is given when a turkey is upset or frightened. It sounds like a pair of two-by-fours being slapped together. I've seen turkeys putt at snakes. I've seen them putt and leave a field as a deer walked into it.

I've watched a turkey walk toward a hunter, see his silhouette, give one or two putts, and walk off. The hunter didn't even move. The turkey didn't know exactly what the silhouette was, but realized something wasn't right. If he had seen the hunter move, he would probably have given several excited putts and either flown or run off.

THE KEE-KEE RUN

A young turkey doesn't come equipped with adult turkey language, and has to use the calls he or she is able to make. The kee-kee run is like the words of a child just learning to talk. It's the call that a young hen or gobbler makes when attempting to yelp, but the sound is more like whistling than yelping.

Young turkeys use the kee-kee to locate their mamas or the rest of the flock. But it's not just a call they use when they're lost. They also use it when they're milling around in a flock together.

Most hunters use the kee-kee run in the fall. They bust up a flock of turkeys, then try to call them together and draw a gobbler into gun range. But I use the kee-kee in the spring as well. It's especially effective for old toms that are reluctant to gobble. A tom will usually gobble in answer to a high-pitched call. When a crow flies over and gives a high-pitched call, a tom will generally gobble to it. Since the kee-kee has a high pitch, many times you can give it in the spring and make an older gobbler croak out a mating call. Also, some young gobblers will still kee-kee in the spring. So it's not out of character for a young gobbler to kee-kee then, and for an old gobbler to answer.

THE GOBBLE

The gobble is the mating call of the male turkey, given in the spring to attract hens. Many hunters overlook the gobble and fail to use it. But any hunter who wants to become a master will learn how and when to gobble.

The gobble is potent on old turkeys and young ones, but seldom effective on middle-aged turkeys. An old gobbler will get jealous when he hears a gobble, and will come in to fight. A young one, when he hears it, will assume there's a flock of turkeys in the neighborhood and will want to join them. A middle-aged gobbler, however, is usually reluctant to challenge an older gobbler or to fool with a younger one. Therefore, when you gobble you separate turkeys into age groups—those that will come and those that won't.

Very few hunters can gobble well with their mouths, but many can learn to gobble with a snuff-box call. By using your throat, your lips, and your finger to strum the inside rubber of the snuff box, you can make a very effective gobble. In my opinion, the best snuff-box call to gobble on is the Morgan call, because it's big enough to put your finger in.

Although many hunters use shaking-type gobbling tubes, the only one I have much confidence in is the Red Wolf gobbling tube. Often, a box caller is a very effective tool for gobbling. A realistic gobble is probably the most difficult call the hunter has to make.

DRUMMING

Drumming is a sound that gobblers make in the spring when they're strutting. It's a mating call. At times, I've been in the woods with hens in front of me, and then behind me I've heard a gobbler drumming. As I watched, the hens would come to attention and go running to him. For that reason, I know drumming is one of the turkey's mating calls.

A drumming call can sometimes be heard 150 yards away in the woods. The sound is made deep in the gobbler's chest and is very resonant and hollow. The best way to describe drumming is to say it sounds like an 18-wheeler shifting gears. Often, I've been in the woods and heard an 18-wheeler several miles away slow down and shift gears, and I haven't been sure whether I heard the 18-wheeler or a turkey drumming. The sound is *vroomm!*

Few hunters use the drumming call. But drumming can be practiced, learned, and used very effectively to take gobblers. The best way to learn what drumming sounds like and how to imitate it is to find a wild turkey in captivity, and watch him and listen to him in the spring. As you listen, practice the drumming sound with your mouth.

Often you can use a drumming call alone to get a gobbler to come to you. It's productive when an older gobbler hangs up 50 or 60 yards from you, and you can't decide whether to gobble at him or not. If he's a sub-dominant turkey, a gobble may run him off. I usually give the drumming call, and many times that will break him out of his strut. Even if he hasn't been strutting, it will bring him in to check out this other gobbler drumming near the hens he thinks he's heard.

Another kind of drumming, which most hunters completely overlook, is the kind a turkey does on his roost. A turkey doesn't have to be in full strut to drum, but he does have to hold his tail at least barely out and spread, and lay his head back. At times, I've seen turkeys strut and drum on the limb.

When the weather is inclement, or when dogs or hunters have harassed the turkeys, often turkeys drum rather than gobble. Most of the time, they'll be drumming on the limbs in the mornings before they fly down. If you listen for that drumming in the morning, many times you can find a turkey without having to hear him gobble.

THE CACKLE

Often, this call is mistakenly labeled the "fly-down cackle." Hen turkeys do use this call when they fly off the roost. But they also cackle when flying across a creek, when jumping from one small depression in the ground to another, or when expressing excitement for any other reason. Turkeys don't have any laid-down, concrete rules as to when they give a call. Sometimes they give one just because they want to.

Cackling is simply excited yelping. A hen turkey shows the degree of her excitement by how she gives her yelps. The cackle most hunters call the fly-down cackle, which a hen gives as she flies off the limb and hits the ground, is just her expression of joy at meeting the new day. She's been awake about an hour, and finally there's enough light for her to fly down and begin to eat, socialize, and mate. So naturally she's excited when she gets to jump out of that tree. To express her excitement, she cackles.

Another reason a hen cackles is that she knows mating time has arrived and she's excited about finding her gobbler. Actually, a hen will cackle

Primos feels the most effective time to cackle is when the gobbler is in the air. In the morning, Primos establishes his presence with the gobbler by giving a few soft yelps and beating a hen turkey's wing in the air and against trees and leaves. Then the gobbler believes a hen is on the ground. When Primos hears the tom fly out of the tree, he gives a strong, loud cackle as if to say, "I'm excited to hear you coming, and I can't wait for you to get here." (New York State Dept. of Environmental Conservation photo)

almost anytime she gets excited about anything. When you hear a cackle, you know that somewhere out there something exciting and intense is happening.

I believe the most effective time to use the cackle is when a gobbler is in the air. When I go to a gobbler in the morning, I establish my presence by giving a few soft yelps and beating a hen wing in the air. Then I beat the wing against trees and leaves so he knows I'm on the ground. And I listen for that gobbler to fly down. When I hear him start to fly I give a loud, strong cackle, as if to say, "I'm excited to hear you coming, and can't wait for you to get here." By cackling when I hear him fly down, I establish a strong bond with him.

I've discovered that by using this tactic I kill more turkeys in the first five minutes of hunting than I do at any other time. The cackle is so strong a gobbler can't resist coming. I've actually seen gobblers start to fly down, turn in mid-air when I cackled, and land right in front of me. So I think the most effective time to cackle is when you hear them leave the tree and they're still in the air.

CUTTING

Cutting is what the northern boys have decided to call what we in the South have always considered to be excited clucking. The call is still the same. Those Yankee hunters just decided to give it a newer and classier name. Cutting is a series of fast, excited clucks put together to show another degree of the hen's excitement.

The best way to explain what cutting means to an old gobbler is to relate it to what can happen at a bar. A man sits there on a stool beside a woman he's trying to pick up, and suddenly she gets excited. She throws her house key on the counter in front of him. Automatically, the man knows what's going to take place. When a hen starts to cut, a gobbler reads her as though she's just handed him her house key. That's the reason cutting is such a deadly call to use for an older gobbler.

THE WAVY CALL

This is another call often overlooked by hunters. I use the term *wavy* because the pitch changes as the call is given, starting on the crest of a wave and then sliding down the side and climbing halfway up the side of the next wave. A hen gives this call when she's extremely content—when the sun is shining on a spring or fall day, and she's way out in the middle of a field, far from danger, chasing crickets or grasshoppers and just happy to be alive. It's a feeding call, and the sound is sort of *pee-uuuu*.

I use this call with the basic yelps when I'm trying to act unconcerned about a gobbler. I want him to think I could care less whether he comes over where I am. Then he'll decide he has to influence me and show me just what a fine gobbler he really is, so I'll get excited and be ready to mate with him. When he comes to impress me, that's when I take him.

THE PURR

The purr is another contented call of the hen. She doesn't think *Now I'm going to give a purr,* but instead just gives it when she's happy. She's really not conscious of giving the purr.

The purr may compare best to a woman's humming. She's not humming because she means anything by it. She's just happy with her situation and her surroundings, and humming is the best way to express her contentment.

Many times, you can use the purr early in the morning to communicate to a gobbler that a hen is contented and has no intention of mating. This call will often cause him to come to the hen and try to get her interested in him.

What you must remember about using hen calls is the two attitudes a hen turkey may take when she hears a gobbler. One attitude is excitement. She's ready to breed and anxious for the gobbler to come and make love to her. The other is a coy, contented attitude. The hen doesn't really care who the gobbler is or where he is. Often, an old gobbler ready to mate will come to this kind of hen quicker than he will to an aggressive one.

But neither technique works on all gobblers. Some like the coy type of calling, while others prefer the aggressive, come-on-let's-get-it-on type of calling. Being able to determine which type of calling is best is what separates the master turkey hunters from the novices.

Gobble

Your Way

to a Tom

with Walter Parrott

A few years ago, two of us were hunting in Tennessee. We heard a turkey gobble, so we moved in to set up on him. I was going to do the calling. I had an older fellow with me who was planning to shoot. After less than five minutes of calling, the gobbler was within 50 yards. Then my hunting partner moved, and the turkey saw the movement. Although he wasn't spooked, he was confused by what he'd seen and wouldn't come on in.

As I continued to call and work him, he began to strut and drum. Then, off to my left about 200 yards, I heard another turkey gobble. The first turkey now seemed more interested in coming to my calling. But instead of trying to call him in, I turned my head slightly to the left and started calling to the second turkey, which I hadn't yet seen. In about five minutes, the second turkey came running toward us in a half strut, but I noticed that turkey number one wasn't coming to my calling. Instead he was heading straight toward turkey number two. As I watched, I figured turkey number one was the boss gobbler, because apparently he was more interested in fighting turkey number two than in coming to my hen calls.

When turkey number one got to turkey number two, they both walked out of sight. Since I didn't hear anything for a while, I began to call and got a gobble out of one of them. I believe turkey number one had run turkey number two off. Turkey number two must have decided the way to avoid getting whipped was to keep his mouth shut and try to find a sweetheart in another area of town.

Since turkey number one apparently wanted to fight, I gave a few hen calls so it would seem a hen was still in the region. Then I gobbled so it would seem another gobbler had moved in to mate with her. I did the gobbling on a snuff can, because I wanted the turkey to think the other gobbler was a young one with a high-pitched voice. Right away, the turkey gobbled back. I felt he wanted me to show myself before he came in, so I

Walter Parrott was calling to a tom that was strutting and drumming when he heard another turkey walking and gobbling about 200 yards away. But when Parrot's calling brought turkey Number 1 to turkey Number 2, they both walked out of sight. ("Bearded Bronze-Wild Turkeys," by Ken Carlson, courtesy of National Wild Turkey Federation, Inc.)

quit calling for about ten minutes. Then the old turkey started gobbling a little harder. I didn't call, because I wanted him to think the other gobbler had left.

Once again the turkey gobbled, and this time he seemed aggressive. I changed to a box call. Previously I'd been giving loud, aggressive hen calls with a lot of cutting and cackling. But now I gave soft, contented calls on the box. I wanted the old turkey to think a young gobbler had come in and taken most of his hens off while he was down the hill. But there was still one hen left that was just so contented she couldn't have cared less whether the boss gobbler was around. I gave some real light calls and then stopped for about ten minutes. After two series of these light calls the old turkey came in, and we took him.

Had we not used the gobble call and had the turkey not believed most of the hens had left with another gobbler, I don't believe he would have come on in.

A gobbling call is not a very safe call to use, especially in an area where there's a lot of hunting pressure. If the turkey you're trying to call is a juvenile, he'll hush and leave rather than come in to challenge an old boss gobbler. You must have some idea about the age of the turkey before you try a gobbling call.

On another hunt, I used a gobbling box to pull an old gobbler out of a flock of hens. I'd heard the gobbler and sat down to call, and then a little hen had come in. At this time I hadn't yet seen the gobbler. When the hen got in closer, I looked behind her. About 100 yards away, a gobbler was strutting on a ridge with four hens. At first I thought he would come on in to me, but then he turned back to his right and took his hens away.

I continued to call for an hour and a half. The old gobbler was fired up. He'd gobble back and answer me. But he had his harem with him, and he wasn't going to leave his home flock to check out a new hen. I

A box call can be shaken aggressively as shown. But you must be careful if you are hunting in areas of high hunter pressure. Sometimes a gobbling call will run a tom off. (Sara Bright photo)

could hear him mating with his hens when I was calling. I continued to call, and he kept on gobbling in answer. Finally, another hen came to me that I assumed was the boss hen. She looked me over pretty good and began to call. Then she walked away from me. When she got out of sight I called, and she cackled. I was playing with her more than anything else, but she was getting irritated and excited.

With all this racket going on, the old gobbler was staying where he was. I took my cedar box out and gobbled on it. I believe I made him think the boss hen had gotten out there and found herself another gobbler. Even though the boss gobbler had all the hens he could tend to, he just couldn't stand the pressure when I gobbled twice. He believed another gobbler had taken over his number-one lady, and his manly pride just couldn't handle that much of a challenge without doing something about it. He came strutting in, and at about 30 yards his ego met with a shot from my 12 gauge.

Most of the time, you shouldn't go into the woods planning to use your gobbling call. It's most effective when a turkey hangs up and you use it in conjunction with your hen calls. Usually, you want to create the illusion that a gobbler is moving in to mate with a bunch of hens just out of eyesight of the gobbler you're trying to work.

The gobbling call is also productive when you've already called up a group of hens and know there's a gobbler just out of sight listening to them. In this situation the hens do all the calling, and when they're not looking, you give a gobble. That gobbler will believe the hens he's been moving with all morning have found themselves another tom. He'll then come in to reassert his dominance over the flock.

The gobbling call differs from most other calls in this important respect: the situation dictates when you should use it. The mood of the gobbler, his age, and the position of the hens are key indicators as to when you should gobble. When all else fails, a gobble will often bring a bronze baron to the place where he can lose his head.

Firing Them Up——————————

with Bill Harper——————————

*I*n the spring, when hunters haven't been fooling with gobblers and trying to call them, my firing-'em-up tactic will produce one pretty quick. When I say "firing 'em up," I mean calling so aggressively and loudly that a gobbler just has to get excited.

Many times I hunt with a client. To fire up an old gobbler for him, I do a lot of loud cackling, yelping, cutting, and purring for two or three minutes. When I start firing one up, he'll often gobble only two or three times, or he may gobble 40 or 50 times. But sooner or later he'll shut up. Then I turn around, walk off, and leave him. Now that the old boy is all fired up, he's ready to mate. However, he's looking for a hen that's not there. And you can imagine what that does to him.

Usually, my client and I will back 50 to 100 yards farther from the turkey. I won't call again until he gobbles—which may be as soon as 30 minutes, or as late as two hours. When he does gobble, I start using some soft purrs and soft yelps. Often, he'll come at a quiet, sneaky run to us. He usually won't make any sound, because he is trying to sneak up.

I use this firing-'em-up technique when I have a client or friend I want to make sure bags a turkey. I'll go into an area, find some turkeys gobbling in the daylight, and do an awful lot of clucking and cackling to fire them up. I'm trying to get them red-hot for mating. Then I walk off and leave them, go pick up my client, sneak back into that area, and do some soft purring and soft calling. Sometimes the hunter will bag his bird within 30 to 45 minutes of the time we sit down.

One example of this technique is a hunt that happened a few seasons ago. Brad Harris, who works here at Lohman's calls, had located a turkey and fired him up one morning. Our sales manager had a client in and wanted him to kill a nice gobbler.

So Brad told the sales manager where to take the client and where to sit, and told him to give only a few light yelps and purrs. Less than ten minutes after the sales manager had begun to call, a 24-pound gobbler ran within six feet of the client, who bagged him. Now that client thinks my sales manager is one of the greatest callers who ever lived. He doesn't know that Brad had been out there firing that turkey up for an hour and a half before he got there.

One of the problems most hunters have with this technique is that walking off and leaving a gobbling turkey is hard. Their minds work like this: *I have the old turkey gobbling now. I know where he is, and he knows where I am. If I keep on talking to him, I'm bound to kill him. If I walk off and leave him, he may not be here when I get back.*

So these hunters continue to call to the turkey and don't kill him. To walk off and leave a gobbling turkey, believing you can come back and kill him later, takes nerves of steel and the kind of faith that moves mountains. But firing 'em up works.

Sometimes the hunter who kills the turkey is not the same one who fires him up. Often you can get your friends to fire turkeys up for you, then build your reputation as a turkey hunter by going in and killing the ones they couldn't kill.

As an example, I'll meet Leroy at the service station about 8:00 A.M., and he'll say to me, "Bill, I've been working this old gobbler all morning out on the back forty. He's gobbled 20 or 30 times, but he won't come in. He's been doing this for the last three or four mornings, and I still can't kill him. Do you reckon you could go down there and take him before he drives me crazy? I'll tell you exactly where he is, and how I've been calling to him."

And I'll answer, "Well, if doing that will help you out, I'll go and see if I can put that old boy out of his misery."

I'll wait for 45 minutes or an hour before I go out where Leroy has been doing all his calling. Then I'll sit down quietly and begin some soft clucking and purring. In just a few minutes, the old gobbler will usually walk up, and I'll kill him. Then everybody will think I'm one of the world's greatest turkey hunters, because I went in and killed the ornery gobbler that Leroy couldn't take. But Leroy actually did all the work, by getting the gobbler all fired up. I just went in and finished the job.

Many times a smart gobbler like this won't call when he walks up. So you have to be ready and looking. But I've taken many turkeys after other hunters have given up on them and gone on home. If you're hunting in an area with a lot of hunting pressure, and you hear a gobbler in a tree and then hear other people trying to call him, let them fool with him the first part of the morning. If they're good, aggressive callers, all they'll do is fire the turkey up for you. Then, when they have to go to work at 7:00 or 8:00 A.M., you can go back to the same area where they've been doing all that calling, and kill their turkey for them.

One place where I've tried to fire up many gobblers is along the Canadian River in Oklahoma, where I hunt the Rio Grande turkey. I once found an island in the river where hunting wasn't permitted and the turkeys

When a turkey gobbler begins to strut, he also makes a sound that is similar to an 18-wheel tractor trailer shifting gears in the distance—*Vutt-V-rooooom*. Even if the hen can't see the gobbler strut, she can hear him telling her just how big and strong he is. (Leonard Lee Rue III photo)

were holing up. So I got on a high ridge close to the river and called aggressively for about two hours. I was able to fire those old gobblers up so much that they flew across the river, where I could bag them.

When you're firing up gobblers like this, you may want to sound like a whole flock of turkeys. One way to do that is to keep switching to different calls. Another way is to use the 836 Lohman diaphragm caller, which can sound like an old hen or a young one and even give a young gobbler's squealing call. By using that one caller and changing the amount of air that goes over it, you can sound like a whole bunch of turkeys in one place.

Firing turkeys up is also extremely effective on rainy days. Turkeys just don't like to gobble in the rain. But if you know where a big gobbler is ranging, then go into his area and do some loud, aggressive cutting and cackling. Generally, he'll gobble at least once in response—although the first response may take an hour or more. After that, if you leave him alone for an hour and then do some soft purring and yelping, many times you can pull him right into range.

Turkeys that strut in fields in the middle of the day often are easy to fire up. In many cases, firing 'em up works when nothing else will. Novice hunters often will slip close to the edge of a field and try to call a strutting turkey into the woods. But most boss gobblers are not going to leave a field where there's safety to go find a hen in the woods. A gobbler realizes that hens can see him in a field strutting, and that they should naturally walk out to him if they want to mate. Therefore, calling him out of that field will be difficult.

However, the tactic that I use to kill a field gobbler is to force him to come after me. I like to get on top of a ridge away from the field. The gobbler can hear me, but may have to travel a great distance to get to me.

When I start all that cutting and cackling, the gobbler is standing down there in the middle of the field wondering what's going on up on that ridge. Many times I've seen a mature gobbler walk out of a field where he has hens and climb the ridge to find that exciting hen. Although the gobbler may require two or three hours to get up to where I'm calling, that's one of the advantages of the fire-'em-up technique. Instead of going to the gobbler, I make the gobbler come and find me.

Yet another advantage of firing up an old gobbler is that you can often take him even when he has hens with him. A boss gobbler may refuse to leave his hens to come find an excited young hen that's ready to mate. But what he will do—if you get him really fired up—is drive those hens toward you. Apparently he's thinking he can keep his harem and still pick up this new girl that's so excited.

Another instance where firing 'em up pays big dividends is when you find an old gobbler in his strutting zone, which may be on the side of a ridge, along the edge of a field, or someplace else where he regularly shows up. If you've hunted turkeys for a long time, you'll know you can often find one in these places around 9:00 or 10:00 A.M., after he's mated with his hens.

The turkey will be strutting, gobbling, and putting on a show. You can slam a car door or toot the horn, and the turkey will gobble. But he won't come to a call. When you find a turkey like that, if you fire him up for 30 minutes to an hour, then walk off, leave him, and come back later with some soft clucking and purring, many times you can kill him.

One of the most effective techniques is to fire up a turkey two or three mornings in a row before opening day. Get him red-hot each time and then leave, making sure he doesn't see you. On opening morning, go right back to that same turkey, fire him up again, and hush. Many times he'll come to you at a dead run, wanting to meet this girl who's talked to him every morning and then run off. This time he's determined to make her acquaintance, but he's likely to meet with lead instead.

So calling up a turkey is not very difficult. All you have to know is when to call, when not to call, and how aggressive or soft your calling should be.

Owl-Hooting the High Country

with Ray Eye

I scout aggressively where I hunt in the Ozark Mountains. By moving quickly from one ridge to another, I cover a lot of ground and find many turkeys. I never use a turkey call to scout. Instead, I owl-hoot. In my opinion, the owl hoot is the most misunderstood and underused call in the sport of turkey hunting. I've killed more turkeys because of hooting than because of turkey calling.

A turkey call invites the gobbler to come to you. When you're scouting, you want to know where the turkey is and you want him to stay there. If you yelp or cluck and the turkey is close to you, he'll come in, see you, and get spooked.

A turkey won't come to an owl call, but he will gobble to it. When he gobbles, you can move close to him and pinpoint his location without fear he'll come in to you. By owling and moving, I discover turkeys all day long—even at high noon. I've learned that a turkey that answers an owl will come to hen calls easier and quicker.

Owling is also safer than hen calling. I hunt areas where there's quite a bit of hunting pressure. Other hunters are looking for turkeys, and I don't want to be moving through the woods giving turkey calls. Once I sit down, with a tree wider than my shoulders at my back and a clear field of view in front, then I'll sound like a turkey—but not before.

One of the most important ingredients in taking a turkey is finding a good calling position. Once I locate a gobbler by owl hooting, I look for open woods where he'll feel comfortable walking. I always locate a turkey from a high ridge and then move down to him. I also search for a spot that won't let me see the turkey until he's in killing distance. When I see him, I want to be able to shoot. If I can't see the turkey, then he shouldn't be able to see me and there's less chance for error. The longer a turkey can look you over, the more likely he is to identify you and run off.

Owl hooting gets a gobbler's attention quickly and will often cause him to shock gobble but will not draw him to the hunter. By owl hooting, the hunter can find a good location at which to take a stand before calling the turkey. (Lovett Williams, Florida Game and Fish, photo)

I never use a hen call when I'm looking for a place to take a turkey. I prefer an owl call. Then I can keep up with his location without his coming and seeing me while I'm looking. I hoot to judge distance, to keep up with his movement, and to find the best calling position.

When I do make hen calls, I'm ready to shoot. If a turkey is visible to me, he should be dead.

Part **3**

TACTICS AND
TECHNIQUES

When the tom steps into his strut zone, the hunter, who has identified various strut zones, hopes to be there waiting for him.

Hunting the
Strut Zones

with Bill Harper

A strut zone may be a wheat field in Kansas, a river-bottom swamp in Alabama, a ridgetop in New York, or a shelf on a mountainside in Missouri. A strut zone is a place in the woods or in a field where a tom turkey likes to strut.

Hunters will always be able to see a tom in a strut zone during some time of the day, since that zone is his hangout. Sometimes he'll be fighting other gobblers there. This strut zone is where he likes to be and where he'll do a great deal of gobbling.

Usually a turkey will be in a strut zone at a certain time of day. He'll generally gobble, but he'll rarely come to calling when he's in the strut zone. It's a place where he likes to show off and display himself, because he feels safe and comfortable there. And he'll usually mate many hens in the strut zone.

In most cases a turkey will have more than one strut zone. For instance, he may have a strut zone 15 or 20 feet from his roost tree, where he likes to fly when he leaves the roost. He'll meet his hens, mate, and do some strutting there.

This tom may also have another strut zone along the edge of a creek, where he walks to get a drink of water after he leaves his roost strutting zone. This second strut zone may be ¼ to ½ mile from the first one. But again this is where the turkey likes to meet his hens, mate, and display.

After a gobbler leaves his watering site, he may like to walk up the side of a hill to a little terrace and strut there. After he's been there for a while, he may go down to a strut zone in a field. So a turkey's having one to six strut zones is not uncommon at all.

If left undisturbed, that turkey may make the same walk every day, going to each one of his strut zones in the morning and coming back through them in the evening, until he ends up close to his roost tree. Then he can fly up to roost just before dark.

I've found that if the turkey isn't interrupted he'll set a pattern of going to these different strut zones at the same time every day during the spring mating season. If you know that the turkey is going to show up in a strut zone, then all you have to do to kill him is be in the strut zone when he appears.

So the trick to successful turkey hunting is to locate the strut zones. And one of the best ways to do this is to spend a lot time in the woods. In disturbed pine needles or leaves on the forest floor, look for a figure-eight pattern made by a turkey dragging his wings as he struts. Also search for broken feathers and gobbler droppings in the area. The gobbler dropping will be shaped like a fishhook, while a hen dropping will be more elongated. When you find a place like this, you can be pretty certain you've discovered a strut zone. And with no other information, you should be able to sit there either in the morning or in the afternoon and have a better-than-average chance of seeing a gobbler walk up on you.

If you find that strut zone on the eastern side of a mountain, then you will pretty well know it's a morning strutting zone, because turkeys like to fly down in the morning on the sunny side of a hill, to warm up as soon as possible. They do most of their morning strutting on the eastern sides of hills, and most of their afternoon strutting on the western slopes of hills.

Hunters can search for a figure-8 pattern in disturbed pine needles or leaves on the forest floor to find where a turkey has been dragging his wings in his strut zones.

But there's a better way to find the strut zone than simply walking through the woods looking for a figure-eight pattern on the ground. I'm convinced you should go into the woods a week before turkey season comes in and get on a high ridge that may have finger ridges running off it. Give an owl hoot or a crow call or whatever you do to make a turkey gobble, and then listen for the turkey to answer back. Using a flashlight to see by, write down on a piece of paper the time of day that the turkey gobbled. Then try to move to within 100 yards of him. If you get within 100 yards and hear him fly out of the tree, put that information on paper.

As the gobbler moves, keep up with his location by either owl-hooting to him or climbing on a ridge above and watching him. I listen for the hens clucking as they come to the gobbler after he leaves the roost. I use my compass to determine which way the hens are coming from, and I write that fact down, along with the time. My entries may look like this:

6:06 A.M.—Tom turkey gobbles

6:15 A.M.—Tom flies down out of tree

6:25 A.M.—Hens come to tom from southwest.

The other piece of equipment I have with me before the season is a topographical map. As I'm determining these different directions with my compass, I mark on the topo map where I first heard the turkey gobble, the direction he flew down from, the direction the hens came from, the approximate place he met the hens, and other pertinent information. I plot all of these facts on the topo map so I begin to have a diagram of the turkey's daily routine.

Generally I continue to follow the gobbler a while. He may go to a creek, get a drink of water, and then begin to do a lot of gobbling and strutting. So on my topo map I note the strut zone and, just as important, what time the gobbler arrived there and how long he stayed. I also note how far this strut zone is from the closest road.

For instance, I may travel ½ to ¾ of a mile to the turkey before I first hear him gobble in the tree. Then I may follow him for ½ mile through the woods. But once I discover his strut zone, I may be only 200 yards from a logging road I can see on my topo map.

Let's say the turkey is in his strut zone until 9:00 A.M. Now I could continue to follow him the rest of the day and try to find all of his strut zones. But most mornings I won't be able to hunt past 9:00 or 10:00 A.M. Since I've already located this gobbler's strut zone and know which direction he comes from and which direction he leaves, what time he comes and what time he goes, I have enough information to kill him.

Once I've done my reconnaissance on a particular gobbler in a strut zone, I walk straight toward the turkeys that are in that area. They usually putt, run off or fly off, and I visually inspect this strut zone. Next I tie a little white piece of cloth to a tree or a bush about eye level right in the strut zone. I take a compass reading to determine the direction to the nearest road. Then I mark my trail with little white pieces of cloth as I walk out of the woods. When I arrive at the road, I lay a limb on the edge of the road or turn a rock over or leave some kind of mark I can see and understand but no other hunter will recognize.

Then the evening before turkey season opens, I go back to the place where I heard the turkey gobble early in the morning, and make sure he's still roosting in the same tree he was roosting in when I followed him. If I go back on opening morning and see a car parked right in the spot where I was listening for that turkey, then I know someone else is trying to hunt the same turkey and putting pressure on him. So I'm tickled to death.

I know that hunter will attempt to get within 100 yards of the turkey and try to call the gobbler to him. And more than likely he'll attempt to call from a direction the turkey doesn't want to go. If the turkey is an old smart one, a boss gobbler, he's probably heard calling before and won't go to this new hunter anyhow.

So all I do is head for the strut zone. I let the other hunter fool with the turkey early. I'm betting he won't kill the gobbler. As I go to the strut zone, I'm careful to remove all the little white pieces of cloth that I left before the beginning of season. Once I'm in the strut zone, I hoot like an owl—just to make sure the turkey is still in the tree. But I never give hen calls until I'm ready to kill the gobbler. I look at my watch. As soon as legal hunting time arrives, I start giving some light hen putts, which are called clucks by many hunters.

I start calling as soon as it's legal because that gobbler may have gotten flushed off the roost by a novice hunter. Instead of taking 45 minutes or an hour to get to his strut zone, that gobbler may show up in ten minutes. Another reason I start calling as soon as it's legal is that there may be another gobbler roosting within 50 yards of the strut zone.

If I don't hear any gobbling after giving a few soft putts and yelps, I become a little louder with my calling. If the old gobbler still doesn't answer, I give a loud mating cackle. If he gobbles back at me, I call with an aggressive cackle—letting him know I'm ready to meet him. When he gobbles back to that, I hush. As long as he's gobbling and walking toward me, I don't call to him. Sometimes that turkey will walk right on in, and I can kill him. But at other times he may stop 50 to 100 yards short of his strut zone and begin to gobble and drum.

Although this behavior makes many hunters think a turkey is hung up, actually he's not. He's just trying to get the hen to come to him. The trick now is to stay quiet and not move. The turkey may walk off to the right and gobble again. Often a hunter will turn to face the turkey, and in doing so will run the bird off. So instead of turning, stay absolutely still. This is the true test of a turkey hunter's nerve.

An eastern turkey may walk around his strut zone before he comes into it. Sometimes I've had a turkey come in from behind me, pass 6 or 7 feet from where I'm sitting, and walk right out in his strut zone. Once more the hunter must have nerves of steel. His instinct, when he hears a turkey behind him, is to turn quickly and shoot before the gobbler can run. But if the hunter stays still, more often than not the turkey will walk right past him and out in front of him. I've had a turkey so close to me that I actually had to squint my eyes to keep him from seeing the whites of my eyeballs.

But let's say that for one reason or the other, I don't kill the turkey. I may have spooked him or someone else may have come in and run him off before he could get to me. However, my day's hunting isn't over. Before the season, when I located this turkey, I also discovered six or seven more in other strut zones at other times. So I still have turkeys to hunt that day.

To find various turkeys in other strut zones, a hunter must scout all day long. I do a great deal of owl hooting. Then, when turkeys answer, say at 10:00 A.M., 1:00 P.M., 2:00 P.M., and 4:00 P.M., I mark their locations and the times on my topo map. Once I have five or six turkeys located in different places at different times, my hunting can really become exciting.

For instance, if a turkey I'm hunting in a strut zone gets spooked at 8:00 A.M. and won't come in where I'm set up, then that hunt is blown. But after consulting my topo map, I see that I have a 9:00 A.M. turkey three miles away. So I leave my small white cloth flags to mark the trail to my 8:00 A.M. turkey. Then I can find him the next morning. I go immediately to my car and drive to my 9:00 A.M. turkey and try to work him. If my 9:00 A.M. turkey doesn't gobble, or I don't see him or get a shot, I've got an 11:00 A.M. turkey six miles away and I can get in my car and drive there. By parking the car at the road closest to a turkey's strut zone, I can easily and quickly get from one gobbler to another.

So if you have seven or eight strut zones to hunt during a Saturday, the chances are about 99 percent that you will bag a turkey before the day is over at one of those strut zones. By keeping your appointment with the turkeys at the times they like to strut, you greatly increase your odds of bagging a bird. Even on a morning that's overcast or rainy, when turkeys don't want to gobble, you still have a 50-50 chance of bagging a gobbler if you have seven strut zones to hunt.

Another advantage to hunting the strut zone with this technique is that the turkey doesn't have to gobble in order for you to kill him. If you know what time he shows up and where, and if you take a stand close enough, you can often kill him without ever calling.

Hunting these strut zones may be the only way to kill an old boss gobbler that's been fooled with and possibly shot at by several hunters over two or three years. And once you spend the time to find a strut zone, you can usually kill a gobbler there every year, because of the pecking order of turkeys.

Once the dominant bird is killed from a strut zone, a subdominant bird will then exert dominance, picking up the old boss gobbler's hens and starting to strut and gobble in the same place where the boss gobbler was strutting and gobbling.

In one strut zone I found at the Lake of the Ozarks, my friends and I have now killed 25 gobblers. I don't know anything in hunting that's more productive or dependable than a strut zone.

In the remarkable photos in this sequence, Lovett Williams has captured first a tense face-off and then some dramatic fighting, which is continued on page 132.

You can think of a turkey's strut zone as being similar to a whitetail deer's scraping area. Year after year, deer will usually scrape in the same place during the rut. And year after year, turkeys will work the same strut zone.

Yet another reason I enjoy hunting strut zones is that I like to do a lot of calling. I've had as many as 12 strut zones to work in a day. So I called

to a different bird just about every 45 minutes if I moved quickly enough.

I like to call and to watch gobblers strut and drum. And I enjoy seeing how close I can make a turkey come to me or my hunting partner before we take him. By hunting a strut zone, I can do all of these things.

Fighting gobblers. (Lovett Williams photo)

Mapping Your Way to Gobblers

with Terry Rohm

Pennsylvania has many state game lands with a lot of hunting pressure. To locate a turkey to hunt, I first have to find an area without many hunters. I use topo maps from the state forestry commission. I look for a spot on the map that has several hollows running together into one large hollow. This spot needs to be 3 to 5 miles from the nearest road, so it's not easily accessible to other hunters.

I enter the woods before dawn to check the spot without anyone having any idea where I am. Once I locate one of these out-of-the-way hollows and find a turkey, there usually will be a turkey in that same hollow year after year and, with luck, no other turkey hunters. I attempt to find several of these secret hollows before the season and make sure they have turkeys.

During the fall turkey season in Pennsylvania, hunters are allowed to take either a hen or a gobbler. As a result, we have fewer hens during the spring season than states that do not permit the taking of hens during the fall. With the hens in short supply, the gobblers start gobbling in February—much earlier than they do in many other states. If they find hens, they'll gobble all day long. Of course, with so much gobbling, the turkeys call in many hunters. Last season I had three turkeys run off by other hunters. That's why I like to hunt remote areas.

I walk and call from daylight until about noon. I cover a lot of ground. I'll call down a hollow and wait a few minutes. If I don't hear a turkey gobble, I keep walking.

One of the biggest mistakes is to take a turkey call into the woods before the season begins. If you call to a turkey and he answers, comes in, sees you and putts off, the chances of calling him again in the same spot are slim. The best calls for scouting are the crow call and the owl call. You'll locate just as many turkeys and spook far fewer by using these two calls.

When I leave to go to my hunting spot before daylight, I may have to walk an hour or two in the dark. But when I arrive, I'll be in such a remote

Terry Rohm has learned how to dodge other hunters. By using a map to reach the most remote part of the woods, at least 5 miles from the nearest access road, Rohm can consistently take more turkeys.

area that I rarely will be bothered by other hunters. Most of the spots I hunt are the same ones I've hunted for several years. I've discovered that turkeys can be shot at, wounded, and killed in a spot, yet the next year there still will be turkeys in these same hollows.

To take a gobbler, I like to get within 100 yards of him. I cluck a little and give a soft yelp. Then I shut up and wait to see what the turkey is going to do. If he gobbles on his own, I'll wait a little while and then call back to him. I want to act coy and flirty. I want him to be more anxious to see me than I am to see him.

So I just keep picking at him with flirty little calls after a long silence. I want my old turkey to be so worked up when he leaves the limb that he forgets his eyesight is ten times better than mine, that he can hear better than I can, and that he's smarter than I am. When I whisper those low, soft, sweet love calls in his ears, sometimes the old gobbler will come running to me with love on his mind and wind up with lead in his head.

If you hunt regions with high hunter pressure, you can utilize topo maps to find the remote areas. Then you can mark the spots where you locate turkeys, and use different marks for the spots where you take one. By using the same map for two or three years, hunting various areas, and taking turkeys from them, you'll soon know where to find turkeys.

Finding
Gobblers
from the Road

with Paul Butski

*T*urkeys gobble a lot during the evening in upstate New York. You can't hunt them in the evening, but you can find them then. A crow call, a gobbling call, or an owl hoot will trigger a gobble in good turkey country in the evening.

In the western part of New York the woodlots are broken up by many roads. About 20 minutes before dark I drive the roads, call, and wait for an answer. If a turkey doesn't gobble, I move on to the next woodlot. By calling and driving I can cover a lot of ground and find many turkeys in a short time.

New York turkeys gobble a lot from the roost. Often I can locate them by driving the roads in late afternoon and just listening. If I hear a turkey gobble close to the road, I give a few clucks and yelps before I leave him. The gobbler is not going to fly down from the roost, but he'll be thinking about that hen all night long and plan for a date at sunrise.

The next morning, I try to take a stand on the same level with the turkey or just above him. I give an owl hoot and hope he'll gobble, so I can make sure he's still where I left him the night before. Next, I tree-call one time. Then I won't call again until he hits the ground. When he does, I really like to get him excited with a lot of cutting and cackling. I believe plenty of calling brings the turkey in fast, and he'll be less wary.

My car-scouting works especially well late in the season, and I think one reason is that the gobblers are traveling—looking for a few hens and trying to get away from the hunters. Most turkey hunters won't hunt the first 200 yards of a woodlot. They want to get the turkeys in the deep woods. But after those deep-woods turkeys have been fooled with a time or two, they move out on the fringes of the woods closer to the road, to escape the hunters. And that's where I find them.

Car-scouting also works in mountainous country. I drive from mountaintop to mountaintop, call down the hollows, and listen for gobbling. Contrary to what some hunters think, a car doesn't seem to bother turkeys.

A flock of hens has a pecking order. When a gobbler decides to move with his harem, he often becomes subordinate to the dominant hen. She decides where the flock will feed, how long it will stay, and when it will leave the area. By understanding this dominant hen's determination to be the queen, Butski tries to lure her to his calling, knowing that if he can reel her in, she may be dragging a gobbler along behind her.

Once a turkey gobbles, I try to get a bearing on his exact location. If he's close to the road—100 to 200 yards—I cluck and yelp to him a few times before I leave. I want him to be thinking all night about the hen he talked to. When I come back the next morning, he'll usually be ready to do more than talk.

Much of the land I hunt is public game land, but I do hunt private land too. I've found that most posted land is posted primarily to keep deer hunters out. If I find a turkey on posted land, I ask the landowner for permission to hunt him. So far I haven't been refused permission to hunt any area where I've located a turkey.

One of the most difficult turkeys to call is an old gobbler with hens. To call him away from them, you must understand the social order of a hen harem. There's always a dominant hen. She's usually the one who makes the decisions for the flock. This matriarch governs not only the rest of the hens, but the gobbler, too, when he moves with them. She's his number-one lady.

To get the gobbler away from her and from the rest of the harem, I use a lot of cutting calls. I think cutting best imitates the sound of another dominant hen. When the old queen hears this younger one calling her gobbler, she'll generally charge to run her off. The gobbler will follow along. Often the old queen will run by me and lead him straight to me. If he doesn't come immediately, she'll start calling from behind me and lure him into my gunsights.

I believe that a hunter who learns to scout from the road will take more turkeys, and take them quicker, than the fellow who walks to find them.

High-Noon Turkeys

Turkeys

with Harold Knight

I do most of my hunting in the Land Between the Lakes region on the Tennessee-Kentucky border. The easiest way to scout there is to walk along the edges of old fields and find where turkeys have been scratching, dusting, and traveling. Also, I try to spot turkeys in fields before the season starts. These will make for easy hunting early in the season, if there's not a lot of hunting pressure.

But later in the season, when the pressure is heavy and the turkeys have been called to and shot at, I do my searching differently. The turkeys have wised up to hunters. Often, gobblers that have been called to continuously in the mornings will stop doing any gobbling then. However, they still may gobble and come to a call in the middle of the day. So that's when I do my searching. From 11:00 A.M. to 2:00 P.M., I locate many gobblers that other hunters may not.

One of the keys to locating turkeys in the middle of the day is to get comfortable so you can sit motionless for 30 minutes to an hour. I generally carry a stool and set up where three or four finger ridges run into a bottom. This way, a turkey has several ridges he can take to come down into the hollow where I'm calling.

In the middle of the day I usually have to do a lot more calling than hunters do in the morning. I do several fast calls and then some cutting, to try to get a turkey to give a shock gobble—which is a reaction gobble, not a deliberate gobble to a hen. Sometimes I hear turkeys answer a hawk call, so I've also started using hawk calls to make them shock-gobble. If I can't make a turkey gobble within 30 minutes or an hour, I move a quarter mile or a half mile, find another hollow with finger ridges, and use the same tactics.

However, I don't have to make a turkey gobble to locate him in the middle of the day. As I move from place to place, I scout with my ears. A turkey strut sounds like an 18-wheel tractor trailer truck shifting gears in the distance—*Vutt-V-Roooom*. So you can often pinpoint a gobbler without

Harold Knight's World's Best Overall Typical Eastern Gobbler with an overall score of 80⅝ points and taken with a tube call at Land Between the Lakes, Tennessee, in 1978. (Knight and Hale Game Calls photo)

ever calling to him. When you hear him strut, you've got to realize he's close. You must be prepared to set up and take him without a lot of movement. I've killed many turkeys in the middle of the day because I heard them strut before I set up to call them.

Although I like to hunt turkeys at any time, I prefer the middle of the day. There's less competition than in the morning or the evening. Since few hunters, if any, are in the woods after 9:00 A.M., I usually can take my time and work a turkey the way I want to, rather than trying to get him in quickly before another hunter kills him.

And I like to hunt those finger ridges that run into big hollows. I generally get up on the side of these ridges to start calling. I've also found many turkeys in hardwood saddles between two mountains.

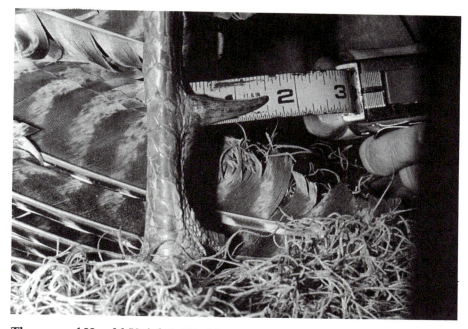

The spur of Harold Knight's World's Best Overall Typical Eastern Gobbler. (Knight and Hale Game Calls photo)

You should be able to call a turkey that gobbles midday into gun range. I believe you need a slate call for clucking and yelping, a tube call to get the volume to make a turkey gobble, a box to change the pitch of your call in case an old gobbler won't come in, and a mouth call to work a turkey in close in open woods. With a variety of calls, you often can bring a turkey into gun range easier and quicker.

If Tom Turkey shock-gobbles to my tube within 100 yards, I usually put the tube down and use my mouth call to bring him in with a few clucks and soft yelps. I hunt that turkey like he has a gun and is hunting me. Even when I move my eyes, I do it slowly. If soft-talking him doesn't work, I may try a box or the slate. Some gobblers will come only to a raspy, coarse call, while others want a call as smooth as molasses being poured over a slick river rock.

I know some hunters don't call much because they're afraid they'll hit a wrong note and spook a turkey. However, some of the worst calling I've heard has come from hen turkeys. To kill turkeys in the middle of the day, you need to call a lot and not worry about hitting a wrong note. The hen you're trying to imitate often hits a wrong note but gets her gobbler anyway, and so will you.

Oftentimes there will be more than one gobbler in an area in the early part of the spring before the hens come into estrus. When you kill that bird, the other turkeys will start gobbling in the same place where you bagged the turkey earlier in the season.

Following
Spring Turkeys

with Tom Kelley

*T*he first thing to remember when you sit down to call a turkey is that you're trying to get him to perform an unnatural act—going to the hen. In nature, most of the time, the hen will go to the gobbler. So from the very beginning when you try to call a turkey, you're at a disadvantage.

The turkey mating program starts in the spring when the old toms begin to gobble. If you watch turkeys long enough, you know the next thing that usually happens is that the hens start flying down toward a gobbler or running through the woods to him. When a tom has gathered enough hens for his morning activities, he'll fly down off the roost and walk through the woods with them. He'll feed along and gobble every now and then. Later in the morning, the hens will start moving away from him.

Normally, when an old boss gobbler has his hens with him and you yelp to him, he'll gobble back and continue walking away from you with them. I've found that if you get up and move closer to him—maybe within 100 yards—and continue to call as he moves away, he'll begin to notice that you're there. He'll gobble back and you'll yelp, but he'll still keep moving off. Every time he moves away from you, continue to slip closer. Every now and then, an older turkey like this will get a notion that he needs to come back to you, gather you up, and bring you in with the rest of his hens. And that's when you can get him.

Even though the turkey has all his hens with him, he starts to believe there's one hen back there he really needs to take into his harem. As long as you follow him, he keeps believing you want to be part of that harem. And later in the day when some of his lady friends have left him, he'll decide to come back to you. That's when you take your shot.

I discovered this tactic through sheer stubbornness and persistence. I just made up my mind that a turkey wasn't going to walk off and leave me. I was going to trail him through the woods until he came back to get me—if the whole process took two or three hours.

I've learned that the most difficult thing in the world is to sit flat on your fanny and make a turkey come to you. For that reason, I move a great deal when trying to get a turkey to come within range. I believe that to be a successful turkey hunter, you have to be aggressive and move a lot. If a turkey doesn't come to you, you've got to get ahead of him or to the side of him and make him come to you. This tactic won't work every time, of course, but nothing else will either.

Turkeys are easiest to take at the beginning of the spring gobbling season. They haven't established their gobbling grounds and are just out walking around. When you yelp to a gobbler then, he may run all over you. Of course you only get one gobbler like that every three or four years, but this type of bird really refreshes you. You feel you're doing a good job of yelping when he comes running in to you, but really you aren't. You just caught one old boy out with lovemaking on his mind, and you were available.

A turkey that stops and gobbles in one place regularly will have hens coming to him. They know where to watch for him, and he knows where to expect them. So when he sounds off in the morning, the hens come to meet him. If you kill one of these old gobblers later in the season by following him or using another tactic, two or three mornings afterward you may hear more gobbling in that same place. But don't worry. It's not the ghost of that gobbler you took home to supper.

There may be several subdominant gobblers in the area where the old boss gobbler was. Since the boss gobbler was dominant, he wouldn't let these others gobble. As long as he was gobbling, they had two choices—

Each spring Tom Kelley (far right) teaches novice turkey hunters how to bag the wily gobblers. But according to Kelley, the only foolproof way to take a tom is to "put out a steel trap and then take a pick handle and beat the turkey's brains out when the trap's jaws catch the turkey's leg." (Westervelt Hunting Lodge and Gulf States Paper Company photo)

either keep quiet or get whipped. Most of them chose to keep quiet. But after you killed the boss gobbler and the younger ones didn't hear him for several mornings, the next gobbler in the pecking order moved into his territory and established dominance.

Sometimes I'll go back to an area and take the next turkey in line. In one spring gobbling season, I took three gobblers out of the same acre of woods—which is not unusual, as most veteran turkey hunters would attest. Once you locate an area where turkeys gobble year after year, you can return to that area and kill one just about every year. And depending on the state's season and bag limits, you can sometimes take two or three turkeys in the same area each season.

One of my secrets for successful turkey hunting is to go to an area after listening to some fellow brag about hunting a turkey for eight, ten, or twelve mornings and then finally killing him. Usually the hunter will tell me exactly where he killed the turkey, and how. He'll assume his gobbler was the only one there, and he'll be off hunting other areas trying to find other turkeys. And generally other hunters will avoid an area like this because they know a turkey has already been killed there.

When those other hunters assume that, they've just opened the door for me to go into that same area and hunt without being disturbed. If hens have been accustomed to meeting a gobbler there, usually when that gobbler is killed another one will move in to pick them up. And probably I'll get him. This tactic is always best at the last of the season when the boss gobblers have already set up their territories and exerted their dominance over the junior gobblers. During the first of the season, when the turkeys are just moving around and haven't set up territories, this tactic is not nearly as effective.

Another secret I've learned, which most old-time turkey hunters completely disregard, is to listen to wildlife biologists. Two of my favorites are Lovett Williams in Florida and Dan Speake in Alabama, both of whom have researched turkeys using radiotelemetry. There is so much research being done on turkeys right now, and so much knowledge being gained, that you can drastically improve your turkey hunting by listening to what biologists say about turkey movement and behavior patterns. Most turkey hunters get their information at the barber shop, which usually isn't worth a damn. To become a better hunter, listen to the biologists who study turkeys. By putting radios on turkeys, they can track them all year long. The radios are so sensitive the biologists even know when a turkey dies.

If you really want to learn more about turkeys and master the sport, go to the people who are getting paid to learn all they can about turkeys. Listen to the wildlife biologists.

When snow covers the ground, finding something to eat can be difficult for wild turkeys. But if there is a dairy farm close by, the turkeys may discover a grocery store that opens daily. When a dairy farmer brings out warm manure from the barn and spreads that manure on his pasture, the turkeys can move into the open fields and peck out the undigested grains from the manure. So often northern hunters who hunt near dairy farms can take toms right after a manure spreading. (Leonard Lee Rue III photo)

How to Hunt Jack-Frost Turkeys

by John E. Phillips

*M*odern fall and winter turkey hunters would not be impressed by the early Pilgrims and their tactics for hunting the Thanksgiving gobbler. By today's standards our forefathers were nothing more than bushwhackers. Their primary tactic was to slip into the woods before daylight, and shoot a turkey off the roost before he ever had a chance to fly down.

The other tactic employed in colonial days was to find a drove of turkeys in the winter, and kill as many as possible before they escaped. They were slaughtered on the ground and in the air. But we must not judge too harshly. Without gobblers on the table, many of the early settlers would not have survived.

In the early 1900s, when there were no bag limits and turkeys were scarce across much of the country, they were still plentiful in Alabama. Roy Moorer and his father, from the town of Evergreen, used to take them regularly during the winter.

"I rarely shot a turkey on the ground," the 96-year-old Moorer remembers. "In those days we didn't feel there was much sport to that. We shot most of our turkeys in the air. Either we'd flush them ourselves, or we'd have a turkey dog that would pick up their scent, trail them to where they'd been feeding, and flush them for us."

I remember my first fall turkey hunt. I knew where turkeys had been ranging. After searching a couple of hours, I found about 15 bronze birds in a river bottom. They were feeding on acorns and apparently weren't looking for danger. I slipped in close to get a shot at an old gobbler just off to one side of the flock. But each time I got ready to shoot, he'd take a step and put a tree between us.

As I tried to move closer, a hen saw me and spooked the whole flock. The turkeys never flew—they simply ran through the woods like a group of frightened chickens. I didn't have my caller with me, so I spent the rest of the day trying to slip up on them and ambush one. Just about the time

I'd get in shooting distance, the turkeys would get out. When the afternoon was over, I understood totally why the Indians had found it easier to call a turkey than to chase one.

Some hunters think there's not much to hunting turkeys in the fall or winter. As an old hunter once told me, "All you have to do is find a bunch of turkeys, scatter them, then sit down and call them back together."

Basically, he's right. Hunting fall and winter turkeys is simple—until you begin to look at questions like:

- How and where do you find a bunch of turkeys?
- What's the best way to scatter them?
- What calls do you use?
- What are the chances of taking a really big gobbler in the fall or winter?

Turkey hunting during cold weather remains simple as long as you don't ask these questions. But if you do ask, the hunting can be rewarding once you have the answers.

The old bronze warlord of the spring woods, who'd rather chase hens than keep his head, changes drastically when the icy fingers of winter begin to claw the leaves from his lofty perch. A mature gobbler is a loner by nature. Although he may occasionally move with other turkeys or roost with them, his main interest is not to be the social director for a bunch of hens and rowdy young jakes. For this reason, the possibility of taking an old gobbler is much more remote in the fall or winter than in the spring.

Of course, before you can decide which turkey to shoot, you must find a bunch to hunt—which may not be so easy a task as it is during spring gobbling season. That is, turkeys don't gobble much in the fall, which makes locating them much more difficult. You must depend on your woodsman-ship to locate turkeys in the fall or winter.

"Mast trees are the key to finding winter turkeys," says Ben Lee, the nationally known turkey caller. "I look for oak, dogwood, cherry, and beech trees first. Then once I find the feed, locating the turkeys is not too hard. They'll be on the ground feeding under these trees, most of the time."

"I kept hearing this racket in a bunch of water oaks about nine or ten o'clock one morning," Danny Fields, another fine turkey hunter, explains. "I slipped over and saw a whole drove of turkeys sitting in the trees eating acorns. They apparently hadn't flown down that morning and seemed content to stay in the trees the rest of the day."

Although locating mast is your best bet for finding wintertime turkeys, mast is not the only feed a turkey will eat. One of the best places to look for turkeys in northern states is right in the middle of snow-covered pastures.

According to Lee, "If there are any turkeys around a dairy farm during winter, you can most always find them in the fields. Although turkeys don't particularly like to be in them, the fields are where the food is.

"Every afternoon or every other afternoon, dairy farmers carry manure from their barns and spread it on the fields. The manure is warm and contains a lot of seeds and grain. So the turkeys dig in and remove this undigested stuff from it.

"A smart turkey hunter will watch the fields on the days the manure is spread and soon locate his turkeys, besides finding which way they come into the field and which way they leave it. Then he can try to call them as they come or go."

But finding turkeys and taking them are not always synonymous. Once a winter flock is discovered, generally the next task is to scatter them. The reason for this is simple. When scattered in the winter, the young turkeys try to flock back to the older ones for security. The hunter who calls in an attempt to get the flock back together will usually bag his turkey. So scattering the flock is critical.

Shooting over the turkeys and screaming and running at them will generally do the trick. Most turkey takers suggest that you allow the woods to settle for a few minutes, while you find a big tree to use as a back blind. Only then do you sit down and start calling.

"Winter turkeys don't talk much," Lee says, "so you shouldn't call a lot. The most effective call for fall and winter turkeys is the kee-kee-run. A plastic coach's whistle is about the best caller you can use. Take the ball out of it. When you blow into the whistle just say, "Boy, boy, boy," and you have a perfect kee-kee.

"For yelping, I use either a box caller or a slate caller. These two types of callers are a little more raspy than a mouth yelper and seem to imitate an old hen better. The best calls to make are the ones you hear. I try to imitate exactly the turkeys I hear trying to get back together."

Roy Moorer explains, "If an old hen shows up first, I get up and run her off. She's trying to do the same thing I am. So I try to get her as far

Locating what the turkeys like to feed on is the key to finding winter turkeys. In many areas if you find mast producing trees, you will also find turkeys. (Colorado Div. of Wildlife photo)

away from me as I can. Then I sit back down, wait a little while, and start calling again.''

Most of the time, the young gobblers will be the first to show up. They haven't really learned what to do in the woods yet, and are still leaning heavily on the hens for an education. For this reason, they'll usually be the first gobblers taken. Old gobblers are much harder to fool in the winter.

"Your best bet for taking a trophy gobbler in the winter,'' Lee says, "is to try roosting him at night and then get close to him when he flies down in the morning. Once I find a flock, I go and listen to them fly up to roost just at dark. The next morning I try to move within 75 yards of the roost. I cluck one time. If the gobbler answers, I may yelp three times on a box caller. But that's all the calling he'll hear from me that morning. Hunting gobblers with a 6-inch beard or better during the winter is one of the most difficult tasks I know.''

The tactics described above are primarily for the hunter who has the woods to himself. But during the fall and winter there often are many outdoorsmen other than turkey hunters in the woods. Small-game hunters and deer hunters may compete with the turkey hunter for space, and sometimes even for the turkeys. The wise turkey hunter will use this competition to his advantage.

If there's a deer drive—by man or dog—through a woodland where you've located turkeys, the additional pressure can be in your favor. When the drive is over, go to the area where you've seen turkey sign, and listen. The drive has probably scattered your turkeys. Once you hear them calling, you can move in close and start to call. Often they'll come right to you, just as if you'd scattered them.

Another clue to listen for is several rapid shots from a shotgun. A rabbit or squirrel hunter often will fire only one shot at his quarry. If he fires more than once, the follow-up shots will be spaced apart as the quarry darts in and out of cover. But most hunters who accidentally walk up on a bunch of turkeys or flush them will throw their guns to their shoulders and fire several shots quickly—most often bagging only air. So wait and listen. If a hunter did flush turkeys, they'll start calling to regroup in a few minutes. Sit down and call, and you may take a turkey home for supper.

The lost call, the kee-kee run, a few raspy yelps, and a cluck are all the calls you need to master for fall or winter hunting. The less you call, the better your chances. For successful cold-weather turkey hunting, ask the pertinent questions first. Then know the answers before you start your hunt.

Keep in mind that fall and winter hunting are different from spring hunting, but just as exciting. Anytime your skill as a woodsman and caller is tested, anytime you see the eyes of the woods monarch searching every twig and branch for danger, anytime you watch the sun dancing off feathers of green, purple, bronze, black, blue, and copper, then making a trip into the forest is well worth the effort—no matter what the time of year.

Hunting
Them Hard

by John E. Phillips

*A*t 24 years of age, Terry Phillips may well be one of the youngest veteran turkey hunters in the state of Arkansas. Although the terms "young" and "veteran" may not seem to go together, they aptly describe him. (By the way, he's not a relative of mine.)

Terry Phillips has been hunting the wild turkey since the mid-1970s and has bagged many gobblers. This Jonesboro, Arkansas, native has won the Southwest Open Turkey Calling Championship, the Alabama State Open Non-Resident Division, and the National Open Turkey Calling Championship.

What makes Terry Phillips unique is that he combines some of the best hunting techniques of the past with his own more aggressive style. Where some older turkey hunters use more patience and skill to lure a bird into gun range, Phillips utilizes his youth, strength, and endurance to hunt the hard places, to cover much ground, and to attack the turkey on the turkey's own territory. Being in condition to walk long distances and being willing to hunt in areas that are too far away for most hunters are the keys to this young man's turkey-hunting success.

Although winning turkey-calling contests is not synonymous with good turkey hunting, Phillips has proven his expertise in both areas, and he especially enjoys hunting wildlife-management areas and national forests.

"One of the big advantages to hunting these places," he says, "is that there are many forestry roads. By using these old roads, I can get far away from the crowds. You'll find the largest concentration of hunters within a half mile of the major roads into a management area. This is where the hunting pressure is heaviest and the competition for the birds is keenest. So I leave these places alone and move deeper into the woods with my compass, along logging roads.

"Then, when I do find a turkey gobbling, I don't have to worry about somebody else spooking him or competing with me. I leave my car 30

When a turkey won't come in where Terry Phillips is waiting, Phillips will follow the tom until he closes within shooting distance.

minutes to an hour before daylight, and get to the spot I want to hunt before the sun comes up.

"Another excellent way to get away from everybody and into places where you can kill a turkey is to follow hiking trails through national forests. These trails are usually about a foot wide and provide easy access to much of the deep woods where most other turkey hunters won't go.

"If I really want solitude, I head for management areas with many mountains in them. Because of the rough terrain, they don't seem to receive as much hunting pressure."

Phillips can take turkeys year after year because he learns an area thoroughly—finds out where the turkeys stay in it—and hunts the same spots year after year. His technique involves much walking. From daylight until 11:00 A.M. he may cover 6 to 8 miles.

As Phillips explains, "Most hunters will go to an area where they think there's a turkey, start to call, then sit down and wait for the turkey to come in to them. But I don't do that. At daylight I begin to owl-hoot. If I don't hear a turkey gobble back to my hooting, I walk 100 yards and then hoot again.

"When the sun comes up, I change calls but use the same basic method. I replace the owl hooting with a mating yelp and a cackle, because a cackle is the most exciting call a hen can give. If a gobbler hears it, he'll gobble back if he's ever thought about gobbling. Even if the gobbler is with hens, he'll gobble back when he hears a cackle if he's close to me. If I don't get a gobble to my cackle, I keep on moving. I feel I'm wasting time sitting in one spot and waiting for a turkey to call back to me. And that's the reason the logging roads and hiking trails are critical. I can move quickly and easily along them and cover enough ground to find a bird.

"When I get a gobble in return, I try to move within 100 yards of the turkey. Even if he's on the ground, I like to get in close and try to call him. I don't want anything to come between us, like a hen or another caller. If the turkey is in the tree, I like to be in position to call so I can see him when he flies down. I try to be as convenient to the old boy as I can. If he does have to go out of his way to come to me, he won't have to go very far out of his way.

"Most of the time, if there's nothing else going on in the woods and I'm calling well, I should be the number-one thing on that turkey's mind when he pitches off the roost. If he thinks there's a hen in close to his roost tree, he'll usually come right on toward me."

Some hunters hide behind trees, using them as blinds, but not Terry. He prefers to set up in front of a tree so there's no obstruction between him and the turkey.

"Since I'm right handed, I always point my left knee at the turkey and rest my gun on my left knee. Then I have maximum field of fire no matter which way the turkey comes to me. Pointing my left knee directly at the turkey minimizes the movement I make when aiming at him."

Another tactic Phillips employs is to call a lot to a turkey. In the past, hunters believed they were better off with the least amount of calling that would bring a gobbler into their gunsights.

But Phillips says, "When I get an old bird's attention, I want to keep him interested in me. I want to build up his enthusiasm and excitement. When he comes in, I want him to be so fired up about mating that he won't be looking for me or any other form of danger. An excited turkey is less cautious and easier to kill. He'll also come in much faster than a turkey that isn't excited and just happens to be on his way by and thought he might stop to check out a hen he heard. I believe that doing more calling will enable more hunters to take more turkeys.

"I do a lot of cutting, cackling, and yelping—not only to get the turkey to come in fast but also to outcompete hens in the area. Often the woods will be full of hens. There may be a hen yelping closer to the gobbler than I am. But if I have his attention, have him excited, and have him moving, he'll come to me before he'll check out that hen."

Phillips has come under criticism from some older hunters who have listened to tapes of his hunts and find it difficult to believe that he calls so much and uses so many varieties of calls.

But Phillips says, "One of the mistakes novice hunters make in trying to call turkeys is that they're afraid to try something new. I use a slate call and a tube call—which is nothing more than a pill bottle—and five different mouth yelpers. I may utilize all of these on the same turkey in the same morning. A hunter should have several calls, because if he spooks a turkey using one particular type, he'll find calling that turkey again with the same call difficult. If I spook a turkey, I change calls and locations. Then he thinks I'm a different hen in a different place. Usually he'll come on in to me.

"I've also found that some turkeys prefer the sound of one call over that of another. Certain gobblers like to hear a high-pitched, smooth call, while others favor a deep, raspy call. They may answer back to one call and not gobble at another. So I try to give the gobbler the call he likes to answer. Then I work him with that call until I bring him into gun range."

The slate caller is Phillips' favorite for clucking and purring. He says, "The slate gives the most realistic cluck and purr a hunter can produce. But then when I start yelping and cackling, I prefer the diaphragm caller. When I guide, I primarily use the diaphragm, because I don't have to use my hands. I can cut down the movement that the turkey might see.

"I like to get my turkey to within 30 steps before I try to take him. I use a 12-gauge magnum with no. 4 shot. And I can take a turkey within that 30-yard range."

One reason Phillips takes more turkeys than most other hunters do is that he hunts more aggressively. He doesn't give up on a bird.

"One day as soon as I got out of the car and owl-hooted, I heard an old turkey gobble," he recalls. "I thought, *This is going to be an easy turkey to kill.* I set up in front of a big tree and started calling to the gobbler. When I called, he gobbled back and began coming to me.

"In my mind, I could already see that bird dead on the ground. But when he was about 40 yards out, a herd of deer broke from cover and spooked him. However, I still felt I could take my gobbler. The process was just going to be a little more difficult now.

"I waited about 15 or 20 minutes and called again. This time, the turkey answered from a high ridge. Immediately I started running to him. I've found many times that you can take a turkey if you can outrun him. Go as fast and as hard as you can in the woods to circle a turkey and try to get in front of him. If you can get within calling distance and be headed in the same direction he wants to go, often you can kill a spooked gobbler.

"I always attempt to think like a turkey. Before the deer spooked him, that gobbler had mating on his mind. I believed that if I could get in front of him in a place he wanted to come to, he would still have mating on his mind. A spooked gobbler can be killed, but you must hunt more aggressively and you must plan your strategy carefully.

"As I ran, I found a small creek at the bottom of the ridge. I had to wade waist-deep water to get to the other side. I owl-hooted again, and the turkey answered. But he was still above me. I knew if I was going to take that turkey, I had to get to a calling position above him where he would come.

"So I ran up the ridge to get higher than the turkey. I came to a small clearing, found a big oak, and sat down beside it. I waited 15 or 20 minutes before I called again. I think a turkey needs time to settle down before you start working him once more. I tried the same caller I'd used on him before, but the old gobbler wouldn't answer.

"I then waited about another 15 minutes and changed callers. But I still heard nothing. I continued to watch the woods and wait. In a few minutes I saw the gobbler coming at about 80 yards. He didn't gobble, strut, or do anything except keep walk straight to me. When the bird was about 30 yards from me, I took him."

Terry Phillips is a young man, but experience does not always come with age. Experience in turkey hunting is a product of spending hours in the woods scouting, locating, calling, working, missing, and bagging turkeys. Phillips has put in hours hunting all across the nation. By utilizing some of his aggressive tactics, you too may be able to bag a bronze baron for a spring dinner.

Double-Circle
Technique

with Brent Harrell

Jay Brown and I heard six turkeys gobble that morning. Usually, when Jay and I hear more than one turkey gobble, we'll split up and try to take one apiece. But this particular morning, this one old turkey just wouldn't shut up. We counted 140 gobbles from him. He was out of his mind.

After we'd fooled with some other turkeys, we agreed we'd try to take this one. But when he flew out of his tree, he didn't come to our call—he went in the other direction instead. He wasn't a really big turkey, but apparently someone else had tried to shoot him before. Still, we didn't believe we were going to have too hard a time bagging him.

We soon realized, however, that he was call-wise and hunter-shy. A smart gobbler like that one usually won't come into gun range unless he sees his hen. Often, a decoy will do the trick. But, since we had no decoy, we tried another tactic that's worked for killing old, tough gobblers—the double-circle technique.

Jay circled the turkey one way, and I circled him the other way. I crawled on my belly, went under fences, cackled, yelped, purred, and clucked, but the old gobbler wouldn't come in where I was.

Jay was doing the same things on the other side of the turkey. We tried to confuse him enough to get him to go one way or the other. But he wouldn't move. He kept walking in one place, drumming and strutting, and wouldn't come to a call. I decided to drum and gobble to him, hoping to make him jealous so he'd come in to take his hens before another gobbler got to them. Often, this tactic is successful—especially in an area with a lot of hens and many gobblers.

But this particular gobbler would have nothing to do with drumming or gobbling. Later, I found out this tactic was the wrong one to use on this turkey. I discovered he was bruised and scarred, so he'd probably been in a fight recently and taken a whipping from a fiercer gobbler. Anyway, he wouldn't come to a gobble or a drum. Although Jay was cackling, yelping, and cutting as I continued to call, the old gobbler wouldn't budge.

When a smart gobbler hangs up and is difficult for one hunter to take, two hunters can double up on the bird, using the double circle tactic. This is designed to cause the bird to go to one of the hunters. Often one hunter can give hen calls, while the other hunter gobbles, gives drumming and strutting sounds. The gobbler has to decide whether to mate or fight.

When you and another hunter try to flank a turkey this way, each of you must be sure to know where the other is at all times. Then, if a shot does present itself, you won't wind up shooting one another.

We continued to work the turkey past 8:00 A.M. We'd first heard him at 5:05, and we still weren't any closer to him than we had been then. But I was determined to keep after him as long as Jay did. I pulled out all the stops. I moved and scratched like a hen. I gobbled and drummed like a gobbler. I clucked and purred like a feeding hen. I cackled like a mating hen, but that tom still stayed in one place.

He reminded me of Uncle Remus's story of the tar baby. I'd done everything I could to make him answer and come to me, but just like the tar baby he wouldn't move.

Finally, at 8:23, I heard the report of Jay's shotgun. I went over and found Jay with a 17-pound gobbler that had an 8-inch beard and 1-inch spurs. Though not impressive in weight or beard, that gobbler was a very knowledgeable bird and a real challenge to hunt. I don't believe I've ever had another turkey as hard to take as the Easter Sunday morning gobbler.

To kill a turkey with the double-circle technique, you must be able to think like a turkey. The situation that Jay and I set up was totally frustrating to the gobbler. He assumed that there was a very desirable hen on either side of him and that both hens were ready to mate. Both were within walking distance, and both were talking to him like they were very excited about the prospect of a date. However, the hen I was simulating had apparently found one boyfriend already. The gobbler assumed this because of the drumming and gobbling I did. If he'd been a boss gobbler, he'd have come running to me to whip the fellow atempting to steal his girl.

But, as I mentioned earlier, when we examined him we found he was bruised and scarred—which indicated he was a subdominant gobbler that may already have been whipped by a boss gobbler. So, when Jay called to him without using any gobbling calls, the turkey probably thought he had two choices. He could go to the hen that had a gobbler with her, and fight him for the right to mate her; or he could go over to the hen that didn't have a gobbler, and avoid a fight.

That being the choice, I can understand why the Easter Sunday morning gobbler went to Jay's calling instead of mine.

When a turkey is this hot and bothered, he knows for sure that his lady friend will show up soon. After all, she has answered him every time he's called. He thinks he just needs to stay in the area and wait to mate. He knows that she is supposed to come to him, and this is why turkeys get hung up. So a smart hunter will let the gobbler cool down. Then the gobbler will search to find out why that hen didn't come to meet him after indicating she would. (Leonard Lee Rue III photo)

Cool 'em Down _____

to Kill 'em _____

with Gary Stilwell _____

I'd been hunting the boss gobbler of Sleepy Creek for about a week. The weather had fouled me up when I tried to take him one morning. Another morning he had hens with him, and I couldn't get him away from them. On several different mornings, he did exactly what I thought he wouldn't do. This old gobbler was really getting to be a pain.

Finally, I had a beautiful, clear morning to hunt him. All I needed to do was cross a little creek and get to him to call. When I stepped into the creek, which had been only ankle-deep the day before, I sank in waist-deep and almost went under. But at last I got in the right position to take the old gobbler. I was on the same ridge with him, and when I called he gobbled. I thought, *Today, old boy, you belong to me.*

The turkey was in open hardwoods. I was sitting just on the edge of a pine thicket that adjoined them. My game plan was flawless. There was an old logging road I was absolutely certain the turkey would have to come down. I figured this hunt should be a piece of cake. But the turkey didn't do what he was supposed to. Instead of coming down the road to me, he went through the pine thicket to a field above him. I continued to call. I changed calls. I went from raspy to sweet and from sweet to raspy, but still nothing happened. I decided that if the turkey wasn't coming to me, I was going to him. I could tell by his gobbling which way he was going, and I got around in front of him.

This time I set up and changed to a friction caller, to make the old gobbler think there was a different hen close by that he could service. When I called he gobbled, and I could hear him drumming. After a while, he stopped drumming. So I decided to move and see what was keeping him from walking where I was.

As I slipped in close, I saw a fence. The lowest strand of the fence was about two feet high and would have been easy for him to walk under. But for some reason, he just didn't want to cross that fence. Apparently he walked on down the fence line and away from me.

I could see which way the big turkey was going. So I circled again and got in front of him. I started calling. He gobbled and moved closer, about 70 yards in front of me, where I could see him. By now, he was really hot. He was strutting, but he wouldn't break the strut and come in to me. The more I called, the more he strutted. I finally decided that I had the old boy too worked up. He was out there strutting and displaying. If there was a hen close by, she should come to him. That old turkey had made up his mind that if she didn't come to him, he wouldn't go to her.

I cooled him down by not talking to him for 30 minutes. Even though he was gobbling and strutting, I wouldn't say anything to him. I really hurt his feelings. He was doing everything a virile, proud, noble gobbler was supposed to do to impress a lady, but I wouldn't even talk to him.

Finally, after 30 minutes of keeping quiet, I started giving some soft yelps that were flat and dull—as though the lady I was imitating was still there but just not interested in him at all. Then I turned my head away from the turkey, down toward the ground, and gave a soft cut and cackle like I was fed up with him and would leave. When I did that, I heard the tempo of his gobble change. And I thought, *He's coming in.* I gave a few more really soft clucks before the gobbler walked right to the spot where I'd chosen to kill him.

This hunt on Sleepy Creek is a prime example of how to cool down a turkey to kill him. Many times, you can get a turkey so fired up and intent on mating and strutting that the turkey really gets prideful. He's so excited about how worked up the hen is that he thinks all he has to do is strut and gobble and she'll come running to him like he was the best-looking bird in the woods.

When a gobbler gets the big head like that, calling him is very difficult. However, that gobbler can be killed if you destroy his ego. I have to use this tactic on a regular basis. I'm a hot dog about turkey hunting. I call a lot and really try to get my gobblers worked up. I go hunting in the spring to hear them gobble and see them strut. I want them to gobble and strut as much as they can before they come to me. But because I call so much, the turkeys tend to get worked up too much and hang up. Therefore, I have to use what I call my cool-'em-down technique if I'm going to kill them.

The first thing I do when a turkey hangs up is to get quiet. Then I look at my watch. And no matter what that turkey does or says, I'm not going to talk to him again for a full 30 minutes. Next, I move laterally, either to the right or to the left, for 50 or 60 yards from where I last saw the turkey. The third thing I do is change the caller I'm using. And then I start the turkey off with some light clucking, purrs, and whines.

If he walks away from me during this 30-minute period, I may move with him. I may slip up behind him, but I'll still go off to the left or right of the direction he's traveling, to give the impression I'm another hen and not the same one who broke his heart earlier.

Also, I change calls. If I've been giving a raspy call, I may go to a smooth one. If I've been using a diaphragm caller, I may change to a friction caller. I want to give some type of call that will make the old turkey think he's not talking to the same hen he talked to earlier. Remember that the gobbler was pretty hot and excited when he was strutting. He was ready to mate, but there was nobody there for mating. He'll be even more ready to mate with the next lady he hears. So finally I start calling with some soft clucks and purrs, to let him know I'm available.

A boss gobbler is much like a body builder on the beach. While he's pumping iron, there are many pretty young things vying for his attention. But there's always one good-looking, well-built girl in a bikini who's not impressed with his physique and who walks away to the concession stand to buy a soft drink while he's showing off. For some reason, this girl who doesn't pay him any attention is always the one the body builder and the boss gobbler are most attracted to. And when that girl walks to the concession stand, the proud male—whether he's clad in a bathing suit or feathers—will hurry over to meet her.

Usually a gobbler knows he can't count on his strutting and gobbling to get this hen's attention. He won't keep trying to impress her with his pretty feathers and his showy walk. After a gobbler like this is cooled down, taking him is much easier.

Birds caught in nets are released in areas where the turkey populations are small. (Michigan Dept. of Natural Resources photo)

How to

Outcompete

Competition

with Glenn Terry

*I*ndiana doesn't have many turkeys, but it does have lots of hunters. So, to take a tom in my state, you have to outhunt the crowds.

In recent years, the first official Indiana turkey season was in 1970. The state conservation department released the turkeys, and most serious hunters knew where those turkeys were supposed to be. But hunters took only six turkeys that year.

Through the years, the released turkeys have stayed close to the release sites. Consequently, the hunting pressure near these sites is extremely high. There probably are at least eight or ten hunters competing for each gobbler. And the hunters start calling to the gobblers and spooking them two or three months before the season begins.

The easiest way to scout is to go into the woods and listen for other hunters calling. When a hunter locates a turkey in preseason scouting he'll usually go back to that same spot every time he goes into the woods, and he'll call to that turkey. Sooner or later, though, the turkey is going to see him and become spooked. For this reason, I try to find a calling spot where I think a gobbler has never heard a hen calling. I listen for other hunters and eliminate the spots they call from. The turkey should then come to my spot because he's never been spooked there. Though this kind of scouting is relatively easy, taking a turkey under crowded conditions is still difficult.

A tougher way to scout, but a way that's actually been more productive for me, is to go to places where the turkeys aren't supposed to be. I use topo maps to locate big hollows far from the release sites, hollows that have several hills nearby to call from. I start scouting these areas long before the season opens. I also talk to landowners and ask their permission to hunt. Most of them don't believe they have turkeys, but they do. I don't find many turkeys by scouting this way, but the ones I do find are usually mine. I can take my time and hunt them the way I want, with a lot of

Released turkeys rarely travel far from their release sites. Most hunters in Terry's home state of Indiana know this. So most of the hunting pressure is concentrated around release sites. Consequently, where you find the most turkey hunters in some states, you will also be in areas with the highest concentration of turkeys. (Lovett Williams, Florida Game and Freshwater Fish Commission, photo)

calling and waiting, working and moving, without interference from other hunters.

Each season I try to pinpoint three or four of these hidden turkeys, so I do have some spares in case someone else happens to get the first one I go after. If I can't find any hidden turkeys and if the season is about to close, I hunt in areas where there are other turkeys and lots of hunters.

When I hunt the heavy-pressure areas, I use my kicking and gouging tactics. I assume that most of the turkeys there have had more calling than they care to hear, and are call-shy. After finding a gobbler and choosing a spot where no one has called to a gobbler before, I set up. Then I cluck three times while he's still in the tree, and never call again. Most of the time, he won't answer these clucks. But in many cases he'll slip in to see what made them. And that's when I take him.

Using this tactic, I rarely hear a turkey between the time he flies down and the time I actually see him. So I'm hunting without knowing where he is. Yet by calling less, I feel I have a greater chance of taking a tom than the hunters who call a lot.

I also try to outlast the competition. When I find a turkey, I go to him every morning. If other hunters continually see my truck parked in the same place, they will get discouraged. So, knowing they'll have competition for the turkey that morning, they'll locate another one to hunt. Endurance will not only win the turkey but also discourage other hunters.

I don't like to hunt the pressure areas. But often, if I refuse to, I won't have a place to hunt. So my formula for these areas, which has proven successful, is to call very little, hunt long and hard, outlast the competition, and hope to get lucky.

Call-less

Turkey

Hunting

with David Hale

I had to go to college to learn how to hunt turkeys. Although I really wasn't much interested in college, I didn't want to go to Vietnam. And a college deferment from service provided the only out for me—just as it did for many boys back in the '60s.

I'd been raised in the woods. But I'd never done any turkey hunting, because the part of Tennessee I'm from didn't have any turkeys. But when I was in college I heard about a place called Land Between the Lakes, often called LBL, on the Tennessee-Kentucky border, owned by the Tennessee Valley Authority. Land Between the Lakes was close to my college and was home to two critters I'd never seen—fallow deer and wild turkeys.

Because I was raised in the country, I always hung out at the country store with the local folks when I had time off from college, instead of the pool hall with the rest of the college boys. Hanging out at the country store came naturally to me, and pool shooting didn't.

In February all the local men at the store started talking about turkeys and turkey hunting. To listen to those men talk, killing a wild turkey was the greatest accomplishment a man could make in his lifetime. Why, there were even some men at the store who had seen, or said they had seen, a wild turkey—which ensured their being looked up to and respected by the store's patrons.

Also, every now and then a man would come through the store who had killed a wild turkey, or said he had killed one. He was immediately recognized as the top dog in the kennel. All the lesser men who had only seen or heard a wild turkey would back off and let him explain just what was required to kill one.

Right there in that country store, I made up my mind to become a turkey hunter. After all, what else in life could give a man the respect and admiration of as many folks as killing a wild turkey? When one of those real wild-turkey killers came in, he always commanded the respect and admiration of all within earshot. So I knew if I could take one of those old baldheaded birds, I could reach heights most men only dream about. I realized the job would be difficult, because turkey hunting at that time was not great at Land Between the Lakes. In a six-day hunt with over 2,000 hunters, the take was only four to six turkeys.

I began to hunt turkeys in 1967. During my first year, I took a turkey and reached the heights most men at the country store aspired to. Only 17 turkeys were killed that year at LBL, and I'd taken one of them. I'll never forget how I killed my first turkey, and how I learned more about turkeys without using a caller than many hunters learn with one.

A buddy from school and I had been going over to LBL but hadn't heard any turkeys. Finally, on the fourth morning I heard a turkey gobble, which was the greatest thrill of my life. Although I never dreamed at the time that I would actually kill a turkey, at least I had heard one gobble and knew what a gobble sounded like.

The reason I didn't have a turkey caller was that I didn't know they existed. And so I didn't know what they looked like, or how they worked. I was just ignorant of calling. But since I was a pretty fair deer hunter, I felt I might be able to slip up on one of those turkeys and shoot him. I was also a good listener and had trained myself to pay attention to different sounds in the woods, to pinpoint them, and to see what animal was making them.

So when I heard that turkey gobble, I tried to pinpoint his location, and then I took off after him. On the way, I began to remember what I'd heard the fellows saying back at the country store. They believed the way to hunt was to sit back 300 or 400 yards from the turkey, and then spend three or four hours calling him up. So I figured that with so many hunters in the woods and so few turkeys to hunt, the only way I could kill one was to get closer to him and get there first—before the other hunters did.

I thought, *If those old-timers are going to wait and attempt to call the turkey from a ridge or two away, I'm going to get on the same ridge with him and try to shoot him.*

The turkey gobbled an hour to an hour and a half. I decided he was staying in one small saddle of the ridge to do all his gobbling and strutting. So I belly-crawled up the ridge. When the turkey moved away from me, I'd crawl in his direction. When he turned and walked toward me, I'd lie flat and not move. I kept crawling until I was within 50 yards of the spot where the turkey would turn to walk back toward me. While he was still going away, I sat down next to a tree and waited for him to make his turn.

After 45 minutes, I knew that sooner or later he was going to walk back past me, or he was going to walk off in the opposite direction. Luckily, when he quit strutting he walked close to me, and I shot him.

When I returned to the store and told my friends about killing a turkey, they were all duly impressed. I continued to use this stalking tactic for five years and was successful in bagging two turkeys and probably spooking at least ten more.

Without using a call, David Hale can slip in close enough to a turkey to bag him as he goes about his daily routine. This skill requires a thorough knowledge of turkey habits and terrain as well as excellent stalking skills. (Dave Kenyon, Michigan Dept. of Natural Resources, photo)

I learned about what turkeys do, why they do it, and what kind of noises they make. I understood that the most important sound to recognize is the strutting, because there are numerous turkeys that will strut and won't gobble. Unless you can identify the sound of a turkey strut, you may walk off and leave gobblers that are within killing distance. Also, when a turkey is strutting, he's absolutely confident there's no danger around. So you can move on him and move around him much easier than if he were looking for you.

In those days, when I heard a turkey strutting, I would try to move within 30 yards—always staying below or above him so that more than likely he wouldn't see me. I never wanted to be on the same level with the turkey. But, I was careful not to slip in too close to him. I always attempted to take the turkey after he'd quit strutting—when he'd decided to walk off. I just wanted to be in the path he'd take when he walked out of his strutting area.

At least, that's the way I started turkey hunting. But the longer I stayed in the woods, the more I understood about turkeys. I learned how to go into the woods early in the morning and hear a turkey gobble, fly down, and walk off. Our turkeys in Tennessee and Kentucky usually walk on the tops of ridges, because that's where they can hear their hens the best. So when I heard a turkey gobble from the roost, fly down, and begin to walk along a ridge, I'd take off running to get ahead of him on the same ridge, and wait for him to walk toward me. Sometimes I'd have to wait two hours. But many times the turkey would just walk along that ridge right into my gunsights, and I never would call. Even since I've learned to call, I don't try to call a turkey that's just naturally and normally going to walk to me. There's no sense in calling if you don't have to do it.

Many hunters would say this is not the most ethical way to hunt, and would label me a bushwhacker. But in my opinion, it's much easier to call a turkey in than to figure out just where he's heading, get in front of him, and be sitting there when he walks up. This tactic works well when many other hunters have been in the woods fooling with the turkeys, or when you're trying to take a call-shy gobbler.

When attempting to get in front of a turkey walking a ridge, remember one thing. Don't take a stand on top of the ridge where you can see him coming for 200 yards—because he can see you for 200 yards, too. Take your stand on one side of the ridge. Then, when you see him, he'll be only 50 to 60 yards away. To hunt this way, you have to be both aggressive and patient. You must go after the turkey aggressively, moving quickly to get in front of him. But once you're there, you must be patient enough to let him walk to you.

After five years of hunting turkeys at LBL and having a reputation as a pretty good turkey hunter, I was embarrassed that I didn't own a caller and didn't know how to call a turkey. However, I met Harold Knight, who had called turkeys all his life. I picked Knight's brain on calling turkeys, and I talked him into making me one of his callers. Then I began to call turkeys.

But I still believe one reason most hunters don't take more turkeys is that they feel they can pick up a caller, make a few sounds, and be an instant success—rather than really learning how to hunt turkeys, and just using the caller like icing on the cake.

It's natural for a hen to go to a gobbler, not for a gobbler to go to a hen. When you call, you're trying to make the gobbler perform an unnatural act. So don't rely too heavily on your calling. You'll be far more successful if you understand that it's easier to let a gobbler do what he wants, and that to kill him you need to be where he wants to meet a hen.

Calling is only 10 to 20 percent of what it takes to bring home a turkey. Learning to hunt without a caller accounts for 80 percent of my success, while my calling accounts for only 15 percent. That other 5 percent, I figure, is just plain luck.

If Too Many
Turkeys and
Too Many Hunters

with Lewis Stowe

South Carolina, where I generally hunt, has an unusual turkey population and also has unusual hunting conditions. There's an excess of hens, so the gobblers don't have to fly down until they actually see one. Some of the big gobblers stay in the trees until 9:00 or 10:00 A.M. When they do fly down, they may stay in a strutting area for two to four hours, waiting for the hens to come in to them. They may gobble for several hours, so they're relatively easy to find.

But taking one of these harem kings is sometimes difficult. He doesn't have to chase the hens. All he has to do is gobble and wait for the girls to show up. Most often, he'll call from his tree and fly to a strutting area where he has a clear field of vision for 100 to 200 yards. A bronze sultan like this is easy to locate but hard to kill. He'll rarely come to a call, because he knows the hens will come to him. And you can't move on him, because he'll see you.

To add to the difficulty, South Carolina has one of the longest deer seasons in the nation—August through January—and deer hunters may flush a turkey two or three times a day and call to him. When I go to hunt in the spring, I've got turkeys that have been flushed and called by deer hunters for six months, and also by turkey hunters who started scouting and calling in February. So these turkeys know what a man is, and they're call-shy.

In woods with high hen populations and heavy hunting pressure, you have to scout well enough to become very familiar with the turkey you plan to take. My scouting consists not only of finding the turkeys but also of learning which ones do what, and where and when they do it. Some turkeys gobble only in the morning; others gobble only at noon or in the evening. By learning where and when a turkey gobbles, I know how to locate him each day. Then I try to figure out where I need to be to take him. Finding a spot to shoot from often requires getting on a first-name basis with the turkey and knowing what he's going to do before he does it.

I've developed a technique for taking a harem king. I work on his ego. When I find him in a tree or on open ground, I walk straight to him so he'll spook and run off. Next, I walk 75 to 100 yards in the direction he went. After 30 to 40 minutes of silence, I start giving loud yelps, cackles, and cuts. I try to sound like a madwoman. That old gobbler has been crowing about his manhood all morning long. Now this hen has come to be serviced, and he isn't here to do the thing he's been bragging about so long and loud. Since she doesn't know the gobbler has been spooked, she's really fussing at him for standing her up.

The calls I give are my rendition of what any female will say to a man who stands her up after she's had her hair done, bought a new dress, and put on make-up. I've found that the old gobbler usually will come running back to prove his manhood and then wind up as dinner at my house. To take a tough turkey in hen country, spook him, give loud demanding calls, and shoot before he runs over you.

Moving in
Front of
Walking Birds

with Ben Rodgers Lee

O*ne of the hardest turkeys in the world to bag is the kind that will gobble while walking away from you. This turkey may have been shot at before, and more than likely has been ambushed by other hunters. He doesn't want to come to conventional calling, and in most cases he simply won't. Often, specialists such as Ben Rodgers Lee of Coffeeville, Alabama, are called in to try to take these bad old birds. Here are the thoughts of Rodgers.*

When you try to hunt a turkey like this, you usually have to make two critical decisions. First, do you want to call the turkey, or do you want to kill him? Most of the time you don't get the opportunity to do both. If you're going to call to the turkey, you're probably not going to kill him. If you're going to kill him, most likely you're not going to call to him; because usually these turkeys are call-shy. So as soon as you call to this kind of bird, he will walk away from you. Try as you may, calling just will not make a bird like this come to you. Therefore, if you are planning to bag a walking/talking tom, do not call to the bird. Instead try and outmaneuver him in the woods, and take a stand where you think the turkey wants to come. Then wait there in ambush.

The next decision essential to bagging this wise old gobbler is whether you're willing to have someone else hunt with you. A turkey that will walk away from a call has been fooled with by so many other hunters that the odds are slim that one hunter can take him alone. But two hunters have a chance.

The tactic that's worked for me is to locate the turkey first, owl-hoot to him, and get him to answer. Then you attempt to get in front of him, going in the direction he wants to walk. If he's walking down a ridge or a bottom or across a field, you can keep track of his location by owling.

Now you're ready to go after him. Leave the other hunter behind to owl about every 15 minutes, so the turkey will give away his position. Take off running and try to get well out in front of the turkey.

Locate a place in the woods where you think the turkey should naturally want to walk. Find yourself a big tree and sit down next to it. Don't call, don't owl, don't do anything—just sit there and wait. Let your buddy continue to owl to the turkey. Then, if you need to change to a better place, you can move and still know where the turkey is.

You have to depend on your woodsmanship to figure out where that turkey is heading and what route he should take to get there. When he comes into view, shoot him. Now there are some hunters who will say this is bushwhacking and not a sporting way to bag a gobbler. But I believe intercepting a gobbler in the woods without calling to him requires far more skill than calling one up.

While one hunter stays behind and owls, as shown, the other hunter should take off on the run to get in front of the turkey that walks and talks. (Sara Bright photo)

For most of his life, Ben Rodgers Lee has hunted turkeys, made turkey calls, promoted turkey hunting, and tried to outsmart wily gobblers. But Ben says that there comes a time when an old gobbler becomes so smart that the hunter must decide to either call the bird or kill it. Very rarely can you do both. (Ben Lee Calls photo)

In my opinion, the hunter who can take a turkey that won't gobble is one of the best turkey hunters anywhere. He has to know more about the turkeys he's hunting and the woods he's hunting in, and be more conscious of what a turkey wants to do, than a hunter who goes into the woods in the spring, hears a turkey gobble, sits down, and tries to call him up.

Just sitting down in the right place doesn't necessarily mean you are going to kill the turkey. You have to remember that old gobbler has dealt with hunters before. Your camouflage has to be right, and many times you've got to sit for a long time without moving. Of course, if killing those call-shy birds was easy, anybody would be able to do it.

Sometimes when Rob Keck naps on gobblers, a tom will walk in behind him. Then Keck must sit still until the turkey walks in front of him. Keck and I recreated this scene for the camera, using a bird I mounted.

Napping
for Gobblers

with Rob Keck

The trick of napping for gobblers is quite simple. All you do is go to sleep and wait for the turkey to show up. You become the hunted rather than the hunter.

Because of my reputation as a turkey hunter and caller, everywhere I go hunters want to bless me with the opportunity to hunt an old gobbler nobody else has been able to kill. In many camps they greet me with comments like, "Boy, Rob, we're really glad to see you. Down here on the branch we've got a long-bearded gobbler with big curved spurs that three of my uncles, both of my granddaddies, and two of my cousins have been working on for two or three years. We've crippled him twice and run him off three times. We sure would like you to kill him, because he's about to drive us crazy."

So I wind up having to hunt old Clubfoot, Slewfoot, or whatever they've named that crazy critter. And my hosts always expect me to bring him back. What these men fail to realize is that all the time they've been hunting that old gobbler, they've awarded him his Ph.D. in Humanology. That gobbler knows more about people and what they do and why they do it than most high-priced psychiatrists. More than likely, I won't be able to kill old Slewfoot either. So my hosts will discover there's no such thing as being able to hunt a turkey on a given day and bag it.

Still, I've often been able to use the napping trick to fool not only the turkey but also my hosts. Most of the time they'll show me about where an old turkey hangs out. Then, by scouting the area, I can often find droppings and feathers and feel pretty confident I'm where the turkey is moving and feeding. Once I've got an idea of where that turkey is going to be, the next morning I go hunt a different one. I don't even bother with old Slewfoot. He's been called to and shot at by a whole family of good turkey hunters many mornings over several years. So I try to find a turkey to call that I can kill.

If I don't get my gobbler by 10:00 A.M. I go back where Slewfoot is supposed to hang out. I believe that turkeys, especially where there's lots of hunting pressure, get accustomed to that surge of hunters from daylight until about 8:00 A.M. Most hunters hunt the first couple of hours in the morning because that's generally when toms gobble the most and come to call the quickest. After 8:00 the turkeys know the hunters are leaving the woods, so they feel more confident about moving. The best time to hunt these tough turkeys is between 10:00 A.M. and noon, or between 3:00 P.M. and 5:00.

If I can find the roost tree and see which direction the turkey goes after he leaves the roost, half the battle is won. Generally the turkey will come back to the roost tree from the same direction. I say ''generally'' because turkeys never, ever, do what they're supposed to.

Next, I locate a tree between the roost tree and the direction the turkey went. I choose a tree that allows me to move around in any direction and see 30 to 40 yards. Then the turkey will be in shotgun range as soon as I spot him. I want the area to be open—but not so open that I can see the turkey coming from 100 yards away.

In an area like this, I feel very confident. The turkey is using it in the mornings when he flies down from the roost, and probably in the afternoons just before he flies back up. I can be pretty sure he hasn't been spooked, shot at, or had an encounter with a predator here. So he should feel relatively secure when he's in my killing zone.

The next task is to make myself a soft place to sit. I may have to spend one to two hours here, and must be comfortable enough to go to sleep. I take extra time to get rid of rocks, sticks, and briars, and then I make a cushion of pine straw or leaves.

I have a vest with a cushioned drop seat and a cushion for my back. I let the seat down and sit back against the tree. Before I get too comfortable, I rake away some of the leaves all the way around the base of the tree, so I can move quietly if the turkey comes up from behind me or from either side.

Then I go into a sequence of mating calls. I do a lot of cutting, and give many single notes quickly in a cackle rhythm. Although many people define a cackle as a fast series of yelps that build up to a crescendo and then drop off with the cackle, numbering as many as five to seven notes, I feel that the cackle is a series of single notes given in rapid succession instead of double notes. Then I break off my cackle with a gobble. After I go through that series of calls, I keep still for three to five minutes before going back into that same routine.

I probably call more than the average caller. I like to hear myself call, and I think that hunters more often fail to bag their birds from too little calling than they do from too much. Usually, if a turkey is going to gobble to my calling, he'll do so when I go through my first sequence of mating calls. But, if he never does gobble, I keep giving this same sequence until

I get tired. Then I lay down my calls, put my gun across my lap, and go to sleep.

I love to sleep in the woods. Many times I don't go to sleep deliberately, but when I've stayed up half the night gabbing with hunters about turkeys, gotten up before daylight, eaten a big breakfast and hunted until 10:00 A.M., taking a nap is about all I can do.

Often I've been wakened by a turkey gobbling only 20 or 30 yards from me. The trick then is to determine whether I'm dreaming, or actually hearing a gobble. Once I decide I'm not dreaming, I open my eyes and try to become fully awake before I move my eyes or any part of my body. The chances are that the turkey can already see me, and the worst thing I could do is to start looking around for him.

Often this is the hardest part of napping for gobblers—waking up, knowing a turkey is close, and having to fight the urge to look for him.

I wait awhile and listen for the turkey to walk, drum, or gobble again. If I'm patient enough, usually he'll give his position away. Only then do I let myself move, look, and take whatever action I need to get a shot.

Sometimes I've awakened simply because I could feel a turkey. I believe that hunters who spend a lot of time in the woods develop a sixth sense, and can feel the presence of a turkey without actually seeing or hearing him.

To sum it all up, napping for gobblers gives you a number of unusual advantages:

- You have the opportunity to hunt turkeys when you are really too tired to hunt.

- If you are short on patience, you can wait unconscious in a good location until a turkey shows up.

- You can spend more time hunting if you take a nap in the woods instead of going home at 9:00 or 10:00 A.M. More time in the woods means more chance that you and a turkey will meet. What's more, you'll be hunting after most hunters have called it quits, when wary old gobblers are more likely to reveal themselves.

- Best of all, though, napping for gobblers is both easy and fun.

Dave Kenyon, Michigan Dept. of Natural Resources, photo

The Big
Seed Turkeys

with Jay Brown

One of my favorite turkeys is Old Wallace. I named this turkey after a karate fighter—Bill Wallace—who's known as Superfoot. Old Wallace has the biggest foot I've ever seen on a turkey. His track is like the track of a small ostrich.

Old Wallace is a tough bird. I've seen him only three times, but a friend of mine missed him at 17 steps. Yet nobody has taken him. Old Wallace travels with a younger bird that I guess is about two years old. I've seen the two together through a binocular. The second lieutenant's beard appears about 8 inches long, while I judge Old Wallace's beard to be between 11 and 12 inches long.

Old Wallace is tough to hunt because he's been called to so many times and so many hunters have fooled with him. There's just not much a hunter can do that Old Wallace hasn't heard or seen before. Old Wallace will gobble good in the morning until he hears the first sound made by the hunter—whether he's owling, crow calling, or hen yelping. When he hears a hunter, he shuts up. But even if he's heard a hunter, he'll gobble again in about ten minutes if there are hens in the area giving light tree calls.

I've been trying to take Old Wallace for two years, and I believe he was at least two years old when I first started hunting him. I've introduced him to several other hunters—good hunters—who haven't been able to do anything with him either. I think the only way Old Wallace will ever be killed is to hunt him in the afternoon. He'll gobble one time late in the afternoon, generally before he flies up to roost. I believe that if I take a slate and try calling him in the afternoons, I may have a chance of killing him.

All I plan to do is cluck and purr very softly. Old Wallace probably won't gobble back to me. I believe he'll slip in behind me without making a sound. The only way I'll be able to kill him is to see him before he sees me. That's what makes Old Wallace a tough turkey to take. I call him a seed turkey, because he'll seed many offspring before he's ever killed or before he dies naturally.

Another seed turkey that's dealt me fits for the last few years is the Garden-Patch Gobbler. There's an old lady who lives way back in the hills and has a garden patch. Really, it's more like a small truck farm than a garden. The patch is about an acre, and an old gobbler lives close by.

Every morning when the turkey pitches off the roost, he flies straight to the garden. He'll strut in the middle of that one-acre patch and stay right there until his hens come to meet him. No matter what call you use or how sneaky you are, you're not going to lure the Garden-Patch Gobbler away from the clear patch.

When that gobbler's hens show up, he'll get right in the middle of them and walk off with them. If you try to call him, he'll go in the other direction. That gobbler is not going to move out of the middle of the garden patch until he sees hens or else has hens around him. I've had absolutely no success in calling him, and I don't know if he'll ever be killed. He's another of those tough seed turkeys.

But the oldest, smartest gobbler I ever chased is the Low-Water Bridge Turkey. I've come close to taking him on a couple of occasions, but after three years of hunting, the score is turkey 3, me 0.

I think this turkey is the oldest one I've ever hunted. He must be at least five years old. He roosts in the same area year after year. I see him every fall during deer season, and once I could have taken a shot at him. But I wasn't sure I could hit him. I inherited the Low-Water Bridge Turkey from another fellow who'd been trying to kill him. After three years of fooling with him, I gave him back to the fellow who gave him to me.

This turkey will gobble two times each day. He gobbles one time when he flies down from the roost, and the other time when he flies back up. I've seen hens really raise Cain around him, but he never will gobble to them. He'll strut and drum, but that's all the noise he'll make. He's extremely call-shy. I don't believe anybody will ever kill him unless they get lucky in the afternoon with a slate call.

Old, hard-to-kill gobblers are much like the most beautiful girl in the high school you once attended. You finally realize that you never really had a chance of getting a date with her, but you always had to go back and try—just to see if there wasn't something you could do a little differently or say a little differently to win her attention. I've known turkey hunters who became obsessed with the thought of taking an old, tough gobbler. Even though there are easier turkeys and often closer turkeys to hunt, one of those seed turkeys that outsmarts the hunter every time is like a magnet that draws him back each spring for another attempt.

These seed turkeys are my nemeses. Even though I'll hunt and take many more gobblers, these three, and eventually others like them, will continue to draw me into the woods each spring. I enjoy a challenge, and I like to take turkeys. So I spend time hunting in the woods where I know

One of the ingredients that is required for good turkey habitat is dusting sites like the one pictured. When a hunter discovers a dusting area, he knows that there are birds in the area and that this will be a prime location for gobblers. (Leonard Lee Rue III photo)

I can kill a turkey. And we are lucky in Mississippi, because we have so much open land in the form of national forests and state management areas.

There are two types of terrain to hunt in my region. First there are the flatlands along the Mississippi River, which are open terrain with mainly cottonwoods and hackberry, and some oaks where the flatlands merge with the hills. In this bottomland you can usually see for 200 or 300 yards. If you hear a turkey gobble, you set up to call him just as you would anywhere else. The biggest problem I have with the flatlands is that you can't get as close to a turkey as you can in the hills. This is one of the reasons I prefer to hunt the hills.

If you understand the lay of the land in the hills, you know which ridges to walk. Then you can position yourself so you can be close to the turkey without his ever seeing you. For instance, a turkey can be just off the ridge on one side of the hill, and you can be off it on the other side. When the turkey flies down, he can walk up to the top of the hill without ever seeing you. When you see him, he'll be within killing distance.

The closer to home you hunt, the more time you can spend hunting before you have to go to work. And luckily, I've found that the terrain near my home is excellent for turkeys. There are rolling hills with steep ridges. On some of these hills are old pastures where cattle graze. The pastures are surrounded by big hardwood trees—oak, sweetgum, dogwood, and red-bud. There's a minimum of undergrowth. The woods provide plenty of feed, while the pastures furnish excellent dusting and nesting areas for the hens. All of this makes ideal habitat for wild turkeys.

Since we have plenty of turkeys in Mississippi and not as many hunters as some of the northern states, I plan to bag my bird each season. But I'll probably still go back and try some of those old seed turkeys again, to see if I've learned enough to take one.

Playing the Game Fairly

by John E. Phillips

We were just outside Liberty, Mississippi. The turkey was gobbling his head off. Even the least-experienced hunter would have known that gobbler was fooled. Still, he wouldn't come to our blind.

"He's hung up," I whispered to Allen Jenkins and J. C. Brown, my two hunting companions.

Although in many situations three's a crowd, when you're turkey hunting three's a mob. But we three wanted to hunt together. And Brown and Jenkins planned to show me just how deadly the old Lynch box caller still is in luring *Meleagris gallopavo* to the hunter.

"Well," Brown answered, "some folks might think the turkey is hung up—but not us. Just be patient, and we'll get that old bird.

"Here's the situation," he continued. "The turkey is on the other side of a fairly deep ditch. He doesn't want to fly across it. And he knows he shouldn't have to, because that hen should come where he's gobbling if she wants to be serviced. So he's trying to gobble, strut, and drum enough to get his lady friend to cross the ditch and come to him like she should."

But after an hour of working the proud gobbler, Brown and Jenkins had lured him no closer than the edge of the ditch—some 100 yards away. Although I had traveled to Louisiana to learn how these men hunted, after an hour of hearing a big tom gobble his head off I felt I had to do something—even if it was wrong. Since I'd hunted turkeys for many years, I could think of several methods to kill one that wouldn't cross a natural barrier like a ditch. I decided that probably the easiest method would be to leave our blind, circle the turkey, get on the same side of the ditch with him, and then call him up and take him. So I suggested that tactic to Jenkins and Brown.

"No, I don't think so," Brown said. "We're not going to bushwhack that gobbler. That's not playing the game fairly."

Bushwhack, I thought. *Why, moving on a turkey isn't bushwhacking. That's just good turkey hunting.*

180

But I was a guest. And I always try to hunt the way my host prefers to hunt—even if I think he's wrong. My patience was wearing very thin, however, after listening to the turkey gobble for an hour.

I was convinced that if I applied the tactics I had learned, I could kill the gobbler. Ten minutes of calling, gobbling, and silence passed before I spoke again. As we sat in the blind, I was studying our situation and the turkey's position, and figuring what other technique I could use to kill him without "bushwhacking."

We were "blind-up" in the woods along the side of a sloping field, close to its upper end. The gobbler was across a ditch about 50 yards beyond the lower end of the field. The way I figured it, I could belly-crawl down through the field, slip into the woods, and move in on the bird, while Brown and Jenkins kept calling. Since the turkey was moving along the ditch, first one way and then the other, I assumed that all I had to do was wait until he moved away from me and then slip into a spot he was sure to walk back to. But after I explained my strategy, Jenkins said, "We're not going to bushwhack the turkey."

By now my two hunting buddies could see my frustration. I knew how to kill the turkey, but my methods were not in accord with the way these men hunted.

"Listen, John," Jenkins told me. "Killing the bird is no sport. Anybody can do that."

Although I had my doubts, I kept quiet. I was hoping to learn why we weren't much concerned with killing a turkey—since after all, we were turkey hunting.

"When you call a turkey within gun range," Jenkins went on, "you make him do something unnatural. The hens are supposed to go to him. He shouldn't have to go to them. If you can fool that turkey into believing you're a hen ready for mating and make him come to you, then you've beaten him at his own game. You deserve to take him. But whether you bag him or not, you've played fairly and won the game. If you can't call the turkey to you, no matter what the reason, the turkey wins. You should have to hunt him another day."

This philosophy sounds noble when you're sitting at a campfire trying to convince others you're the greatest hunter alive. But when a hot turkey has been gobbling his fool head off 100 yards away from you for over an hour, playing the game fairly doesn't seem nearly as important as killing him.

Besides the problem of the ditch the turkey had to cross, Jenkins and Brown were determined to call him with a box caller, one of the first modern callers developed for turkey hunting. I had used a box caller to take turkeys. But my increasing prowess as a turkey hunter had made the box seem a tame means of calling, not quite as glamorous as a diaphragm mouth caller.

"Okay, John, here's what we're going to do," Brown said. "Allen and I will start cutting and calling at the same time. That old gobbler will think there are two or three hens here. He won't be able to stand the thought of all those hens waiting to be mated. So he'll walk all the way to the end of the ditch, around the ditch, and come up through the woods on the opposite side of the field from us. Then we'll call him across the field. When he's 30 yards out, you can shoot him.''

I couldn't believe Brown thought he and Jenkins could make that turkey go through all that trouble to mate a hen. ''Don't you think you're asking a lot of him?'' I said.

''Sure we are,'' Brown whispered. ''But that's what makes calling turkeys so much more fun than hunting turkeys.''

I found that the two men were really enjoying the hunt, although they knew I didn't have much faith in this sit-and-wait tactic. But when the cutting and cackling started, Jenkins said, ''Okay, the turkey's coming.''

I had a hard time believing what I was hearing. The turkey continued to gobble as he walked around the ditch, then up through the woods on the far side of the field.

''Better get your gun up, John,'' Brown instructed while grinning from ear to ear. ''The turkey will be here in just a minute.''

And just as though he were following a script, the longbeard walked out on the opposite side of the field—strutting and drumming while moving straight toward us. When he was 50 yards away, Jenkins cackled to him. The turkey blew up like a toad—strutting and gobbling all the way. When he was 40 yards out, Jenkins asked me, ''Do you want to shoot him?'' Again, I couldn't believe what I was seeing. There was a fine 9- to 10-inch beard on a fully mature turkey that we'd been calling for an hour and 45 minutes, and my host was asking if I wanted to shoot the turkey.

Trying hard not to be rude, I asked Jenkins, ''Do you want me to shoot him?'' Then I thought, *Did I really say that?*

Jenkins allowed that the turkey was a big one and the beard was nice. Judging from the spurs, though, he thought the turkey was only a two-year-old. ''But take him if you want to,'' he said.

I must be losing my mind, I thought. *There's a turkey strutting and gobbling at 30 yards that we've called for almost two hours, and now we're discussing whether or not to shoot.*

''What do you want me to do?'' I asked.

Gobble, gobble, gobble, the turkey retorted.

''We may be able to find an older bird close to another field,'' Brown whispered.

''No, let's let John go ahead and take this one,'' said Jenkins. ''If we find another gobbler, we'll call him up and let John take a look. Okay, John, take him.''

When the turkey dropped strut and craned his neck, I squeezed the trigger on my 3-inch-magnum Remington SP. The turkey went down, and I raced across the ground to cover him just in case he decided to get up.

''That's the first time I've ever seen a fellow jump on a turkey and pick him up in less than a minute after the shot," Brown observed as he and Jenkins approached.

The gobbler weighed 19 pounds and had a 10-inch beard. But downing him was not the end of the hunt or the end of what I would learn from Allen Jenkins, president of the Lynch Turkey Call Company, and from J. C. Brown, one of the company's key men.

During the next two days, we called six more gobblers within range but never fired a shot.

"J. C. probably has 50 gobblers on his land," Jenkins said. "But he won't allow more than eight or ten birds to be harvested a year. He wants plenty of old gobblers to hunt and likes to see them in his fields. J. C. will hunt almost every day of the season. He'll call maybe 10 to 20 turkeys within range. He may let his friends bag some, but he'll only kill one or two turkeys a season himself."

Beating the turkeys at their own game is what qualifies Brown and Jenkins as masters of the sport. "The reason so many hunters don't kill turkeys is that they don't give them time to come to their calling," Jenkins explain. "Although some gobblers will run to a caller like a race horse, those are usually the younger ones. The older gobblers will be much slower and much more cautious. The hunter who beats the veteran turkeys has to play the game the way they do, or he can never win fairly."

Then Jenkins mentioned another aspect of the sport that I'd never really thought about: "John, the bird you took makes a good case for hunting the old way. We had the opportunity to work with that turkey for almost two hours. We were able to hear him gobble, figure out what he was doing and where he was going, and watch him strut and drum. Then we still had plenty of time to shoot if we so chose.

"If we'd moved on the turkey like you suggested, or if you'd crawled to him, more than likely you'd have spooked him or taken him quickly and missed all the fun of listening to him and watching him work. No matter what tactic we might have used, we wouldn't have had as much fun as we did by being patient, letting the turkey work, hunting the old way, and playing the game fairly."

Deep down inside, I knew Jenkins was right.

To further prove the case for hunting the old way, Jenkins let Brown use his mouth caller to try to call a gobbler. Just like the tar baby, however, the gobbler didn't say nothing. But when Jenkins cackled on his foolproof box, the turkey gobbled.

Sometimes only a box call will force a turkey to gobble. Many hunters don't realize that a box call sounds exactly like a hen at 30 to 50 yards. The old-fashioned boxes call up many gobblers for hunters even today.

According to Jenkins, "If you want to call more turkeys, enjoy the sport more, and play the game fairly, then try the old way."

Jenkins says the greatest challenge of all is a special kind of turkey called a hermit: "To be classified as a hermit, a gobbler must be at least

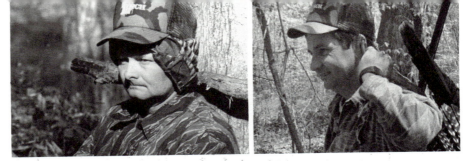

Fair players Allen Jenkins (left) and J. C. Brown.

five years old and should travel by himself. As the turkey gets older, he'll rarely be with hens. A hermit tom will usually gobble very little, if at all. In most turkey-hunting circles, these birds are classified as silent gobblers.

"Also, a hermit turkey should have an unusual track. Then the hunter can keep up with him and learn his movement patterns. Some of the hermits I've hunted have had clubfeet, crooked toes, or bent toes.

"I'll never kill a hermit even though I may have many chances, because hermits are the smartest turkeys in the world. If you find one and kill him, you may never be able to hunt a turkey like that again. Locating a hermit tom is the true test of a master hunter. If you beat a hermit, then you can truly be classified as a champion turkey taker."

When Jenkins speaks of "beating the turkey," he doesn't mean killing the turkey but instead is referring to getting him within killing range and then allowing him to walk off.

"Each time you work a hermit gobbler, he gets smarter and smarter," Jenkins says. "The longer you fool with him, the more challenging the game becomes."

Jenkins told me about the School-Bus Hermit that would gobble only at 7:36 A.M., when a school bus went down a dirt road and hit a certain bump that jarred its windows. As he spoke of the School-Bus Hermit, I could tell he was talking about an old friend he'd met on the field of combat many a spring morning. Although the duel between them could have been to the death, each combatant played the game nobly. And when the contest for the day was over, each knew more about the other's strengths and weaknesses.

"If J. C. comes to work at 9:00 A.M. on a morning during turkey season and says that he beat an old gobbler that day, he doesn't have to have a dead turkey in hand to prove that he won the game," Jenkins says. "If J. C. says he beat the turkey, then I know, and J. C. knows, that he could have taken him if he wanted to, but he left the gobbler so he could hunt him again another day."

Playing the game fairly—hunting the old way—does not mean taking a limit of turkeys each season. Playing the game fairly:

- does not require the hunter to win every time,
- does allow for more enjoyment of the sport of turkey calling,
- does build memories that last,
- may not be as swift as the modern way of hurrying up to take a turkey and
- doesn't have to result in a limit of turkeys being taken for the season.

But hunting the old way still works, just as it did in the old days.

Part **4**

SPECIAL
SITUATIONS

Fred Darty says his trophy turkey success depends 20 percent on calling ability, 30 percent on detailed information about a particular turkey that he gathers from every possible source, and 50 percent on his ability to sit still and remain unnoticed or to move and outflank his quarry.

Fred Darty: Trophy Hunter

by John E. Phillips

A trophy turkey hunter hunts legends, not just turkeys. Gobblers no one else can kill are his quarry. When everybody has given up on one of these old turkeys, a veteran hunter like Fred Darty of Jasper, Alabama, often hears about him and takes him on. To such a hunter, the weight of the turkey and the length of his beard and spurs are not nearly so important as the stories of other hunters pitting their skills against him and losing.

"To qualify as a trophy," says Darty, "a turkey must be at least five years old and must have encountered many hunters. He'll rarely come to a hen or a caller. Caution has superseded his sex drive, and he may well be the wisest creature in the woods."

Darty is a tall, quiet man. I first met him one morning at the Southern Sportsman Lodge in central Alabama. I'd heard that he was almost sure to bag a turkey every day he hunted.

"Shoot one for me," I told him as a joke early that morning.

"Sure," he answered quietly, and left the lodge.

Dressed from head to toe in camouflage, he melted into the darkness. Later, I met him for lunch. He reported that he and his son had heard some turkeys and would try to take one in the afternoon. That night, back at the lodge, Darty sauntered over to my table.

"Your turkey is in the cooler. Keith and I both got one this afternoon. So I went ahead and cleaned the one I shot for you."

"You're kidding," I said.

"You said you wanted a turkey, didn't you?" he asked.

No one had ever given me a wild turkey before. I've never given one away or known of anyone else who has. Turkeys come too hard to be given away, but that's not true where Fred Darty is concerned.

"Taking young turkeys before they get their education is not difficult," Darty explained. "You can get in close, set up, call, and they'll come. But once a hunter has gone after a turkey and failed, the odds change heavily in the turkey's favor."

Fred is the most meticulous hunter I've ever met. Nothing is overlooked in his preparation for a hunt. Nothing goes unnoticed when he's afield. He runs all available information through his computer until he conceives a viable plan.

Careful, early training in the woods accounts for much of Darty's hunting expertise. He turkey-hunted for the first time in 1945. "I was only six years old," he says, "but my dad was a superb turkey hunter. He taught me what he knew."

Years later, while practicing dentistry in Warner Robins, Georgia, Darty really began to concentrate on trophy gobblers. Knowing Darty loved to hunt turkeys, his patients and friends often told him about wary gobblers that had fooled them for years. Many offered him a chance to hunt a trophy turkey. As Darty's reputation grew, hunters all over Georgia and Alabama began to call him when they were forced to give up on an old turkey that had outsmarted them time after time. And he often succeeded when no one else could.

According to Darty, his trophy turkey taking depends 20 percent on his calling ability, 30 percent on detailed information about a particular turkey that he gathers from every possible source, and 50 percent on his ability to hide, sit still, move, and outflank his quarry.

Darty attempts to avoid the errors the other hunters have committed. "Before I hunt a trophy turkey," he says, "I talk to all the people I can find who have tried and failed to take him. Maybe they got too close, shot too quickly, or called to him too much. If they've shot at him in a particular area, I try not to set up there because I think turkeys soon learn to avoid dangerous places."

Lengthy preparation and investigation paid off when he challenged an old turkey on a heavily hunted wildlife-management area. "A friend of mine told me about the turkey. He'd wounded him slightly the year before, after hunting him for a couple of years. The turkey had plenty of hunting pressure every season and was really wary.

"After collecting all the information I could, I hunted this cagey turkey for seven mornings before I found out how to take him. He gobbled readily at a long distance in answer to my calling, but he would come no closer than 150 yards and then stop gobbling. No amount of calling would pull him within gun range. I decided that this smart turkey knew from past experience how close he could safely come. He apparently gobbled early to let the hens know where he was. After he flew down from his roost, he walked within 150 yards of where he thought the hens were, and waited for them to show up.

"I'd found some big turkey tracks on a logging road while scouting. They seemed to go directly to the turkey's roost tree. When the woods started to wake up, I gave a short, fast, excited fly-down cackle about 300 yards from where I thought the roost was. The turkey double-gobbled. He sounded like he was choking, he answered so fast. I turned and headed down the logging road at a dead run. When I was within 100 yards of his roost, I stopped and sat down next to a large oak but didn't touch my call. My heart was still pounding when I saw the turkey coming up the road. When he walked within 20 yards of me, I fired."

The Wildlife-Management Area Turkey weighed 20½ pounds and had 1⅜-inch spurs. He carried two old shotgun wounds, one in his chest and one in the root of his tail.

Moving up on old gobblers is one of Darty's favorite tactics: "I've learned to call less for trophy turkeys than I do for younger ones. Getting to a spot an old turkey will come to is far more important than calling. Good calling will bring young turkeys in, but a veteran turkey has heard and answered good calling before, and he's had problems with hunters. He won't come in like a young turkey. You have to meet him at a spot in the woods where he feels safe and where he normally wants to go. Knowing that spot, getting there quietly, and staying hidden long enough for him to show up are the top requirements for bagging a boss gobbler.

"Another tactic I use, once I find out where a trophy turkey is roosting, is to move in close and yelp to him as the hens are flying up in the evening. As soon as he gobbles back, I leave. The next morning, I try to get between him and the hens and give a few light tree calls as the hens fly down. I use the same call I used the evening before, a light yelp. Then I wait.

"One morning, before the old gobbler I'd yelped to could arrive, a jake moved in. Knowing the jake might spook the trophy gobbler, I waved my gloved hand. The jake saw the movement and left. A few minutes later, the big turkey I'd attempted to outmaneuver for a week came into range, and I bagged him."

Most hunters believe their hunt is over once a gobbler finds his hens, because calling him away from his harem is extremely difficult. Darty, however, doesn't give up: "Sometimes I deliberately call hens I think are escorting an old gobbler. The hens may bring the trophy to me, if I'm camouflaged well and I sit still enough. A gobbler feels safe with a flock of hens. There are more eyes and ears to look and listen for danger, so he feels much more secure than he does when he's by himself."

Darty is a camouflage expert. "I hunted a piney woods gobbler for three years," he says, "and had him in range once but never was able to shoot. Finally, on a drizzly day, the turkey stood 25 yards away. But my gun wasn't pointing right, and I couldn't move. He looked around a tree straight at me. I was convinced he couldn't see me. I was perfectly camouflaged, and I was motionless. I even squinted my eyes so the whites wouldn't show. But I know he saw me. He putted and left.

"I was confused and frustrated. I went to the spot where the turkey had been and looked back at the tree I'd been sitting against. In the rain, the trunk looked very dark and the foliage looked almost black. I walked to the tree and propped up my hunting coat against it. When I moved where the turkey had been and looked at my stand again, I saw what he'd seen. My green camo shirt stood out like a neon light."

Selecting the right camouflage to blend with the cover you're hunting is a must. Darty purchased three different suits of camouflage clothing before he finally matched the cover where he was setting up. He waited for the next rainy morning, and took the Piney Woods Gobbler that had eluded him so long.

Darty has discovered that rainy days are better than average for trophy turkey hunting. Because most hunters stay home on rainy days, old gobblers have few if any encounters with them then, and feel more adventuresome. "Turkeys are less skittish and easier to call when the weather's rainy than on bluebird days when most hunters are out."

Darty thinks the traveling turkey is the hardest kind to kill: "A traveling turkey is an old gobbler that answers your calls but moves farther away at each call. If you try to move closer, he just backs off more. But by calling only once or twice, changing calls, and getting in front of this kind of turkey, I've been successful.

"If you call and get an answer, call again a bit later. If the turkey answers, you know the direction he's going and have some idea of the path he'll take. Circle and get in front of him, but don't call. Listen and look for him to walk by. You may score, but some turkeys simply can't be killed."

One of these invincible turkeys was the Clear-Cut Baron. "I hunted him for several seasons," Darty says. "Other hunters had tried to shoot him off the roost and had set up three-man ambushes. But they couldn't get him, no matter what they did."

For more than six years, the Clear-Cut Baron eluded them all. Not even Darty could outsmart him: "That turkey could almost read property lines. He knew where there was sanctuary and how to fool hunters. The last time I saw him, he was strutting on a knoll out in the center of his clear-cut kingdom. There was so little foliage for 300 yards in all directions that there was no way to approach him without being seen. And he sure wouldn't come to a call."

Because rifles are forbidden for turkey hunting in Alabama, the turkey was out of range. And he seemed to be aware of that fact. "You could call all day long." Darty goes on, "and he never would leave his barren home. He drummed, strutted, and waited for a hen to find him in the open, where he could see a great distance. As far as I know, the Clear-Cut Baron died of old age. I never heard of anyone who killed him."

Fred Darty is like an Olympic athlete. He trains, he studies, he polishes his skills. He wants to compete against the very best adversaries he can find. He doesn't always win—but that's what makes the sport of hunting trophy turkeys worthwhile.

Pasture and Field Gobblers

with Seab Hicks

One of the toughest turkeys to kill is a gobbler with a lot of hens that roosts on the edge of a pasture or tilled field. Since he roosts near the hens, he can see them fly down to that pasture or field in the mornings. All he has to do is fly down with them, then gobble, strut, mate, and feed in the open, where he can see danger coming a long way off.

I've known turkeys like this to drive a whole town crazy. Any morning you go by the field you can see the gobbler and his hens. You can try calling him, but he's not going to come. Why should he? He has all his hens with him. There's no way to sneak up on him, because he stays in the open. And there's no reason for him to move into heavy cover because everything he needs is in the field. Hunters may spend weeks trying to bag an old bird like this and never take him.

Before daylight, however, I try moving within 75 or 100 yards of where the gobbler is roosting, just on the edge of the field. I want to be between the gobbler and the field, or on the edge of the field where I can see anything that moves in it.

Once I'm set up I don't owl-hoot, tree-call, or use any of the accepted tactics to make a turkey gobble. I wait for the light to begin to appear on the pasture. For a while after it does, the woods will still be dark. The turkeys will be asleep in the trees, and the songbirds won't even have started singing yet.

When there's just enough light to see in the pasture, I start to call aggressively to the gobbler. I do a lot of cutting, cackling, and yelping, like a really demanding hen. An old gobbler that hears all that racket out in the field really gets shaken up. I guess he thinks a new hen has come to the field, or one of the hens in his harem has gotten to the field and is anxiously waiting for him to arrive.

Whatever he thinks, he doesn't want to disappoint the first lady to come calling. He likes to get to the first hen in the field in the morning

When there is just enough light to see in the pasture, Seab Hicks starts to call aggressively to the gobbler. He does a lot of cutting, cackling, and yelping, imitating a demanding hen. An old gobbler that hears all that racket out in the field gets mighty interested.

and breed her. Those other hens he's roosting with haven't even awakened yet, so I know they won't keep him from coming to me.

When that old gobbler answers my call I get my gun up, because he's probably coming at a run. As he moves out into the field, he's easy to see. He can't spot me, however, because the woods are still dark, the background I'm sitting against is dark, and the camo I wear is dark. This tactic has really worked for me on field and pasture gobblers.

It's also productive at times on turkeys roosting next to clear-cuts. In almost every locality where timber companies manage land by clear-cutting, there's a legendary turkey nicknamed the Clear-Cut Gobbler. He flies down in the morning right in the middle of the clear-cut, for all to see, and hangs up there most of the day. This pasture prescription may be just the medicine to take the old bird for the table.

Remember, however, that no tactic will work on every gobbler every time. That's the reason old *Meleagris gallopavo* is such a great challenge.

Bad-Weather Birds

by John E. Phillips

Most turkey hunters would have gone back to sleep after looking out from under the covers and seeing a moonless sky and heavy overcast. But not the Gulvas brothers. Denny and Ed Gulvas of Dubois, Pennsylvania, are tough hunters.

The two of them had come to the Fairfield Glade Resort in Tennessee, for the Levi Garrett/All American Turkey Calling Championship. Denny is a nationally known competition turkey caller. He's won the U. S. Open Turkey Calling Championship three times, and the Masters' Turkey Calling Championship twice. He's also won scores of state and regional contests. Now, while he and Ed were in Tennessee, they wanted to work in some turkey hunting.

The day before, the weather had been far from typical of spring. The wind blew so hard it broke down trees. Rain came down in sheets, and the temperature dropped into the 30s.

In the darkness of the morning after, as Denny and Ed headed for the woods without hesitation, it appeared the weather might improve. But probably not much.

All the conditions were wrong for bagging a turkey. "The weather made hunting a real challenge," Denny says. "We'd scouted an area and found a lot of turkey sign. If we could get to that area, we felt we should be able to kill a turkey."

Before first light, Denny and Ed made the two-mile hike from their vehicle to the spot they'd chosen.

"As it began to get light," Denny explains, "I made a few calls from a couple of high spots, but got no response. We finally moved down a ridge. I went out on a point and made a few calls. Although I didn't hear a gobble, I saw some movement about 80 yards away. In the soft light I could tell it was a turkey. The area was kind of thick. The turkey moved off to my left. He never answered my call, but I felt he'd heard me. He began to work around the point of the ridge we were on, and met up with another gobbler.

"I don't know where this second turkey came from, because I never heard or saw him until the first one rendezvoused with him. As soon as the two met, they began to fight. They ran at each other, jumped three or four feet into the air, and tried to spur each other. They also wrapped necks and tried to peck each other into submission.

"While the fight was going on, Ed and I tried to get into position to kill one of the turkeys. They were fighting 75 yards away. I knew that if we tried to back up against a stump or tree, they'd see us. So we simply sat down where we were. Since I didn't even have my head net on, I pulled my hat down close to my eyes. But I could still see. Although we were caught out in the open, we felt that anything we might try other than sitting down and being still would spook the turkeys.

"When the fight was over, I waited a few minutes and then gave some calls, thinking both turkeys would come running in to us. But they didn't. For some reason they just didn't have mating on their minds. After a few minutes, the dominant gobbler began to strut."

For what seemed like hours but was only a few minutes, the Gulvas brothers sat frozen as the two turkeys moved within 50 yards of them. The dominant gobbler occasionally would strut, while the younger one stayed about ten yards away from him, casually feeding. They walked off the side of the ridge and into a little bottom 60 to 70 yards from the hunters—out of sight and out of range.

While the turkeys were out of sight, Denny and Ed put on their head nets. Denny took three mouth yelpers out of his pocket and laid them on his knee. Next, he made a few clucks and purrs to get the attention of the turkeys and bring them into range. But they wouldn't fall in love with his calling. For 45 minutes the two men stayed wadded up, their muscles screaming for relief, their eyes straining for the cottony head of the bronze baron.

"I tried a few feeding purrs, thinking that if the gobblers weren't interested in mating I might talk them into coming to feed," Denny remembers. "That didn't work either. All the things you're supposed to be able to do with turkeys at close range didn't work."

So Denny employed his next tactic, using three different calls—an old hen, a young hen, and a middle-aged hen. Working with these, he hoped to imitate a flock of hens feeding in the area just above the gobblers. But they failed to gobble and wouldn't come into sight.

Having seen the turkeys fight, Denny thought he might make them jealous enough to come in: "I took out a gobbling device and prepared my next tactic. I yelped like a hen with my mouth yelper, and then gobbled right on top of the yelp. I did this two or three times, to make the turkeys down in the bottom think another gobbler was on the ridge, escorting those hens that were clucking and yelping."

Yelping and gobbling with aggressive turkeys in the area usually will bring one in—to fight, if for no other reason. The trick should have worked, but it didn't. Denny occasionally could see the white of the turkeys' heads bobbing up and down in the bottom. So he knew they were still in the region, but they wouldn't budge. They'd decided how close they were going to come, and they weren't coming any closer. Hens are supposed to go to gobblers, not gobblers to hens.

"In a case like this, the best thing to do is just wait the turkeys out," Denny says. "Sometimes two or three hours will pass before they finally come in to you. Generally, if you wait there long enough and don't spook them, they'll present you a shot."

After waiting 45 minutes, he went back to the three mouth yelpers. He'd placed them on his knee earlier, to minimize movement when switching from one to another. But still the turkeys failed to gobble or to move any closer.

"Finally, one of them clucked back to me," Denny remembers. "When I heard that one cluck, I knew there was a chance I could get them up to us. So I started doing some hen yelping. In about 15 minutes, I could hear one of the turkeys strutting below me. Then I saw his head moving toward me. He was about 30 or 40 yards away when I saw him—well within killing distance."

In the spring when the sun is warm and the turkeys are really gobbling, sometimes you find two gobblers together and can call them both into range. Denny wanted two gobblers that morning—one for Ed, and one for himself. But the old gobbler began to move in alone, very cautiously, within 22 yards of where they sat.

Denny knew the other turkey was only 10 to 12 yards farther out: "I thought if we sat still and stayed quiet, both turkeys would come within killing distance. Then Ed and I both could bag our gobblers when I gave a signal. I was going to let Ed take the first one, and I planned to shoot the second turkey when he came over the ridge.

"The first one moved off to the right. Ed had his gun aimed straight for its head, while I waited for the second turkey to come into range. For seven or eight minutes, we stayed still. The first gobbler was now within 20 yards. He was looking hard for the hens he'd heard on this ridge. He was really getting nervous because he couldn't find them. Luckily, we'd had enough time to put our face masks on before he'd come into view. He stayed out there at 20 yards and stared at us for a long time.

"Finally the old gobbler moved away from Ed, toward me. I knew he was spooked. He'd come to meet his hens, and they weren't there. The turkey behind him hadn't come over the ridge, and he was ready to leave. I realized I'd have to go ahead and take him and forget about the second one, or neither of us would have a shot all day. So I fired, and the gobbler went down in a heap."

The turkey weighed 17¾ pounds, had a 10-inch beard, and was the only gobbler killed that day by any of the 33 turkey hunters, the nation's best, who had come to the area to compete in the calling championship.

Many hunters stay home on cold, cloudy days when the chances of killing a turkey seem slim. But even though the turkeys may not gobble or be interested in coming to a call, they can still be killed.

"The best thing to do in bad weather," says Denny Gulvas, "is to move into an area where you've seen good turkey signs, do a little bit of turkey talk—clucks, purrs, and light yelps—and be aware of everything around you. A turkey can come in from any direction, and you have to be constantly looking."

Instead of listening for a gobble on bad days, he advises hunters to listen for a turkey to strut: "In fairly open woods, you can generally hear

Ed Gulvas (left) and Denny Gulvas hunted turkeys under the worst conditions possible to bag a gobbler. Denny Gulvas stayed with his tom and continued to try different calls until the turkey came to where he was. Oftentimes a hunter will get up and leave a turkey too quickly, not giving the bird the time required to come.

a turkey strutting 50 to 60 yards away. On bad mornings when they won't gobble, most of the time they'll go into small struts as they drum. Even if a gobbler is not interested in mating, he'll usually service a hen if she comes to his drumming and strutting. So that's what to listen for on bad-weather days. Patience is necessary for success. You've got to be willing to sit for an hour or two, in a spot where you can neither see nor hear a turkey."

Proper calling technique is vital on bad days. Many hunters start off too loud and continue too long. Denny recommends the following:

"Begin with a few low clucks. If you've observed turkeys much, you know that a hen always starts calling slowly and softly. There's a good reason for this. She's not going to call any louder than necessary to interest a gobbler. So your first series of calls should be slow and soft, to get the attention of any gobblers in the immediate area.

"Next, yelp a little louder. Your second series of calls should be some medium-volume yelps, followed in a few minutes by yelps mixed with clucks. This is to reach the gobblers that may be a little farther away. After 30 to 45 minutes, increase your yelping if you still have no response.

"Then begin yelping and cackling loudly. Again, you're trying to reach a little farther and bite off a little more ground where a gobbler may be listening. These yelps are more exciting and are usually in a series of 14 to 16. These are the same calls you'd use if you had a turkey on a far ridge gobbling to you. After 15 or 20 minutes without a response or without seeing a turkey, leave the area and try calling somewhere else.

"If you go into an area and start with loud yelps and clucks, you'll scare gobblers off. They know that a hen starts calling softly and works into louder calling only after failing to locate a gobbler."

Another problem that plagues many bad-day turkey hunters is not believing in themselves long enough. They won't stay in one spot long enough to call a turkey, because they can't defeat the notion that another spot would be better. Once you have scouted a region and know there are turkeys in it, set up and keep calling there for a long time.

As Denny explains: "I've stayed in one area as late as 11:00 A.M. or noon, because I knew the turkeys were there. Often—especially on bad days when turkeys aren't gobbling—the longer you play the waiting game, the better chance you have of bagging one.

"Bad-day turkeys are not easy to take. They don't like to gobble when it's cold, cloudy, or rainy. Male turkeys don't really want to mate during inclement weather. They hang up easily. The turkey is one of the most aggravating of all game species in bad weather. But bad-weather birds are takable. They can be hunted and killed, but not by fair-weather hunters."

Hunters like Denny and Ed Gulvas have learned how to hunt birds on a bad day. Their techniques work for them and will spell success for you. So instead of rolling over and going back to sleep when the rain clouds build, the wind blows, and the temperature falls, try some of these bad-weather tactics yourself.

Writer Jim Zumbo (left) and Billy Maccoy of Southern Sportsman's Lodge, located in the swamps outside of Hayneville, Alabama, show that a hunter usually must get wet to bag a crafty swamp turkey.

How to Take Swamp Turkeys

with Nathan Connell

I rarely miss more than two or three days of turkey hunting each season. I do most of my hunting in the Tombigbee swamps of southwest Alabama.

What makes turkey hunting in the swamp different from turkey hunting in the hills is the water. Ninety-five percent of the gobblers in a swamp will fly up and roost over water.

I've heard two old tales as to why turkeys like to roost over water. The first is that they feel more secure there, since the water prevents predators from coming under the roost trees. The second is that they like to hold their breath until they hear their droppings hit, and they can hear them hit the water more easily than they can hear them hit the ground. Seriously, I believe turkeys like to roost over water because they do feel more secure there.

The big problem in hunting turkeys over water is that you don't know which side of it a turkey will fly down on in the morning. When you hear one gobbling, you just have to guess. Then you go to that side and give your most seductive calls, trying to lure him to fly down there. If he does come to your side, you have at least an even chance of calling him in. But if he goes to the opposite side, the chances are about 95 percent he won't fly back across to meet you. The only way to kill him then is to wade to the side he's on.

To take a turkey in a swamp, you must expect to get wet. You also must expect to move. Once a turkey flies down, you can seldom call him back. Most of the time you have to determine which way he wants to go, then try to get in front of him so he'll walk toward you as you call. When you move on a turkey, you're really playing a guessing game. You surmise where he's going and where you have to be to call him. At the same time, you have to guess which way you can move without being seen. Really, swamp hunting for turkeys is a big crap game. Most often, the turkey wins.

I believe that Westervelt has some of the most educated turkeys in the nation, since they're hunted just about every day of the season. A prime example is Old Mossy Head, a turkey that would gobble his head off on the roost. As soon as you'd get to him, he'd fly down in the opposite direction. Several of us tried to kill him, but none of us could. I believe he'd been shot at and maybe wounded, and I know he was smarter than anybody who tried to take him.

Finally, one morning, I went to him. This time when he gobbled, I didn't say a word. I let Old Mossy Head gobble for a pretty good while on the roost. Then, instead of yelping, I gobbled at him. He gobbled back. I gobbled at him once more, and he gobbled back. We went back and forth four or five times. I thought Old Mossy Head was the dominant gobbler in the area, and I knew he couldn't be called in with hen calls. But by challenging his manhood and calling him out to fight, I thought I might be able to pull him off that limb. I guess he'd wakened ill-tempered anyway, because when he flew off that roost he came straight to me. And the hunter I was guiding killed him.

When you can't lure a tough turkey in with sexy calls, often you can challenge him to a fight and he'll come running. Of course, gobbling doesn't always work. If you gobble at a subdominant turkey, you can make him shut up. Before you start gobbling, you've got to know you're dealing with a boss turkey.

But water is still the number-one problem in hunting turkeys in any swamp. As a rule, if there's water between you and your turkey, he won't come on in to you. I've called turkeys across water on two or three occasions, but that's a rare happening. Other guides at Westervelt have actually seen turkeys wade 3 or 4 inches of water to come to what they thought was a hen. But to do that, an old gobbler really has to be charged up and ready to mate.

I remember calling one morning to a gobbler on the other side of a slough. Before I could get up and move toward him, he started coming to me. So my hunter and I had to sit still. When the turkey got to the edge of the slough, I whispered, "That's it. He's not coming across." But the old turkey squatted, jumped, flew across the slough, and landed about 40 yards from us. He walked right on in and got his head shot off. But this occurrence is really an exception to the rule.

I've also seen turkeys wading out in sloughs and eating crayfish. One morning when I was slipping down the side of a slough, I spotted two jakes eating crayfish in it. I yelped to them. They lifted their heads and looked, but went right back to eating. So apparently younger gobblers would rather eat the crayfish than come find a hen.

We check the crops of all turkeys taken at Westervelt, and I've seen many crayfish in them. So I know turkeys eat crayfish. They also eat a lot of insects, grasses, and seeds. We plant a good deal of food for turkeys at Westervelt, including wheat and crimson clover. The crops of turkeys taken in the afternoon are crammed full of wheat and clover, so we know these are excellent foods. Also, the clover has many insects in it during the spring. Insects contain a large amount of protein, and are especially important for young turkeys.

In many areas, chufas are planted for turkeys. But we don't plant them at Westervelt, because they're terribly expensive and we have high coon and squirrel populations. The coons and squirrels would wind up eating more chufas than the turkeys would.

There's plenty of natural food, in addition to the planted food, for turkeys in swamps. The turkey is one of the most adaptable creatures in the world. He'll eat almost anything. Listing what he won't eat would probably be easier than listing what he will eat. So even though the planted food helps, swamp turkeys would still have plenty to eat without it.

Feeding turkeys, though, is the easy part. Killing them is the hard part, and to me they're all hard to kill. I was guiding a hunter one stormy morning. Just at daybreak, the rain really started to pour. And as we heard thunder in the distance, a turkey triple-gobbled. I said, "Lord have mercy, if he's triple-gobbled, he's ready to die. Let's hurry up and get to him."

We took off running. When we got closer to the turkey, the thunder rolled again. I could tell there were three gobblers, not just one, sitting together about 25 yards apart. Every time thunder rolled or an owl hooted, all three of them would gobble. My hunter and I sat down next to a big tree. The time was late spring, so the mosquitos were bad. They formed small black clouds over our heads and chewed on our hides. Even though we were saturated in insect repellent, we could hardly stand them.

My hunter said, "I'm going to slip up on that turkey out in that tree and kill him."

"No, you're not," I told him. "That turkey will see you as soon as you move. Just sit still, and we'll try to call him in here."

After some arguing in whispered tones, I convinced him to stay put. I gave the turkeys three really soft yelps and all three of them gobbled. I said to myself, "Oh mercy! We're gonna get run over by all these turkeys."

I made two more soft tree yelps, and all three of the turkeys pitched out of different trees at the same time. From the sound they made when they hit the ground, I guessed they'd landed about 80 yards away. When I looked up, all three turkeys were coming straight at us on a dead run. They were shoulder-to-shoulder and bumped each other as they ran. Now, these were not young jakes. All three were mature gobblers. When they were 25 yards out I told the hunter to shoot, since I knew they couldn't come any closer without seeing us. When he fired, two gobblers fell, and the third flew away. He'd shot one time and killed two turkeys.

I'm also a deputy game warden, so I had to arrest him. In Alabama, you're allowed only one turkey a day. This hunter had two turkeys dead on the ground—which wasn't his fault, my fault, or the turkeys' fault. The law was broken, however, so the hunter was arrested and the fine paid.

I'd seen a situation before where two turkeys came in, the hunter waited until they crossed, and then he killed them both with one shot. There's no excuse for that type of greed. But on this occasion the three turkeys were coming hard and fast, with blood in their eyes and rape on their minds. If the hunter hadn't fired, I'm not sure what would have happened to us. He had never hunted turkeys before, and was so happy about killing those two the way we did, he paid his fine gladly. We shook hands and left as friends.

On another morning, I got to see one of the rarest sights in nature. I sat down with my client next to a big tree and tried to call a turkey. As soon as I yelped a few times, a hen answered. I really didn't mind her answering, because many times a big gobbler will be walking with a hen.

This turned out to be one of those times. When the turkeys were 75 yards from us, the hen stopped and began to feed. The gobbler went into a full strut. He displayed there for a few minutes, and the hen just kind of ignored him. Eventually, however, they got around to business. He jumped on her, pinned her head down with his beak, got on her back, and quivered a little for about 30 seconds. As soon as he got off, she shook herself and started to walk away.

When that happened, I cackled. That old gobbler turned and came straight toward us at a dead run. He stopped about 15 yards out. My hunter had his gun to his shoulder. Then the gobbler walked right by us, and went on out of range and hearing distance. The hunter asked, "Why didn't you tell me to shoot?"

"I thought you'd know enough to shoot," I said, "when the turkey was standing there at 15 yards waiting to get his head blown off. There was no way I could communicate with you when the turkey was that close. If I'd blinked my eyes, he would have seen me."

I tried to work the turkey back, but felt sure he'd seen us. That had to be the most exciting and frustrating hunt I had every had. Exciting, because I saw a wild turkey mate. And frustrating, because my hunter failed to shoot when the turkey was at 15 yards.

But things like that happen in turkey hunting. When I guide hunters in the swamp, many times the hunter, not the turkey, creates the problem. Turkeys are run off because the hunter is swatting mosquitos or pulling out his insect repellent when the turkey is looking right at him. When you hunt swamp turkeys, you sometimes have to compete with the insects as well as with the turkeys.

Weather deters many hunters from hunting swamp turkeys, especially in the early spring when the water is still chilly. Although most of my hunters will hit the water to go after a turkey, some ask me to carry them across a slough. If they aren't too big and the slough isn't too wide, I try to accommodate them. If they're not willing to cross water, we really have a hard time killing a turkey in a swamp.

Hunting turkeys in swamps is usually more mental than hunting them any other place. You have to decide that no matter where the turkey is, you're going to him—whether you have to swim a creek, wade a slough, or cross four sloughs. You also have to decide that no matter how many mosquitos there are or how badly they bite, you won't swat them. Regardless of the type of insect repellent you use, a mosquito will usually test it. Naturally, he almost always comes when a turkey is looking right at you—when you need nerves of steel and the patience of Job.

Hunting the Rio Grande Turkey

with Dave Harbour

*H*unting the Rio Grande turkey differs from hunting the eastern turkey mainly because the terrain the Rio Grande inhabits is more open. Since there's less cover to conceal your approach, you must call from much greater distances. And once the sun comes up, moving to different locations to call is almost impossible.

I've hunted Rio Grande turkeys in Texas, Oklahoma, and Hawaii, and taken them in all three states with a shotgun. Though some hunters prefer a rifle, I feel killing any turkey with a rifle is almost a sin. If you can't call a turkey close enough to kill him with a shotgun, I don't think you ought to take him. But that's just my personal belief.

To get a Rio Grande turkey into shotgun range, you must scout before the hunt. Especially important is finding a roost tree, which is relatively easy since there are fewer areas for roosting than there are in the East. Usually a roost tree will be on the edge of a gully or creek. If you can find it, generally you can get within 200 or 300 yards of it before daylight. Once you're hidden in a depression or by a rock or tree, a Rio Grande turkey is fairly easy to call into range.

That's the easy tactic for taking Rio Grandes. Often, however, you locate an old gobbler high on a rimrock and can't get above him. The Rio Grande, like the eastern turkey, would rather walk upward to a hen than fly down to her. When getting above an old gobbler is impossible, I try to locate him with a crow call. I've found that Rio Grandes seem to gobble better to a crow call than to an owl call.

Once I have the turkey located and realize he's above me, I know there's no way I can get to him. So I start using some of my most demanding calls. I do a lot of cutting, cackling, and loud yelping. But I don't want to sound like just one hen. I want to sound like a bunch of hens, all of them excited. So I use several different calls—the more the better. The faster I can use them and change them, and the louder I can work them, the greater my chances of pulling that old gobbler off the rimrock.

If I'm hunting with a partner I want him to use many different calls also. We'll both be cutting, cackling, and yelping loudly, and changing calls as fast as we can. When that gobbler hears all that carrying-on below him, he just can't stand it. He thinks there's a whole harem of hens down there just waiting for him. He'll come off that rimrock like a helicopter and often land within 10 or 20 yards of you. When he hits the ground you'd better be ready to shoot, because he won't stay fooled long.

I usually prefer to hunt by myself. But sometimes, especially when trying to call a gobbler off a cliff, you're more effective with a hunting partner who can use four or five different calls at the same time you're using several.

When I go after Rio Grandes, I carry several mouth yelpers, friction calls, and tube calls. Lately, I believe I've killed more turkeys by using a tube call than by using any other type. I think the reason the tube is so effective is that it's not used quite as much as the others.

One of the best things you can do to bring in an old gobbler is to sound like the new girl in town. You'll get his attention much more quickly with a different call than with the same types that have been tried on him before.

The good news about hunting the Rio Grande is that there isn't as much competition as in hunting the eastern turkey. Also, more and more western states are eliminating the use of rifles for turkeys in the spring. For that reason hunting Rio Grandes is a bit more difficult than in the past, but westerners are beginning to adapt to the shotgun.

When I first hunted in the West, many ranchers thought my companions and I were a little weird when they saw us dressed in camouflage, carrying shotguns, and calling turkeys. But in recent years more western hunters are buying camouflage and shotguns, and finding out how much fun calling a turkey into close range can be.

Western camouflage differs greatly from eastern. Western patterns have more brown, since this blends effectively with the rocky terrain. But there are many places where you may need some green, at least a green jacket or shirt, to blend with a juniper or some other type of shrub.

There's much discussion about the type of shotgun to use. If you call a turkey within 20 yards, where he really should be if you're going to kill him, then the type of gun you have doesn't matter. I shoot a full-choke 12 gauge, because I like a little extra pattern and reach. Although I shoot either no. 6 or no. 4 shot, my favorite is no.4.

I've found that hunters can get a Rio Grande within that 20-yard killing range easier than the eastern turkey. The reason is not that Rio Grandes aren't as intelligent, but that in most areas they haven't had as much hunting pressure. If you put the same amount of pressure on a flock of Rio Grandes and a flock of easterns, I believe they would be equally difficult to kill. As the sport of turkey hunting develops and the pressure increases on the Rio Grande turkeys, I think that one day they'll be as difficult as the eastern turkeys are.

Western hunters have just begun to find out it's more fun to call a turkey into shotgun range than to shoot him with a rifle at great distances.

Dave Harbour has bagged Rio Grande turkeys in Texas, Oklahoma, and Hawaii. (Dave Harbour photo)

The turkey once was a meat bird in the West, but now is starting to gain his rightful position as a sport bird.

All the techniques I've described up to this point have been for the average hunter. Most of the time, one of these will work. A big exception, in my experience, is when people discover an outdoor writer is coming to town, and they bless him with the opportunity to try for an old gobbler no one else there can kill.

When hunting this type of turkey, I change tactics. I set up, then I give one loud call, or a series of calls like an excited yelp, or a bit of loud, excited cutting, so the turkey can locate me. Then I shut up and just barely cluck, spacing the clucks well apart. If the turkey doesn't have hens with him, he'll usually come. But getting him in may take from one to three hours. With an old, tough gobbler there's no shortcut—you just have to wait him out. If he hears several calls sounding from one spot, you can bet he won't come in.

There's one other option for a wise gobbler like this. If you can get into a ravine and do some movement calling, you can pull him in pretty easy. Most callers who have fooled with him probably haven't moved, for fear he'd spot them. If you can move and call at the same time without being spotted, he won't be nearly as suspicious as normal. Just move in any direction where he can't see you—toward him, away from him, or parallel to him. If you can add a few yelps to your clucks as you go, you can get him even more excited. Usually you'll be able to reel him into your gunsights.

The toughest Rio Grande gobbler I ever had to hunt was the Cliffhanger I went after with my son, Doug. This old gobbler would stay on top of a 500-foot cliff all the time. We spent three days trying to get him off it, but he wouldn't budge.

One morning about daylight, Doug and I went in and decided to try the flock-of-turkeys technique on him. We carried plenty of different callers, and both started calling and changing calls as loudly and quickly as we could. We decided to go with this tactic because we'd already tried several loud calls, clucking, and waiting, none of which worked.

After 30 minutes or so of our racket, the turkey flew down and landed about 100 yards away from us. To get him in close enough to shoot, we started our soft clucks again. Sure enough, he walked right to us. A turkey that tough to call, I decided, deserved to live. So I decided not to kill him.

However, I wanted to show my son just how long you can hold a turkey, once you have his attention. We kept that bird there for about an hour. He'd strut and walk off, then we'd call him, and he'd come back and strut some more. To keep him coming back, I'd just use a little cluck and a little whine to tease him. This turkey was the toughest one Doug had in his woods, and one he'd been trying to kill for a long time. But both of us enjoyed seeing that turkey put on a show far more than we'd have enjoyed killing him.

I've hunted turkeys long enough and taken enough turkeys that I now have my own code of ethics. I only take one turkey in one region—no matter what the legal limit is. After I get that one turkey, I just play with the others or enjoy seeing them until the time arrives to go home.

I enjoy calling for beginners, especially kids, and letting them take their first turkey. But I'll call only one time for a person, because I feel that once he's killed one turkey, he'll enjoy the sport more if he learns to hunt and call for himself. And that's a rule I never break.

Hunting the Merriam Turkey

with Jim Zumbo

In the Northwest, the most plentiful turkey is the Merriam. It seems to be the hardiest of all turkeys, surviving in deep snow and sub-zero temperatures in parts of Wyoming, North Dakota, South Dakota, and Montana.

For the Merriam turkey, the big problem is not the winters but the poor nesting conditions in the spring. In high areas there's usually too much rain or lingering snow. Even if nesting occurs, the wet weather may kill the poults.

The Merriam is hunted in much the same way other turkeys are hunted in the East and South, with seasons varying from state to state. One difference is that it tends to be a mountain turkey, so the hunter often must climb more. Another is that white camo clothing is better in many areas than green or brown, since there's usually snow on the ground when the spring season opens. And another is that instead of leaning against a tree or sitting by a bush, you may be able to hide in a snowbank.

The same calls that work on eastern turkeys will work on Merriams. But Merriams use regular trails much more frequently, so calling may be unnecessary. If you can find a trail they're using to get to water or feed, you can sit nearby and wait for them, as you would for deer.

During blizzards, Merriam turkeys may stay on the roost all day, or get on the lee side of a mountain or ridge, or stay in thick timber where they're protected. They move less in snowstorms than in better weather.

Instead of calling a turkey into shooting distance, waiting on a trail for one to walk down, or figuring out where one will walk up and down a ridge, you may be able to track a turkey in the snow. But this is not an easy method. An old Merriam gobbler is much like a smart deer. When you're trailing him, he'll watch his back trail and often spot you before you see him. Rarely can you get a turkey this way, but often you can track one to a ridgetop, then peer over it and spot him before he sees you. If you're a good rifleman, you may be able to bag him.

I know hunting turkeys with a rifle is considered a sin by some eastern hunters. But many westerners don't own shotguns and don't know how to shoot them. Their whole sporting life revolves around the rifle, which is the hunting gun of the West. They see nothing morally or ethically wrong in taking a turkey with a rifle. For this reason, many times the Merriam is taken at distances of 100 to 200 yards.

Merriams seem to form bigger flocks than eastern turkeys. In a single flock I've seen as many as 30. There may be two or more dominant gobblers in a large flock, and calling one of them away from it is extremely difficult. I suspect they think that if they leave to find that lonely hen, one of the other dominant gobblers will take over the hens they've been courting. Your best chance of taking a Merriam is to work a lone bird rather than a flock.

Generally, Merriams are less wary than eastern turkeys. The reason may be that they haven't had as much hunting pressure. Their eyesight is just as keen as that of eastern turkeys, however, and they're able to hear just as well.

One reason the Merriam is tough to hunt is lack of cover for a blind. Concealing yourself when hunting eastern turkeys generally is easy, but many times when you attempt to work a Merriam you get caught flatfooted in the open. He may sound off only a short distance from you, and there won't be any cover you can get behind. Before you can run to any, he'll spot you. Other times, though, you may have a few seconds to put on some camo netting before he arrives.

Carry white netting and the regular green netting when you hunt Merriam turkeys in the spring. In the West you'll find ridges that are snow-covered on one side and summerlike on the other. By carrying both the white and the green camo netting, you'll be prepared for conditions on either side.

Usually I just drape the netting over me so I look like a snowbank or a bush. If the turkey comes in, I shoot through the netting. Using this technique I've called turkeys within 10 or 15 yards before taking them.

Westerners who hunt the smaller upland birds generally have a standard 12-gauge shotgun, and this is what they use if they go after turkeys. Similarly, those who hunt deer will use whatever deer rifle they have. In my opinion, however, the best rifle for turkeys is the .222. Murry Burnham, a turkey-hunting buddy of mine, also prefers a .222. He handloads his shells with less powder than factory loads have. The lighter load seems to kill a turkey just as quickly, but doesn't do as much damage to the meat.

Merriam turkeys are different from eastern turkeys. And they're hunted in different terrain, in different weather, by a different type of hunter. Merriam turkeys are becoming more abundant, as are the hunters.

Merriams

Could Be

the Easiest

with Doug Harbour

*T*he big difference between Merriam turkeys and eastern turkeys is that Merriams like to talk much more. A really hot Merriam may gobble 100 times in an hour. Working one when he's talking like this is a real pleasure. And the hunters I guide get all fired up too. When I yelp, cackle, or cluck and the turkey gobbles or double-gobbles right back, I believe the hunter gets just as excited as the turkey. He can follow the turkey's movements and hear him coming closer and closer, which makes for exciting hunting.

I think one reason Merriams like to talk so much is the lack of hunting pressure on them. Only in recent years have hunters with mouth callers or box callers tried to get them to come in. I'm sure many Merriams I call have never heard a caller or seen a hunter before. Because of this lack of pressure, the Merriam may well be one of the easiest turkeys to call and the most fun to hunt.

Colorado has two different types of terrain where I find and hunt Merriams. Near Colorado's Oklahoma border, there are rolling juniper hills and big canyons with cottonwood trees in the bottom. That's where I do most of my hunting, but I also hunt extensively in the mountains. When hunting in the mountains, I usually find turkeys below 8,000 feet, in areas with scrub oak and Ponderosa pine. I rarely find them in Engelmann spruce or the big, dark timber of the higher country.

No matter where you find Merriams, they seem much easier to call and come in much straighter than eastern turkeys. Rarely will they come in behind you, or fishhook you and come in by the side. Most of the time, if you're positioned right, you can call and the turkey will walk straight to you.

Even though Merriams are easier to call, they're not stupid or blind. To hunt them you have to wear full camouflage. Out here, however, you still wear brown camouflage in the spring, while hunters back East are wearing green. You also tape your gun with brown camouflage, and wear a full face mask or a head net.

To locate Merriams, one of the easiest methods is to drive or walk old creek bottoms and look for tracks or droppings. Usually the turkeys water not far from their roosts. You can search for roost trees in cottonwood bottoms or in Ponderosa pines. Once you find a roost, you're on the way to killing a turkey. Unlike eastern turkeys, Merriams tend to roost in the same tree all the time. Rarely will they change to a different one.

On the ranch where I guide, I've located about 12 roost trees. I can almost guarantee that on any morning in spring you can go close to one of them and hear a turkey gobble. The roost trees draw gobblers like magnets. When a gobbler is taken near one of them, before long another gobbler will be in that same tree.

One spring on opening morning, I heard an old boss gobbler in a particular roost tree I'd been watching. He had about 12 hens with him and was really a fine bird. My client and I set up about 300 yards away and began to call him. He came right on in, and we killed him. Two days later there was another boss gobbler in that same tree, with those same hens. We called him up and killed him. Before the season was out, we took a third gobbler from the same juniper blind I'd built, hunting in the identical roosting area.

So when one turkey is taken from his favorite roost tree, another will move in to fill his place. Year after year, you can pretty much bet there will be a tom in that same roost tree.

When hunting Merriams, you often depend on a binocular. If you haven't killed a bird by midday, you can climb to a rimrock and glass up and down the canyon for a flock of turkeys feeding. Once you spot them, you must determine which direction they're moving. Then you can circle in front of them, set up a blind, and call, hoping to take one that way.

Merriams seem more forgiving than eastern turkeys. Because Merriams aren't hunted so heavily, they're not nearly so alarmed by movement. When you see an eastern turkey, in most cases, you'd better have your gun to your shoulder. But when you see a Merriam, he'll hesitate long enough to let you get your gun up before he runs.

Like eastern turkeys, however, Merriams learn quickly. Remember that spring turkey hunting is still a relatively new sport in the West. Already, Merriams are about ten times smarter than they used to be.

A few years ago, I had a hunter who missed a gobbler but just sort of singed his tail feathers. I spent the rest of the season trying to kill that gobbler and never could. He wised up quickly. I studied him, though, and by the following season I'd learned so much about him I found a technique to take him. I knew he would feed up a certain ridge just about the time the sun was coming up over it. So I took an experienced hunter I was guiding, put him on the ridge, and told him to occasionally give a few quiet yelps and clucks. The big gobbler was moving up the ridge with his hens. And when those hens heard that other hen ahead, they naturally wanted to go to her. In doing so they pulled the gobbler along with them, and my hunter was able to take him.

The Merriam differs from the eastern turkey in its daily movements. Eastern turkeys just wander at random through the woods until they fly up to roost at night. But Merriams where I hunt will fly down to the bottoms in the morning, feed there until an hour after sunup, and then start climbing to the mountaintops, where they spend most of the rest of the day. An hour or two before sundown, they'll come back down the mountains and stay until the time arrives to fly up to roost.

You actually have three times a day to hunt turkeys. In the morning you can hunt them coming off the roost. In the middle of the day, if you haven't taken a gobbler, you can get into your vehicle, go to the top of a mountain, and start calling up there. Often Merriams are as easy to call on mountaintops at midday as they are in the bottoms in the morning. Then, if you fail to get one in the middle of the day, you can go back into the bottoms, start calling and try to take a turkey before he flies up to roost. So actually western hunters have three times and methods of hunting the Merriam.

If you miss or spook a turkey in the morning, you have a good chance of taking the same one in the middle of the day. Also, if you miss a turkey in the morning or afternoon, you have a reasonably good chance of calling him up if you wait a day or two and go to the mountaintop where he normally travels.

One of the most difficult turkeys I've ever led a client to should have been the easiest. I'd guided this man to his first big Merriam a year before. So this time he brought his wife, and wanted her to take her first one. Earlier I had located a big tom and went before daylight to set up on him. When I heard him fly down, I started calling. He came running.

There was an old jeep trail 40 yards in front of our blind where the turkey started strutting. I wouldn't let the lady shoot him, because I wanted him close enough for a clean kill. There was a cactus at 35 yards. As I kept working, I got the turkey to the cactus. Then there was a smashed beer can at 30 yards. When he got to the beer can, I told her to shoot. Just as she started to squeeze the trigger, the turkey started to strut. So I whispered, "Don't shoot him. Wait till he quits strutting, so you'll have a bigger target to shoot at."

When a turkey is strutting and has his head and neck laid back into his feathers, the chances of killing him are reduced by 50 percent. But that turkey must have strutted for a full five minutes. He strutted longer than I had ever seen a turkey strut before. Finally he stopped. So I told her to shoot. Well, she took a full count of ten to aim again. Just when she was going to squeeze the trigger, the turkey once more started strutting.

"Don't shoot. Wait until he quits strutting," I said.

This procedure went on for about 45 minutes. Every time the turkey would drop strut, she would get ready to shoot. Then the turkey would begin to strut. Finally, when I could stand the suspense no longer, I told her to get ready, I was going to make the turkey stop strutting, and when I did she was to shoot him.

I gave the turkey an alarm putt. He dropped strut and stuck his head straight up where she had a good, clear shot. This time she took a count of five to aim and shoot. The shot blew dirt up in the turkey's face, and he took off running.

The next year this same woman came back by herself. We found a big turkey that took us three hours to work. But when she shot this time, he never quivered. He was graveyard dead when his head hit the ground.

The good news for first-time Merriams hunters is that you don't have to be an expert caller to get a turkey to come. Usually four yelps will call a gobbler. And more good news is that the turkeys have gotten a break in recent years, since some western conservation departments have restricted the hunting to shotguns in the spring. More and more first-time Merriam hunters are learning to enjoy the sport.

Part **5**

BOWHUNTING

Turkey hunting with a bow and arrow is not for everyone. But it does present a challenge for even the best of shots. With the right equipment, skills, and dedication, the few who accept the challenge may be rewarded with the most satisfying trophy of all. (Dave Kenyon, Michigan Dept. of Natural Resources, photo)

Should You
Bowhunt Turkeys?

with Charles Farmer

*F*ew hunters will dispute that taking a wild turkey is the ultimate bowhunting challenge. The wild gobbler is highly regarded as a trophy, and the challenge it presents is just as stimulating as a confrontation with a bull elk or a heavy-beamed whitetail buck.

But what actually happens when a bowhunter sets his sights on harvesting a turkey? Can the average bowhunter, or even the expert, enjoy regular success?

With a bow, it's actually more difficult to kill a turkey than to kill most big-game mammals. Guy W. Tillett, a premier turkey hunter and archer from Rapid City, South Dakota, explains why:

"In mammals such as deer, antelope, or javelina, an arrow in the chest and lungs is extremely life threatening—not only because of bleeding but also because of damage to the respiratory system. The rise and fall of the diaphragm, critical to mammalian respiration, is disrupted. Air entering the chest cavity collapses the lungs, the lungs separate from the walls of the chest, and breathing stops. Most chest-wounded mammals die quickly and can be recovered.

"An arrow in the chest of a turkey will not have the same results. If a lung is hit, the internal bleeding will be profuse, but a turkey wounded in the chest can outdistance and outlive the hunter's attempt at recovery. It's seldom possible to locate an arrow-hit turkey by tracking or following a blood trail. Only a hit that damages the central nervous system directly or indirectly through spinal or skull trauma is likely to put a turkey down on the spot. The kill zone to aim for is the brain and spinal cord, which is a target beyond the ability of most archers."

Tillett has killed a 19-pound tom with the bow and arrow, but still contends he's not enthusiastic about the sport or about encouraging others to take it up. Yet he admits that the urge remains, because bowhunting for turkeys is such a terrific challenge.

Some hunters, though acknowledging the difficulty of making a kill,

Many bowhunters use string trackers such as this to aid in recovery of arrow-hit birds, whether the bird runs or flies. (Sara Bright photo)

are not discouraged from trying. Dick Mauch of Bassett, Nebraska, has been bowhunting for turkeys since Nebraska's first archery season, in 1964. One of his specialties is guiding bowhunters. His personal hunting record amounts to four arrow-hit turkeys that went unrecovered, and another that was found after two days but couldn't be salvaged for the table. Nonetheless, Mauch remains high on the sport:

"Should someone bowhunt for turkeys? You bet! The things to be seen, learned, and enjoyed make it the greatest of all hunting experiences. Sure, there are some cripples, but no more excessive than those left from shotgun seasons in Nebraska."

Mauch believes the average archer can shoot and recover turkeys. "What you need most," he says, "is common sense and the persistence to keep looking for a turkey that runs or flies after you hit it. Wounded turkeys can be tracked. They leave blood trails, feathers, and tracks. They take the path of least resistance."

A turkey is easier to recover if the arrow stays in it rather than passing on through. Devices called arrow stoppers can be used on the arrow shaft just behind the broadhead, to limit penetration. Often, however, these keep the broadhead from penetrating as far as it should. "A solution I had in mind several years is now reality," says Mauch, "thanks to Bob Jackson's Viper broadhead. This has an aluminum extender that puts the head itself an inch or more ahead of the stopper. It really does the job."

Many hunters recover their turkeys by using a String Tracker—a light string which is attached to the broadhead and which flows out of an aluminum cylinder fastened to the bow. Robert Eastman, president of the company that makes it, feels the String Tracker is the key to regular recovery of arrow-hit turkeys, whether they run or fly. "If more hunters were aware of the Tracker's potential," he says, "fewer turkeys would be lost."

Cliff Dewell, a well-known bowhunter and turkey stalker from Redding, California, believes that a hunter's dedication to the sport plays an important part in finding a wounded turkey. Dewell says, "I know of several instances where hunters who had given up on cripples returned to the woods, encouraged by dedicated hunters who wanted to help them search. I do not encourage any but the most dedicated bowhunters to try shooting a turkey with a bow."

Dewell offers these tips: "Use sharp, wide broadheads. Try to shoot the turkey in the center of the chest. Avoid letting him see you after the shot, since an arrow-shot turkey may be more alarmed by a rushing hunter than by the arrow. If he runs, try to get in a position—off the crest of a ridge, for instance—where you can watch for him as far as possible. Don't give up the search easily. If you feel you've done everything possible, get help. Two or three additional hunters can cover a lot more ground. Where legal, a dog with a good nose for birds can be a help.

"I've taken 11 elk with a bow," Dewell concludes, "but I'd put any of my four arrow-shot gobblers at the head of my list of trophies."

Ben Rodgers Lee of Coffeeville, Alabama, is a famous turkey hunter and call maker who's killed dozens of turkeys with bow and arrow. Lee believes the right equipment, including special broadheads like the Viper, helps increase the recovery rate. He prefers a bow with a pull of 40 to 45 pounds:

"A light bow works best, because the chances are good the arrow will stay in the turkey. When this happens and the Viper does its cutting, recovery rates are good. Ideally, a turkey bow delivers an arrow so it penetrates 3 to 4 inches. This is one type of bowhunting where the heavy, powerful bows are a disadvantage to the hunter."

A light bow also enables the hunter to hold longer at full draw, until the turkey is in just the right position. Lee uses turkey decoys and believes they help immensely, keeping the gobbler's attention while the bowstring is pulled to the critical full draw.

"Try to stay calm," Lee says. "Don't rush the turkey. He may not know what hit him, and will often walk away or stand still rather than run or fly."

Turkey hunting with bow and arrow is not for everyone. The opportunities for a clean shot at close range are slim. Even the best archers cannot regularly hit the brain or spinal cord. Yet the possibility of a quick, clean kill is there. And no one can deny the challenge. With the right equipment and the desire to keep searching for a wounded turkey, the few who accept that challenge may be rewarded with the greatest trophy of all.

Hugh Blackburn (left) is a master archer, as well as a successful turkey hunter. As an instructor at Westervelt Lodge's Bowhunting School in Aliceville, Alabama, Blackburn teaches students how to aim and shoot.

Bow Tactics
for Turkeys

by Hugh Blackburn

*T*he big problem in taking a turkey with a bow is the amount of movement required to draw, aim, and shoot. A turkey is extremely wary, and the slightest movement will alarm him. When you consider how much movement it takes to shoot, you can understand why the turkey is one of the most difficult critters in the world to take with a bow and arrow. Killing a turkey is one of the highest accomplishments for an archer.

Another problem is to hit the turkey with enough force to kill him, but not so much that the arrow zips through him without stopping him. When modern archers began to hunt turkeys, we could get shots and could make hits, but the turkeys would run off because the arrows went completely through them. I've always hated to waste game. I believed there was a better way than shooting a turkey with an arrow, watching him run off, and not being able to recover him.

So I took a Bear broadhead and soldered two fishhooks on the back of it. When the arrow penetrated the turkey, the hooks would hang and the arrow would stay in. Using this specialized broadhead I was able to recover all the turkeys I hit. With the broadhead stuck and held by the hooks, the turkey couldn't fly or run. I had time to get to him and dispatch him before he flew away to die where I couldn't recover him. I believe this is the most effective way to take a turkey with a bow and arrow.

Of the seven turkeys I've hit, only one was shot through the head. The rest were hit in the body. A hunter who wants to take a turkey with a bow must realize he'll have to do a great deal of hunting, a lot of missing, and very little turkey taking. The turkey presents an illusion. Although he looks like a large target, underneath all those feathers is a small body. So the target you see is not the target you're shooting at. If you're lucky enough to hit the turkey, you must be fleet of foot to recover him, because when the arrow strikes home the turkey will try to run, flop, or fly away. You may have to sprint 20 or 30 yards.

One of the best ways to get into position to take a turkey is to hunt

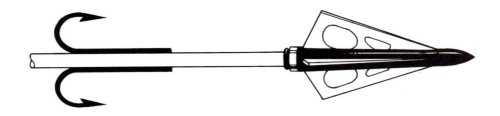

Hugh Blackburn used a broadhead and a soldering iron to create this turkey arrow. Blackburn soldered two fishhooks onto the shaft of the arrow to help hold turkeys fast until he could recover them.

with a partner. Concentrating on more than one thing at a time is very difficult. You have your hands full just trying to figure out when to stand, when to draw, and when to shoot while you watch the movement of the turkey. In gun hunting for turkeys, the shot is the easiest part of the hunt; in bowhunting, it's the most difficult part. So the best tactic for taking a turkey with a bow is to have another hunter do the calling.

Usually the caller should set up 20 to 50 yards behind you. The caller's responsibility is to bring the turkey into bow range, and bring him to a spot where he won't see you making your draw. The lay of the land is critical. Ideally, the turkey will come over a rise or from behind a tree or other cover. The caller's ability to put the turkey in a good spot is just as essential as your ability to draw and shoot accurately. Nearly always, a successful bowhunt for turkeys takes two highly competent people.

I realize there are bowhunters who can call a turkey in and then shoot him on their own. But these individuals are a rare breed. My hat is off to the few who are that highly skilled in turkey calling, woodsmanship, and archery.

The two best shots you can make on a turkey are the back shot and neck shot. Let's discuss the back shot first. If the arrow is placed directly in the back, the force of it will break the turkey down and make him much easier to recover. Also, with the turkey's back to you, there's a better chance you can draw and shoot without being seen.

The head shot is the ultimate. A turkey's head is only about the size of your fist and is constantly moving. And his neck, the size of two or three fingers held together, isn't stationary either. When your arrow arrives, the chances are slight the head will be in the same place it was when you shot. That's why I've killed only one turkey with a shot to the head. The head was what I was aiming at, but I feel extremely lucky it didn't move.

It's a big advantage to have a blind. In a blind it's far easier to move,

Hugh Blackburn says that having a blind behind which to move, draw, and shoot improves success. (Sara Bright photo)

draw, and shoot without being seen by the turkey. A gun hunter may get by in the open, but I believe the bowhunter must have some kind of blind to shoot through.

Bowhunters often contrast deer and turkeys. The big difference is that the deer are more forgiving. If a deer hears an unusual noise when you move or when you release an arrow, there'a good chance he'll stop and give you a second look. He usually won't bolt until he hears something else or sees some movement. But a turkey is different. As soon as he spots a movement or hears an unusual noise, he's gone.

Turkeys are especially wary in the spring. Fall turkeys seem less cautious and are easier to take. All my bow-shot turkeys were taken in the fall.

I consider bagging a turkey with bow and arrow one of the greatest challenges in all the outdoors. Remember: When you hunt with a bow, you'll scare a lot of turkeys and you'll miss a bunch. If you're very, very lucky, you'll wind up taking a few.

If you're bowhunting, wait until the turkey turns his back to you. Then shoot for the base of the tail.

Turkey Decoys:
The Bowhunter's
Best Bet

by Kelly Cooper

*T*he most important ingredient in taking a gobbler with a bow is a good decoy. I believe that a mounted hen turkey is the best decoy for bowhunting. If taking hens is legal in your state, then harvest one. If not, find a domestic hen about the same size as a wild one, and ask the taxidermist to paint the tail and wing feathers brown, so they look convincing. (But first be sure that using decoys is legal in your state.)

Make sure the taxidermist does not mount the turkey on any kind of stand. Instead, there should be heavy-gauge wires, 6 to 8 inches long, coming out of the feet. When forced into the ground, these wires will support the mounted turkey.

To save money, find a taxidermist who's just learning his craft. The mounting does not have to be top quality. All that's needed is to get the feathers in place and the head stuck on the correct end of the bird.

Another necessity is a blind. This can be camo netting, or you can build a blind on the site if you find enough bushes. Personally I prefer the netting, since it's quick and easy to use. With bow and arrows, a turkey decoy, camo netting and a good call, you're ready to hunt.

When you hear a turkey gobble, move into position just as you would if hunting with a shotgun. Choose a tree with a trunk wider than your shoulders to hide behind, and set up your blind beside it. Then you can step from behind the tree and into the blind to shoot.

Place the decoy 8 to 10 yards in front of you. It should face toward you, so the gobbler won't be able to see its eyes. You have to bring the gobbler in close, and he won't continue to come if he sees the eyes, since they lack that live sparkle.

Next, tie a piece of black string to the wires on the feet. This allows you to give the decoy some movement. Let out enough string so you can get behind the tree and work the decoy.

Now you're ready to start calling. You should be able to call the gobbler close enough for him to see the decoy. When you think he's spotted it,

Even the ugliest, rattiest, garage-sale mounted turkey can provide a good decoy. Cooper uses a mounted bird in conjunction with a camo blind to bowhunt turkeys. (Sara Bright photo)

pull the string gently. The movement of the decoy will drive him crazy. He'll think, *Why won't that goofy hen come on out here and mate? We've already talked about it, and she said okay.*

But the stuffed hen will just stay where she is. And before long the gobbler will come in. I've had gobblers jump on top of my decoy. But usually they came in and started strutting really close to the decoy, often only 5 to 10 yards from it. In bowhunting, unlike gun hunting, you do want to shoot the gobbler when he's strutting.

The shotgun hunter's best target is the tom's head and neck, because when small shot is put in this area, the bird will go down quickly. When a turkey is in the strut, his neck and head are laid back into his feathers. Therefore the target that the gun hunter has to shoot at when the bird is strutting is much smaller than if the bird is not strutting. So for this reason, most shotgun hunters prefer not to shoot a turkey in the strut but wait until the turkey breaks strut and has his head and neck fully extended to expose more target area.

However, for the bowhunter, the best shot for you is when the gobbler is in full strut, tail fanned and back to you. Then he can't see you draw. Also, he'll think the noise you make stepping from behind the tree to shoot is the hen. Aim for the base of the tail so the arrow will pass through the whole body.

I've taken several gobblers by using a decoy, and I believe that decoying is your best bet for taking a gobbler with a bow.

Again, check to ensure that decoys are legal in your state.

Part **6**

SHARING
THE SPORT

Billy Maccoy and his friends tell the owner of the nearby country store where they will be hunting to ensure that hunters don't crowd each other.

Staying Friends
Though It's
Turkey Season

with Billy Maccoy

*A*t one time we had many problems among the turkey hunters around my home. We'd walk in on top of one another, lie to each other about where we were hunting, and always wind up mad at each other because of some turkey-hunting problem.

So a few years ago 12 of us who hunt about the same area of national forest got together and agreed on the following:

- We would start telling each other the truth about where we were hunting, and about the turkeys we were hearing.
- We wouldn't go into an area someone else was hunting on that particular day.
- If someone wasn't hunting a particular turkey that day, then that turkey was fair game for anyone else who wanted to hunt him.
- We all would check in at the local country store, and tell the proprietor where we'd be hunting the next day. Then no one would come into the areas we'd selected.

Most everyone in our region who's going to turkey-hunt comes by the store each morning before first light, to let everybody know where he'll be. If a member of our club comes by and doesn't know where he can go to hunt a turkey that morning, we'll all suggest places we know turkeys are. Some members can't hunt through the week, so when they come in on weekends we tell them where we think their best bets are.

The advantage to this system is that we can all stay friends through turkey season. There's no sense in a bunch of guys who are friends all year winding up mad at each other when turkey hunting starts. We've found that telling the truth and working together to take turkeys are much better for all concerned.

In our best year of team turkey hunting, ten hunters in our club bagged 48 turkeys. I believe that if more hunters would use our system—especially on crowded public lands—more friendships would be saved and more gobblers bagged.

Another agreement we have is not to go on the same land the club members hunt when we're taking an out-of-county hunter after turkeys. This keeps harmony in the group, and requires us to hunt for turkeys other than those we've already located.

We work to help all the members of the club bag a turkey. We'll call for each other or put a fellow who's having a hard time bagging a turkey on a really hot gobbler that one of us has found. Also, we share turkey-hunting information and calling techniques. For instance, up until a few years ago nobody in our part of the country had ever heard of cutting, but now every member of the club has learned to cut, as I'll explain now.

I attend many turkey-calling contests—even up North. One time I hunted with two callers from New York State who were using a new technique named cutting, which is a series of loud, fast stutter yelps and clucks much like the beginning of the cackle but not going all the way through the cackle. This cutting sound imitates a hen turkey that is very excited and ready to mate. This sound is heard just before the hen gives the fly-down cackle when she is standing on the limb in the early morning and is excited about leaving the roost and going to the ground to meet a gobbler. But when a hen is cutting, she doesn't cackle at the end, and she usually gives this cutting sound much longer and much louder than the fly-down cackle.

As I learned this technique and tested it on the gobblers in the national forest near home, I found it one of the most effective calls I'd ever used. When I discovered it would work, I began to teach it to other members of our club.

Not many callers in Alabama were cutting at that time, and only a few competition callers were using the technique. Most of the folks who were cutting had been up North and learned how to cut from the northern callers. In many of the turkey-calling contests up North, cutting is a required call. From traveling around the country, I know there's plenty to be learned from hunters in other states.

The rule of thumb I was taught at home was that when you heard a turkey gobble, you clucked three times and yelped three times. Then if the turkey answered, you sat down, started to call, and didn't move. But since then I've found that moving on turkeys is one of the most effective ways of bagging them. If an old gobbler won't come in when I call and he's out of sight, I'll move to the left, the right, forward, or back. I've come to realize that hen turkeys don't stand still—they move around. So moving around when you call is only natural.

I don't think you can wait for a turkey as you once could. We've got more turkeys and more hunters in the woods than we've ever had. If you're sitting there waiting for a gobbler to come to you, a hen may go to him or another hunter may get to him. So I've learned to do a lot more moving on turkeys.

Also, I've learned that many good turkey hunters take more than one

Sharing wisdom on turkey sign and sightings can actually increase the number of turkeys hunters in a locale may take. (Sara Bright photo)

call into the woods. I usually carry a double-reed, a triple-reed, and a single-reed caller, as well as a slate, when I'm going after a gobbler. I change callers when I move, so the old gobbler thinks there's more than one hen in the area, and comes in more quickly.

I studied buddy-hunting tactics with northern hunters. Turkey hunters up North seem to do more buddy hunting and more calling than we do in the South. One tactic that I've seen work extremely well in New York, which has been effective for me in southern hunting, is double cutting.

Two hunters set up with one in front of the other. They both start cutting at the same time. They call as long as two minutes and then stop. Usually the gobbler gets so excited he can't wait. He begins to gobble and comes on in where the hunters are. But if he doesn't come immediately, the hunter in the rear can cut for a few minutes and then give a few clucks and yelps to bring him in. Double calling is a tactic few southern hunters are using now, but it works.

Calling contests have always helped me. And I believe the interest stimulated by contests and seminars is one reason turkey hunting is growing so rapidly across the country. I don't feel, as some do, that the increasing number of hunters is detrimental to the sport.

I believe we have better turkey hunters in the woods now than we had in years past. We've got more turkeys than ever before. And there are still places like the national forests where you can go and be alone with the bird. The national forests have rough terrain in many places. The turkeys there require much harder hunting—more walking and climbing—than turkeys in flatwoods areas.

Also, timber companies across the country have good turkey hunting on their lands. The hunting permits for these lands usually are inexpensive and easily available. And many states have excellent wildlife-management areas where the state conservation departments work hard to ensure good turkey hunting.

I believe that much of the concern about the numbers of hunters in the woods stems from the first week or two of turkey season. Sure, there are many hunters the first two weeks of the season. These folks get that early-season urge to go bag a bird. But by the last two weeks of the season, there are relatively few hunters left in the woods. The deer season is similar: At the beginning of the season, all the world seems to be deer hunting. But by the end, there are only a few serious hunters left.

Something most southern turkey hunters don't consider is that there's plenty of good hunting left after 9:00 A.M. Northern hunters stay out all day long, and they've found that an old gobbler can be called and killed after he's been with his hens.

In years past, I went into areas with high hunting pressure and got shoulder-to-shoulder with other hunters trying to take turkeys. I was secretive and sly, attempting to outfox the hunters as well as the turkeys. I turned friends into adversaries, and had to spend the time after turkey season rekindling old friendships and mending broken relationships.

But in recent years, I've found a better way to take turkeys and a way to help other hunters. By sharing information and learning from each other, we all become better turkey hunters. I know I've learned a lot about hunting Alabama turkeys from folks above the Mason-Dixon line, and hope I've taught them a thing or two about the way we take gobblers down here.

The Day

Patience

Nearly Died

by John E. Phillips

"These songbirds will hush in about ten minutes," Billy Maccoy said. "They usually sing for ten minutes just at the crack of day. During that time you can't hear a turkey gobble even if he's only 20 yards away. But when the songbirds get through singing, the swamp will be quiet and we'll be able to hear a turkey gobble."

"Yeah," I answered.

That was the only word I had the energy to speak after a mile-and-a-half forced march through a muddy swamp before daylight. Although I'm accustomed to walking in the woods early in the morning during turkey season, Maccoy's normal gait is only a half step short of a flat-out run. And no matter where he starts hunting, he always feels he must travel at least one and a half miles farther to be in just the right place.

As Maccoy explains, "Often hunters are too lazy to take a turkey. They drive their vehicles too close to the birds, to save some walking. But I believe a better tactic is to stop well away from the turkey and walk to where you plan to hunt, so your noises at the vehicle won't spook him."

Maccoy and a friend of his, Mike Colburn, had come down from their homes in Lineville, Alabama, to hunt turkeys at the Southern Sportsmen's Lodge near Selma. Colburn and I had hunted the morning before. Only through their wiliness had two turkeys escaped. The first one we tried to work double- and triple-gobbled.

"That turkey wants to die," Colburn whispered. And I agreed with him.

But when the turkey was only 50 yards away, he hushed. And he never came in. Apparently he met some hens before he got to us. Then later in the morning we attempted to work another turkey on the edge of a field. The only approach we had to him was along a rocky creek. Though we tried to move quietly, I'm sure our big feet on those small rocks signaled our approach. Still, we had an enjoyable and, thus, successful day of hunting. We'd just been unsuccessful at taking a turkey.

But this morning Maccoy and I were to hunt together.

"I believe we can get a bird down in the swamp," Billy had surmised. "But we're going to have to get there early."

And to get there "early" meant the long walk through muddy terrain at a forced-march pace. Fifteen minutes had passed when Maccoy broke the silence: "Let's see if we can't make an old bird talk."

Hoot, hoot, hoot, Maccoy owled.

Two turkeys gobbled in answer.

"Let's be sure we've got them located," Maccoy said, and owled again.

Once more the turkeys answered.

"Okay, let's go to the closest one," he suggested.

We walked a foot log across a stream and then half trotted through a field of palmettos until we came to a creek about 20 yards wide.

Hoot, hoot, hoot, Maccoy owled again.

And this time when the turkey answered, he was only about 75 yards away.

"I can try to call him up to the edge of the creek," Maccoy offered.

But both of us realized that any time a hunter allows an obstruction like a creek to come between himself and a turkey, he reduces his odds of taking that turkey by 50 to 75 percent.

"Let's get on the same side of the water the bird is on," I said.

Maccoy smiled in agreement. We waded the waist-deep creek to get to the other bank.

"Listen," Maccoy whispered. Then he gave a series of soft yelps.

The turkey gobbled once more. We made the decision to try to take him.

"He should come right through those palmettos into that clearing," Maccoy said. "John, you lean against the big tree in front of us. I'll get about 15 yards behind you and do the calling. When you see the bird, you can take him."

The clearing extended about 30 yards directly in front of the tree where I sat. On either side of the clearing there were palmettos creating a natural blind. All we had to do was call the turkey into the open and take him.

One of the most critical ingredients in successful turkey hunting is selecting a good stand. Maccoy and I had eliminated the water between us and the bird. We had set up in a clearing where the turkey should have felt comfortable walking. And we had moved close enough to call him, but not so close that we would spook him.

All the elements of a successful hunt were there. And I thought this hunt should be relatively simple, because every time Maccoy called with his diaphragm caller, the turkey gobbled and moved closer. When the turkey was about 40 yards from me and gobbling, I could tell by the direction he was taking that he wouldn't come into the opening, but would come in behind the palmettos to my right. I slid around the base of the tree to face him and listened to Maccoy call.

The turkey gobbled yet another time and began to walk toward me. I could hear him moving now behind the palmettos. At 25 yards I could see his white head darting through the broad leaves of the palmettos. If I shot now, I wouldn't be sure of a clean kill. I decided I wouldn't shoot until the turkey presented an open target.

Many turkeys are missed because the hunter shoots as soon as he sees the head—even if the pellets must travel through brush. But to ensure a clean kill, you should wait till the head is clearly visible and away from any obstruction.

Finally, when the turkey was 12 yards from the tree where I sat, he began strutting and gobbling. But between him and me was a blind of palmettos 12 feet long and 6 feet high. I could hear the turkey strut. I listened intently as his wings dragged the ground. When Maccoy called softly, the turkey gobbled so loudly the ground seemed to shake. As he ended the gobble with his head low to the ground, an echo came back from the forest floor making him sound as though he were in a box. From time to time I glimpsed his white head as he darted back and forth on the other side of the palmettos.

Time dragged. With my gun on my knee and my head down—looking along the barrel of my shotgun—I wondered if I should shoot.

There's no way we can get the turkey any closer than he is right now, I thought. *But if I shoot now without being able to see him totally, chances are extremely good I'll miss him. I wonder how much lead the leaves of the palmetto will absorb? I wonder if Billy wants me to shoot? What's Billy thinking?*

If you've ever hunted with a partner on a turkey, you know how much communication goes on between the hunter and the caller without a word being spoken. I diligently tried to read Maccoy's mind. And he told me later he tried to read mine.

Don't shoot, John, he was thinking. *Let me try to work the gobbler around that bunch of palmettos. If I can't get him in, I'll let him cool down and walk off. Then we'll move in closer and call him back. We can kill this turkey if you won't shoot before you can see him. Just sit still, John, and quit trying to squash those stupid mosquitos with your finger. I hope you'll sit still long enough to let me work the bird the way he should be worked. If you'll just stay still, we'll kill the bird. Lord, please help John not to move.*

Maccoy continued trying to communicate his thoughts and hopes without speaking. And remembering that he's a patient hunter, I decided I wouldn't take a shot unless the turkey came full into view, not strutting, and presented the shot all turkey hunters hope for.

The time had been 7:55 A.M. when the gobbler had first walked behind the palmettos. It was now 8:20, so he had been right there for 25 minutes. I felt as though a lifetime had slipped by. The bronze swamp baron was still drumming and strutting when I heard a rustle in the leaves behind me.

Now what's Billy doing? I asked myself. *Does he want me to turn around so he can point out an area for me to move to? I can't move, because the turkey will see me. If Billy moves, he may be able to get a shot that I can't. Whatever he's doing, he'll just have to do it. And whatever happens will happen. But I'm not going to move, and I'm not about to shoot until the turkey comes out from the palmettos.*

From the start, Maccoy had been using a diaphragm caller. It had pulled the turkey within 12 yards of me. And the turkey was doing everything he was supposed to. By strutting and drumming, he should have been able to make his lady friend walk around the palmettos to meet him. There was no reason for him to come out. The hen should have gone to him, in the natural order of things. But she hadn't, and nothing he could do—including flaunting his manhood—would entice that coy girl to move.

As soon as Maccoy began to call again, I knew what the rustling in the leaves had been about. The change in the sound of his calling told me he had switched from the diaphragm to a slate caller.

Later Maccoy told me that he always carries at least three callers: a diaphragm, which is the one he has the most confidence in; a slate, for clucking and purring; and a box, to use when all else fails. Many times, when a turkey hangs up, Maccoy can pull him into gun range by changing callers.

And Maccoy's soft clucking and purring on the slate really seemed to set that gobbler on fire. Every time the cedar peg crossed the slate, the turkey gobbled or double-gobbled. I saw his ivory head moving toward the end of the palmettos. My head was down, my cheek against the stock of my Remington 1100, with the barrel aimed at the spot where the old boy would appear.

With the morning mist dissipated, the harsh rays of the new day's sun illuminated the very spot where the climactic shot would be aimed. Finally, as the old boy came into the killing ground with the sun backlighting his feathers, the beautiful hues of green, bronze, black, purple, and brown were iridescent.

I squeezed the trigger. The turkey was blown skyward. Because I'd been sitting in a cramped position for over 45 minutes, I was slow to get up. But Maccoy, agile woodsman that he is, was on a dead run once the shotgun cracked. He covered the bird like a pointer retrieving a bobwhite.

As we sat there later—finally able to swat mosquitos—the two of us discussed the long wait we'd endured.

"I was praying you'd hold your shot," Maccoy said.

"And I was hoping you'd keep on calling."

"John, let's see just how close that bird was before you shot." Maccoy had a big smile. He paced off the distance from the downed turkey to the tree where I'd sat. "Eighteen steps."

"Wait a minute," I said. "That's where the turkey landed after he'd been shot." I walked to the corner of the palmettos the turkey had walked around."This is where the old bird was standing when I shot him."

Billy Maccoy (left) and the author show off the turkey they took the day patience nearly died.

This time Maccoy paced off the distance from the tree to the spot where the turkey had taken lead. "Ten steps," he announced. We looked in the leaves behind the palmettos and saw where the turkey had dragged his wings when he was strutting.

"There's only one thing wrong with this hunt," Maccoy said. "Nobody's going to believe we had a gobbler drumming and strutting at 12 yards for 30 minutes before we took him, and he never saw us."

That's one of the things I like most about buddy-hunting turkeys: We got our turkey. And we got a great deal more. We had the opportunity to live through an adventure that few other hunters experience—attempting together to outsmart a turkey, communicating without words.

While sitting there waiting for that turkey to come out, I'd kept thinking, *I really don't believe Billy wants me to take a shot until I can make a clean kill. I believe he'd rather let the turkey go than have me miss it or booger it up.*

And I'd read him right. That was just what he wanted.

When buddy-hunting turkeys, you have to reason like your partner and sense what he's going to do. This silent communication makes the sport of turkey hunting far more exciting and challenging. And, if your patience holds out, you'll bring back a turkey for the pot and the memory of a hunt the two of you can share a lifetime.

There are many tactical advantages in teaming up to take a bird. But the main reason for two hunters trying to take one turkey is to allow the two friends to share the sport.

Teaming-Up
for Turkeys

by John E. Phillips

*T*hough turkey hunting is usually an individual sport, there are several reasons two people will hunt turkeys together. Foremost, for many hunters, is the fellowship that comes from sharing the experience of calling, watching, and bagging a turkey. In addition, there are tactical reasons for teaming up. Old gobblers that have been shot at may be call-shy and man-shy but can often be outsmarted when two hunters combine their skills and knowledge. As well, a hunter who's filled his season limit can still get out if he takes a novice hunting. By making tactical decisions, calling, and telling the novice when to shoot, he can sharpen his own skills and still participate in a hunt.

Ben Curry of Carrollton, Alabama, has guided turkey hunters for 16 years and has killed a world-record turkey. Curry is a proven veteran of the two-man hunt. "I have a buddy I enjoy being with," he says, "and each year we hunt together. We decide beforehand who will call and who will shoot. Taking turns on turkeys has developed into a lot of fun for us both.

"Heck, we even listen for each other. If it's Bubba Gray's turn to kill a turkey and I'm out scouting and hear one, I'll put Bubba on him. Then he does the same for me. Using this method of buddy hunting, we both usually get our five-turkey limit each year."

Of course, having two people in the woods at the same time has a few disadvantages. More twigs break, and there are more people to hide and twice as much movement. "But if both people know how to hunt," Curry says, "they can overcome these obstacles and still get a turkey. One of the keys is to set up in front of a turkey, so he'll naturally walk right to you. Calling one back from where he's already been is really difficult. Behind him is his escape route, and he rarely goes back that way unless he's alarmed.

"Kenny Pool and I had a friend who told us about a big old turkey that had been shot at several times. The men who'd hunted him had seen him at about 75 yards, but could never get him close enough for a shot. They were tired of fooling with him. So they told Kenny and me where he was.

"For two or three mornings we tried to call the turkey. He'd answer, walk down the ridge, and stop. At 75 yards he always strutted and drummed, but he came no closer.

"Well, we tried letting one person sit in front and the other call from behind, but that didn't work. After we'd exhausted all our tactics, we thought we had nothing to lose by attempting something new.

"The next morning, when the turkey gobbled I called. Kenny moved quickly and quietly around him. After Kenny was 75 yards in back of him, he started calling. Both of us worked that old turkey back and forth on the ridge that morning. But he never came into gun range.

"On the following day, we tried another wrinkle. The turkey gobbled, and Kenny got behind him. Kenny and I both started calling. Then we hushed. The turkey gobbled close to me. I could barely see him out in front. Kenny had now moved up to the spot where we'd first heard him gobble that morning. I took my mask off, stood up, and started walking straight toward that wise old turkey. Figuring I hadn't seen him, he sneaked back the way he'd come and right into Kenny's gunsights. Since then, we've often used this technique to kill cantankerous turkeys."

Other hunters have perfected other ways of teaming up for turkeys.

When a turkey is reputed to hang up and not come close enough to the hunter to be taken, a second hunter with gun can set up 25 yards in front of the hunter doing the calling.

For example, one hunter can set up 25 to 40 yards from the other. Then the first hunter starts calling. If the turkey come into range, the first hunter kills him. But if the turkey hangs up, the second hunter begins to work.

"Number-two hunter has a gobbling box or tube," Curry explains. "After the turkey comes about as far as he's going to, the first hunter yelps. Then the second hunter follows the yelps with a gobble. Now the turkey is upset. He has to decide whether he wants to fight or mate, and either choice he makes will be his downfall. This technique seems to work better than just one hunter making both calls. The calls are heard in two different locations, so they're more believable."

One of the biggest challenges for an experienced turkey hunter is to take a novice into the woods. "I explain that once we get out of the truck we won't talk, smoke, or eat," Curry says. "The hunter follows me, and I try to locate a turkey. By owling or using a crow call, I try to get a bird to gobble. Once we hear him, if it's still dark, we get within 75 to 100 yards of him before we set up. If the turkey is already on the ground or if it's late in the morning when we hear him, we usually set up right where we are. I try to find a big tree in a fairly open area. Once we hear the turkey and get ready to set up, I allow my hunter to load his gun."

Curry, like most seasoned turkey guides, prefers to have his hunters sit in his lap. "The hunter sits in a crouched position with one knee up," he says. "He can then prop his gun on his knee and lean back against my chest. This position is almost like sitting in a lounge chair. A hunter can sit motionless like this for a couple of hours, if need be." This position also allows Curry to whisper instructions in the hunter's ear, and to tap him on the shoulder when the turkey is close enough to be shot.

Seeing the excitement on a new hunter's face when he bags his first turkey is a thrill that lasts long after the feathers and meat are gone. But whether you call for a new hunter, or hunt with a buddy to outsmart a keen old bird, teaming up for turkeys is a lot of fun for both of you.

Harold Knight called with a push-button call as John Phillips Jr. sat between Knight's legs and watched for the turkey. By placing John Jr. between his legs, Knight could whisper instructions and explain the hunt.

A Boy's
First Hunt

with John E. Phillips, Jr.

The sun was high in the sky when my dad, the author of this book, woke me up. I asked him why he hadn't gotten me up for school.

"Because we're going hunting," he answered. "And I wanted to surprise you."

I couldn't guess what we were going to hunt. It was mid-March. Couldn't have been deer or squirrel. Finally Dad told me we were going turkey hunting. I had only hunted turkeys once before with Dad, and although we called a bird, I hadn't seen it.

I wasn't sure what equipment we'd need for turkey. In all of my hunting for deer, squirrel, quail, dove and duck, I had never seen a wild turkey. I was about to pick up my 20 gauge, when Dad said he thought I should shoot his Remington 1100 3-inch magnum, Special Purpose shotgun.

"Son, I think you should shoot this gun, because your 20 gauge may not be big enough. These turkeys are large and hard to knock down. You probably won't get a second shot."

I wasn't worried about shooting the 3-inch magnum, because I had used my dad's as well as my uncle's at different times when we were squirrel hunting. So I was familiar with the gun. Besides Dad explained that we would practice-shoot the gun before we hunted. I knew the 3-inch magnum would kick, but I also realized I need to shoot only once to bag a turkey. I was ready to take the gun's kick to bag the bird.

We packed up and started down the highway but stopped at Tuscaloosa, Alabama, where we went into Shoney's and sat down to wait. My dad said, "Son, you are about to meet two of the greatest turkey hunters who ever lived."

The men I met were David Hale and Harold Knight, who are both well-known guides and the owners of Knight and Hale Game Calls in Cadiz, Kentucky. Harold Knight also holds the world's record for the best overall typical eastern wild turkey. When I first met them, I could not believe that I was going to hunt with them for three days.

We had our hunt planned for the fertile lands of Bent Creek Hunting Lodge in Jachin, Alabama. These lands had never been turkey hunted by the public. Arriving at 11:00 A.M., we unpacked and prepared to hunt that afternoon. In Alabama, each hunter can take as many as six gobblers per season but no more than one gobbler a day.

After lunch, I went with Mr. Knight to an abandoned cornfield that had been bushhogged and picked the previous fall. Only the stubble remained, but Mr. Knight explained that in the afternoons, many times turkeys would come into an abandoned field like this to eat the young grasses that sprout up in spring.

As we came up to the field, Mr. Knight took out his binoculars, looked over the field and said, "Okay, John, I see two nice gobblers and some jakes. They are feeding up the field toward the sun. We are going to go around the field and try and call them to the top of the field, because that seems to be the direction they want to go. The easiest way to take a turkey is to attempt to call him to a place he prefers to go."

We slipped around the field as quietly as we could. When we arrived close to the top, I could see some of the turkeys out in the field.

"Get down on your hands and knees, John, so we can crawl to the edge of the field. Be careful to hold the gun out to your side. Make sure your safety is on."

We needed 20 minutes to reach the place we needed to be. We set up in a gully where we could see out in the field. Mr. Knight gave the tom a soft yelp, and the turkey gobbled. The flock fed right up to us just as we expected them to. As the gobbler came into sight, I looked at his giant wings and long beard, while he slipped along taking a little bite of food and then looking up to check the outskirts of the field.

I was observing for the first time a beautiful wild turkey. As I watched in amazement, the gobbler stopped. He looked startled—I had forgotten to cover my bright green collar with camo. I could not get off a shot, and because of a little pine tree that was shielding me from the bird, I whispered to Mr. Knight that since I was unable to have a clear shot for him to go ahead and take the bird. I didn't want to wound the gobbler. I felt I'd have a chance to bag a turkey in the upcoming days.

Although I had spooked the gobbler, Mr. Knight took him as he began to run off. I ran out into the field and looked at the great bird. I had wanted to kill him myself, but as long as we got the turkey, that was fine with me.

I knew that Mr. Knight and I were a team. And just like on my basketball team, the player who makes the basket is just part of the team. We all get the satisfaction of watching the ball go through the hoop. I learned from hunting with Mr. Knight that when a turkey is taken, both hunters are successful. And we can both say, "We got a turkey today," no matter who pulled the trigger. I was willing to wait, and we still had two more days to hunt. That bird weighed about 18 pounds and had a nine-inch beard. Just being able to see a wild turkey was very exciting.

When we arrived at the clubhouse, Dad and Mr. Hale had not seen a gobbler. That night as I lay in my bed I thought about the day's events. I would be ready next time.

The next morning I got up early and dressed. I made sure I was well camouflaged. We decided to go back to the same field. We knew there was one more good gobbler, and there were some jakes too. But this time instead of hunting the field, we stayed in the woods next to the field.

Mr. Knight let out a cluck, and then there was the beating of wings as a dark figure floated down to the ground from a nearby tree. After a while we called, and the turkey gobbled back. A few more calls later, and the tom was close. But then there was the rustle of feet as a deer ran and startled the gobbler.

Immediately the gobbler rose up and flew away. I was disappointed, but there was still plenty of daylight left. As we came out of the woods to the field, we saw a turkey fly over. We searched and called but could not find another bird that morning. When we returned to the clubhouse, we found that Mr. Hale had killed a turkey. That afternoon I went with Dad, but we did not spot anything. After supper that night, Mr. Knight gave me a push-button turkey call and spent an hour teaching me to use it.

"John, I don't want you to just learn how to hunt turkeys," he said. "You need to learn to call. This push-button call is probably the quickest and easiest to learn how to use."

Mr. Knight also gave me a mouth diaphragm call. After practicing some, I decided I'd need a long time to learn how to blow that thing.

The third morning I got up early, because Mr. Knight and I were going deeper in the woods. We arrived at a natural gas line and got out of the truck. Mr. Knight owl-hooted. Three birds gobbled. We went toward one bird and sat down in groves of pine trees. The turkey was behind a ridge. I realized that unless the turkey moved directly into my grove, there would be a slim chance of my bagging this bird.

We called, and the bird gobbled. He continued toward us, until I caught the sight of his blue-colored head looking around the edge of the ridge. He kept walking carefully, searching for a hen so he could show off. The gobbler walked a little closer, but I still did not have a shot.

I had told Mr. Knight ahead of time that whichever one of us got the shot at the turkey, that person should shoot. Since the turkey walked into Mr. Knight's grove, he shot the gobbler. As we carried the turkey to the road, Mr. Knight explained "John, I know we're going to bag you a turkey, because the time is only 6:30 A.M."

We went back into the woods and heard a bird putting. I had a chance to take the gobbler, but I didn't take the shot and explained to Mr. Knight that I wanted a prize gobbler. Then I heard a hawk cry out, and a big turkey gobbled. Mr. Knight called, and the big tom answered. We were excited as we tried to set up. There were cut pine trees around us.

"John, I hear him strutting," Mr. Knight said.

I waited patiently as the gobbler came from behind the trees. I saw the bird was definitely a trophy, and he was in full strut. His beard almost dragged on the ground as he displayed for the hen he thought was there. But the gobbler was headed the wrong way. As Mr. Knight let out a soft yelp, the gobbler turned around and started toward us. Mr. Knight put his gun down. ''This one is yours, John,'' he said.

I had not been nervous until this point. I knew that if I missed the

John Phillips Jr. (left) and Harold Knight combined a youth's enthusiasm and a veteran's skill to take a fine gobbler. But to teach turkey hunting, the veteran must be willing to sacrifice time and his own hunting.

turkey that Mr. Knight could not kill it for me. I put the bead on the bird's head—even as it was tucked down in a strut.

I waited until the gobbler was within 20 yards. He was in full strut. Mr. Knight had told me earlier that usually a hunter shouldn't shoot a turkey in full strut, because not as much of the bird's neck is exposed. But the bird looked straight at me. I could see all of his neck and head. I knew I could take him. I squeezed the trigger.

I sat down, laid flat on my back, and for a few seconds remembered how that strutting gobbler had looked. I got up and went over to that beautiful bird. He weighed 20 pounds and had a 10-inch beard. I hugged Mr. Knight and thanked him for helping me kill my first gobbler. As we walked back to the road, we talked about the two turkeys, picked up our first gobbler and waited for the truck to come back for us.

The truck came toward us, and Dad jumped out as he asked, "Did you get one?"

Dad took pictures of all of us with our turkeys.

Then that afternoon, Mr. Knight and Mr. Hale worked with me some more on my mouth yelper and push-button box call so that I could call my own turkey the next time. That afternoon I went by myself to hunt on some land close to the club. I wasn't planning on seeing anything. I just wanted to practice my calling. But I failed to hear a bird.

I still had one more morning to hunt, and I was going to try to kill one more turkey. Mr. Knight and I were going to hunt by the Tombigbee River. We parked the truck, and Mr. Knight owl-hooted. Immediately a turkey gobbled. We moved in and set up. We were in a hardwood bottom that had ridges on both sides.

I heard a hen on the far ridge. Two gobblers looking for the hen came down into the bottom as they heard the calls made by Mr. Knight. The toms turned and saw each other. Mr. Knight called once more. I watched in amazement as the gobblers started fighting. They fought for about five minutes.

Finally as if nothing had happened, the toms headed to where Mr. Knight had been calling from before the fight. As both birds went over the ridge, there was the boom of a shotgun. Mr. Knight dropped one gobbler. As I ran to see the prize bird, I saw he was about three years old and had a nice beard and long spurs.

We went back to the clubhouse and packed up to leave. On the way home I lay back in the seat, I thought about the hunt:

I had killed my first gobbler.

I had seen the beautiful strutting and moving of the great bird.

I had hunted with one of the best turkey hunters.

And I understood that I had probably been on one of the best hunts I would ever experience. Here, I had seen four gobblers die in three days—more than many people see in a lifetime.

If two disabled hunters can compensate for one another's disability, the result can be a successful outing.

The Disabled Can Hunt Turkeys

by John E. Phillips

Charles Dorsett of Birmingham, Alabama, is legally deaf, although he can slightly hear some sounds. One recent February, his father, Glenn, suffered a heart attack. Only six weeks after Glenn left the hospital, he and Charles combined their outdoor skills to perform one of the most amazing feats in turkey-hunting history.

It was the first week in April, and the Dorsett clan was meeting for its annual family reunion and turkey-hunting trip in a national forest. Glenn's brother, Toxey, a veteran hunter with more than 80 turkeys to his credit, and Toxey's nephew David, dubbed the Woods Wizard, were excited about the hunt. Both of them felt sure they would score. They reckoned, however, that Glenn and Charles had little chance of bagging a turkey.

"Glenn had left the hospital so recently we figured he probably wouldn't come to the hunt," Toxey says, "but he knew how anxious Charles was to take a turkey. Two years before, Charles had killed one that David called in, but he'd never killed one that he called in himself. So he'd bought a mouth yelper and been practicing on it for a year." (Because Charles made the sounds with a mouth yelper, he was able to feel vibration and slightly hear the sound.)

Ignoring the odds, Glenn and Charles put together their own unusual game plan for hunting. They decided to drive their car to a hilltop and listen for a turkey to gobble. Glenn would hear the turkey, determine the area where it was, and direct Charles to it. Although Glenn was still under his doctor's care, he'd walk into the woods with Charles if the turkey wasn't too far away. Charles, of course, would do the calling and shooting.

The Dorsett men left camp on a Wednesday morning. When Toxey and David returned a few hours later, Glenn and Charles were already there—with a gobbler. The game plan had worked.

When they'd stopped the car on a ridge that morning, Glenn heard a turkey gobble not far from the road. They walked in the direction of the gobble and then set up. Charles called, and Glenn whispered into Charles's ear loud enough for Charles to hear him every time the turkey answered. As the turkey moved in, Glenn reported the distance. Finally, the turkey was in sight and close enough for Charles to shoot. Bagging the bronze baron of the hardwoods was a dazzling accomplishment for the two disabled hunters.

On Thursday morning, amazingly, Glenn and Charles repeated their performance. They came back to camp with a second turkey.

Then, on Friday, both Toxey and David scored. Excited about calling and killing their own turkeys, they weren't prepared for what met them at the camp: Glenn and Charles with a third gobbler. Those two disabled hunters had now scored three for three on turkeys—probably the most difficult game in America to hunt.

"When the turkeys came in close and gobbled loud, Charles could actually hear them," Toxey says. "But most of the time Glenn was telling him which direction the turkey was, how close he was, and when he was answering the call."

Taking gobblers on three consecutive mornings is an achievement few veteran turkey hunters ever manage. And the achievement is even more significant when the caller usually cannot hear the gobbler answer and when the other hunter is unable to walk more than 100 yards at a time. For three glorious April mornings, Glenn and Charles Dorsett refused to let disability interfere with their family reunion and their turkey-hunting.

Part **7**

TURKEY
TALES

Uncle Roy, behind camo netting, coaxes a displaying gobbler to gun.

Uncle Roy
Talks Turkey

by John E. Phillips

The first rays of light were beginning to part the green spring leaves and dance on the forest floor when young Roy Moorer and his father slipped into the woods on the backside of the plantation.

The stillness was broken by the raspy gobble of a turkey. Roy's father whispered, "He's your bird, boy. Go get him."

Stalking with the poise of a sure-footed cat, 15-year-old Roy moved toward the turkey perched high on a limb. The shot would be about 30 yards, but he thought he could make it.

The report of the shotgun sent the gobbler reeling. He pitched off the limb and ran for a canebrake. Roy fired again. Though hit, the gobbler vanished. Once again Roy approached. As the white head darted out of the green riverbank cane, Roy squeezed the trigger a third time. With that killing shot, Roy Moorer began writing a legend in the annals of turkey hunting.

"I started out right," he says. "That bird had a 12-inch beard, which was the longest I've ever taken."

The year was 1905—the year Einstein formulated his theory and Ty Cobb began his illustrious baseball career. Theodore Roosevelt was President.

Ever since then, Roy Moorer of Evergreen, Alabama, has hunted the elusive eastern wild turkey. He has bagged more than 500 and probably has stored up more knowledge about turkeys and turkey hunting than any other man alive.

In their mid-90s most hunters would resign themselves to tale telling from a rocker on the front porch, but not Uncle Roy, as he's affectionately called by family and friends. Each spring, with the 12-gauge Winchester automatic that's been his companion for so many years, he moves through the southern swamps and bags another in a long line of gobblers.

Born in 1890, Uncle Roy remembers times before Henry Ford sold his first car and before the Wright brothers flew their first airplane. In Roy's boyhood, the general eastern turkey population was depleted, but the land around Evergreen was still heavily populated with turkeys.

"In the old days one of our favorite ways to hunt in the fall was with our turkey dog, Bob," he says. "When Bob smelled a flock, he'd follow the scent like a bird dog trailing quail. When he got close to the turkeys, he'd go on point. But since turkeys won't hold like quail, old Bob would move in closer and closer. Then, when he caught up to them, he'd flush them and we'd start shooting."

In one season when Uncle Roy took 16 turkeys, 13 of them were shot on the wing. "In the fall, if we didn't get a turkey when a flock flushed, we'd sit down and call them back together. Daddy would take a burlap bag and put it over Bob's head so he couldn't see. When the turkeys moved into gun range, one of us would shoot. Old Bob would bust out from under that bag and run and grab the turkey to make sure he didn't escape."

Those were the heydays of turkeys and turkey hunting in Alabama: "For several years in the early 1900s, the turkey season ran from December to March. The limit was two gobblers a day, but we never killed more than we wanted to eat."

Still, the availability of turkeys was only partly responsible for Uncle Roy's lifetime harvest of gobblers. Just as important was his marksmanship, which he learned from his father, Jim.

"A fellow named Adolph Topperwein, one of the best shots in the country in the early part of the century, came to Evergreen representing the Winchester Arms Company. He was going to put on a shooting demonstration and was looking for someone to compete against him. Several of the men around town told him, 'Jim Moorer is the best shot around here.' So Topperwein invited Daddy to shoot against him. Topperwein broke 24 out of 25 clay pigeons. When it was Daddy's time to shoot, he shattered 24 clay pigeons and knocked a piece out of the 25th."

As Uncle Roy's father trained him, so has Uncle Roy passed on his shooting and turkey knowledge to several family members, including his younger cousin Robert Moorer. "I've tried to teach Robert how to walk quietly in the woods, stalk with patience, and stay with his turkey until he can take him."

"There was one turkey I'd been trying to shoot for a long time," Robert says. "I called Uncle Roy and got him to go with me. I did the calling, and Uncle Roy sat back hoping to get a shot if the turkey outmaneuvered me and came where he was." But the bearded baron fooled them both that morning.

That evening, Robert phoned Uncle Roy to say he was planning to hunt with a friend at another place the next day. "Well, Robert, as sure as two and two are four, I'm going back to our spot and kill that gobbler in the morning," Uncle Roy answered.

Just after Uncle Roy got out of his car the following day, he saw the gobbler fly up into a water oak about 75 yards away. "I don't like to get too close to a turkey before I call to him, because I might spook him,'' Uncle Roy says. "I usually back up against a tree with my gun on my knees, about 75 to 100 yards from the turkey. I don't drive in close to the area in my car. I'm afraid my headlights will scare the turkeys. I generally walk at least a quarter of a mile to where I've got my gobbler located."

After getting situated that morning, Uncle Roy yelped three times and clucked once. Then he put his double whammy on the turkey. He patted

Born in 1890, Uncle Roy Moorer has bagged over 500 turkeys during a hunting lifetime that began when Teddy Roosevelt was President. Uncle Roy was still taking turkeys in his 90s. *Photo inset:* **In World War I, Roy Moorer found his shooting skills came in handy.**

his gloved hands against his pant legs four times. The muffled sound was a perfect imitation of a hen flying down out of a tree.

"When a gobbler hears that fly-down imitation," Uncle Roy says, "he just can't stay on the limb. He's got to come down. But this turkey stayed out about 40 yards, so I had to put my treading note on him."

Uncle Roy believes that next to the fly-down call, the treading note is his deadliest weapon. Made by moving the lid of a box caller very slowly, it sounds almost like a purr. The note is interrupted, however, like a series of putts.

And sure enough, the mystical power of Uncle Roy's playing the love notes on his box lured the big gobbler into range of his 12 gauge. When Robert called that night to ask about the hunt, Uncle Roy said, "I told you I'd get that gobbler."

Robert was only seven years old when Uncle Roy started him hunting. "Uncle Roy was my hero when I was small. He was bigger than life-size. Everyone I knew said Uncle Roy was the greatest turkey hunter in these parts."

If a gobbler was particularly tough to call, Uncle Roy would keep trying even if he had to hunt on Sunday, but he never missed church to do it. "I always asked the Lord to go with me and protect me in the woods. He always has, and I feel I ought to be in His church on Sunday."

And an old gobbler might fool Uncle Roy for a day or two, but there never was a turkey he couldn't take, once he set his mind to it.

"Uncle Roy was usually the first person to find out about any innovations in turkey hunting and try them out," Robert recalls. "When a Dr. Pepper salesman came to the grocery store where Uncle Roy worked and showed him a mouth yelper, Uncle Roy not only learned how to use one but also found out how to make his own."

Uncle Roy interrupts: "I used to be a whole lot better with my mouth yelper than I am now. The call just doesn't seem to sit as good in my mouth when my false teeth are in as it did when I still had my real teeth."

Uncle Roy's mouth yelper, his Lynch's World Champion box caller, and his ability to owl are a few of the reasons for his legendary success. Robert explains another big reason: "Uncle Roy knows turkeys. He knows more about what a turkey is going to do and when he's going to do it than the turkey knows himself. He has a sixth sense that allows him to be in the right place at the right time. He's always thinking, What would I do if I were that turkey?"

One of the hardest turkeys to call in the spring is a boss gobbler with a harem of hens. Many hunters give up immediately, feeling that trying to call him away from his harem is impossible. However, Uncle Roy is convinced that a good hunter can do it.

"You can kill a gobbler like that," he says, "but you've got to stay fairly close to him and to his hens without being seen. Sooner or later during the morning, he'll breed one or more of the hens. You don't have to see this to know when it happens. You'll hear the hen's high, shrill squeal. That's when you start calling immediately. The old gobbler will leave those hens and come in to you. This whole process may take two or three hours of slipping through the woods and watching the turkeys before you have an opportunity to call, but if you stay with them you can bag that big turkey.

"Many hunters give up too easily. I've seen some people who approached turkey hunting like they were hunting a tiger. They were afraid to do anything and were almost terrified of the turkey. Bagging a gobbler does require a lot of time and skill, but it's not as hard as many people believe.

"Once you've called that turkey in close enough," he continues, "you must be able to shoot quickly and accurately. I bought the first 12-gauge Winchester automatic that ever came on the market, back in 1911. That old gun can really shoot. I always put no. 6 shot in it to start. I get as many pellets in the air as possible when the turkey is close. Then, behind the no. 6s, I use no. 4 shot. These heavier shot follow in case the turkey doesn't drop instantly. I only shoot 2¾-inch shells, because I feel if you use a bigger load it may cause you to flinch and miss the turkey."

Uncle Roy says that luck does play an important role in turkey hunting, but he believes a hunter can do a lot to alter the odds in his favor. "If you can determine where a gobbler wants to go and then get between him and his destination so he doesn't have to go out of his way to come to you, he's much easier to call. Consistently bagging turkeys comes only after learning the woods you plan to hunt; studying the feeding, mating, and other habits of turkeys; and spending years learning to think and call like a turkey."

When I first heard about Roy Moorer, I expected to find an elderly man who could barely walk. But he's actually as alert and as young looking as he was 20 or 30 years ago.

"Uncle Roy's slowed up a bit now," Robert says. "He may take 20 minutes to cover a quarter of a mile. Instead of relying on his ability to walk and call, nowadays Uncle Roy depends more on his knowledge of the turkey to put himself in the right place at the right time."

When I asked Uncle Roy if he liked to hunt as much as he once did, he answered with a grin and a chuckle.

"When you get to be 96 years old, you lose a little of your zip. For the last three years, I've been saying I was going to quit. But then someone will start talking turkey. He'll mention a place where he's seen or heard a gobbler. We'll discuss how to hunt that gobbler, and the next thing I know I'm off on another hunt."

Eddie Salter shows off a fine gobbler that flew into my gunsights.

Luck May
Intervene When
Skill Fails

by John E. Phillips

*E*ddie Salter of Evergreen, Alabama, has hunted turkeys most of his life. When he decided to become serious about turkey calling, he kept wild turkeys in a pen at his home—to understand not only what turkeys say but also why they say it. Through study and practice, Salter has learned to speak the language of the turkey as though he were born to it. In 1985 his expertise as a master caller was recognized when he won the World Turkey Calling Contest.

Salter is a quiet man, not given to boasting. So when he told me to "come on down home, and we'll take a turkey together," I knew that bagging an old longbeard with him should be as easy as ordering a turkey from the local food store. That was my first mistaken assumption. No matter how much experience a hunter has or how well he calls, turkeys are anointed as hunter humblers. Just about the time you believe you can go out on any given day and put a boss gobbler in the bag, the turkey will invoke his powers from on high and crush your pride.

Salter and I hunted on some of the best private lands in Alabama. And the only turkey we had seen was a crippled tom that the landowner had taken. I could tell Salter was frustrated and upset. Although he was a very proficient caller, and the land had turkeys on it, we had struck out. We were not able to call or see a turkey in two days of hunting. We went to another location and did spot a few jakes but were unsuccessful in calling them.

I was due to leave for home at noon on the third morning. At 10:00 A.M. Salter and I were desperately driving down country roads looking for turkeys in fields. Salter is the barber in his town and so knows almost everybody in the county. He has obtained permission to hunt many privately owned woodlots and fields. We finally passed by a large pasture.

"There's some birds," Salter observed. "Check them out, John, with your binocular."

While the car continued to move, I looked the turkeys over. "There's one longbeard and the rest look like hens."

257

I could see the turkeys in the field but knew I had no way of slipping up on them. (Gulf States Corporation photo)

"I have permission to hunt that land," Salter said. "So let's try for the longbeard."

"Do you really think we can call that gobbler away from his hens and out of that field into gun range?" I knew Salter was a great caller and a master woodsman. But I felt he was asking a great deal of that gobbler. He knew it, and so did I.

"Since that's the only gobbler we have to work, we can either try him or give up," he explained.

"Let's try him," I said with a sheepish grin.

We parked the truck on a dirt road just past the field where we had seen the turkeys. Quietly we slipped along on the edge of the woods. The turkeys were under a slight knoll about 150 yards from the tree line. Just before we sat down to call, we used our binoculars to take one last, long look at them. I could easily see the longbeard. His cotton-white crown glowed in the sun, and his big, thick beard dragged the ground.

While I admired the beauty of that noble fellow, a strange thing occurred. From 200 yards away, someone shot—probably a hunter who thought his shotgun had the killing power of a high-powered rifle. At least, his shot to the turkeys was 100 yards.

Needless to say, all the would-be hunter succeeded in was flushing the flock from the field. As I watched through the binocular, I saw the gobbler spread his wings and beat the wind to bring his huge body off of the ground. Once airborne, he split away from the hens, gained altitude, and headed straight for us.

"Get ready," Salter instructed.

There was no question that in this last hand, it appeared that fate was going to deal us an ace.

"You'd better shoot," Salter murmured as the bird closed in.

"Not yet," I whispered.

Finally, when the gobbler was straight in front of me, in full flight only 20 yards away, I squeezed the trigger on my Remington 1100 three-inch magnum. The gobbler folded stone dead.

We had hunted hard for three days. We had used every tactic we knew. We had paid the price for success, only to be unsuccessful.

But when all else had failed, sheer luck intervened.

Jim Beam's Unforgettable Gobblers

by John E. Phillips

Jim Beam lives in Cherryville, North Carolina, but does most of his turkey hunting on the Broad River Management Area in South Carolina. He's nationally recognized as a competitive turkey caller and has won numerous contests. He has years of turkey-hunting experience and can speak volumes on turkey hunting.

The turkeys that Beam remembers most vividly are not the ones that have fallen to his 12 gauge, but the old gobblers that have gotten away. Nine years have passed since he and the Cow-Pasture Gobbler rendezvoused with destiny. Today the bird probably is dead from natural causes, but the memory of one spring afternoon keeps him alive for Beam.

"I dreamed about that turkey at night, and I still haven't gotten over it," he says. "And I know that as long as he lived the Cow-Pasture Gobbler never forgot the day he met Jim Beam."

The story begins on a typical spring morning back in 1975 when Beam and a friend went into an area where Beam had located some turkeys. "I put a friend in a spot I knew was really hot. I'd heard many turkeys gobbling in this place, and I wanted him to kill one. I went off in the opposite direction to call.

"As luck would have it, the place I'd chosen was quiet as a tomb. Not a single turkey gobbled all morning long. I'd set up not far from the edge of a pasture. So after the sun was well up, I moved down closer to the pasture and started to call again. After I'd been sitting for about an hour and calling every 15 to 20 minutes, two hens walked into the pasture. The morning's prospects were looking up. The two hens were coming right toward me, but they slowed down and began to feed in the pasture.

"After a little while two jakes came out into the pasture behind the hens. Their beards were 3 to 4 inches long. Then a few minutes later, the biggest gobbler I'd ever seen walked out of the woods behind the jakes. That old boss gobbler had a beard more than 11 inches long. Any time the jakes moved close to the hens, the boss gobbler would run at the jakes, peck them, and run them away from the hens. He was the king of the flock, and he didn't mind showing his superiority over the juvenile males.

"I realized there was no point in calling any more, once the turkey was in the open. I knew my only chance of bagging that old gobbler was to get in close enough to shoot without spooking the rest of the flock. I noticed a hedgerow growing through the middle of the pasture, and running inside the hedgerow was a small stream about 6 inches deep. I decided to try to ambush the boss gobbler. I thought if I could get into that stream and crawl to the center of the pasture, I could possibly get close enough.

"So I got inside the hedgerow and put my knees and elbows in the stream. I carried my gun in one hand and slid through the water on the other hand. I noticed that the turkeys were headed toward the center of the pasture. So every 10 or 20 yards I peeped out of the ditch to make sure they were headed to a point where I thought I could intercept them. I knew that if I could get to the center of the pasture before the turkeys I might get a shot at the boss.

"Next, when I sneaked a look, the turkeys had turned and were coming straight toward me. I couldn't figure out why. So I peeped over the bank again and saw that some cows had come out of the woods and started in the direction of the turkeys. That had turned the birds.

"I waited a few minutes and looked over the bank again. I couldn't believe it—the big gobbler was leading the drove straight toward me. Sitting there in the ditch—wet from my knees to my toes and from my elbows to my little fingers—I made a decision. The next time I peeped up that big old gobbler I'd searched for all my life should be in range. So I decided I would come up fast—gun to my shoulder—and fire the instant I saw his head."

Much like a matador in the bull ring, preparing for the kill, Beam waited in the creek. There would only be an instant to down the gobbler. Everything would have to happen with split-second timing. There could be no mistakes. His aim would have to be perfect. The turkey would have to be within range. Beam would have to make sure there were no limbs or bushes in front of the shot. The turkey was just on the other side of that small bank.

"I pushed the safety off and came up quick. The gobbler was standing tall at about 20 yards. I was shooting no. 7½ shot. When I fired, the old bird flipped on his back and started flopping. I knew I had him dead. I laid my gun down on the streambank and ran into the pasture to get my trophy. When I was within 10 feet of him, he jumped up and started to run. But that turkey wasn't going to get away from me. I took off running right behind him.

"For 75 yards I ran as hard and fast as I could. But he stayed just a few yards out of reach. There's no doubt in my mind I could have caught O. J. Simpson that day, but I couldn't get to that turkey. I estimate I was equaling about an 8-second, hundred-yard dash, but the turkey was covering the same ground in about 7 seconds.

"Finally that big old bird got airborne, and I closed in on him. As he flew, I jumped. Each time I reached for his feet, he drew his legs up. I thought I'd be able to catch him in two or three more jumps. But in the midst of my frenzy I caught an ominous sight just in front of me. There was a five-strand barbed-wire fence dead ahead. I had to decide what to do within 20 yards. I contemplated jumping the fence, but it was too high. Then I thought, *Well, I can roll up under the fence, get back on my feet, and still catch the turkey.* But the last strand of wire was too close to the ground for that.

"By the time I was 15 yards from the fence and out of oxygen, the turkey was gaining altitude. Although he must have weighed well over 20 pounds, he sailed over that fence like a giant bomber airplane. All I could do was stop at the fence and watch him fly into the woods.

"I can see that old turkey flying into the woods until this very day. And in my mind I constantly go over all the things I should have done to prevent him from getting away. If I hadn't aimed too low, I'm convinced that some of the shot would have gotten into the turkey's head and killed him. If I'd carried my shotgun with me from the ditch, like anyone in his right mind, I'd have had an easy shot when he got up at 10 yards.

"If I'd run a little faster, jumped a little higher, or dived for the bird, I just might have been able to grab a foot. There should have been a little more speed in my reserve that would have helped me catch that turkey. Each time I jumped I was within 2 inches of grabbing his foot. And if that fence hadn't been in front of me and I'd had a little more running room, I could have gotten the bird.

"But then I also recall standing at the fence and praying that the turkey wouldn't die. I feel sure I didn't put any shot in his head or neck. I don't believe he'd have been able to escape the way he did if he'd been wounded very badly. I think the shot hit his feathers, knocked the breath out of him, and put him down.

"I never heard of anyone else ever taking that turkey. And even though I went back several times, I never saw him again. I believe he left that area and died of old age. He was the most magnificent turkey I've ever seen. He had a long beard, he weighed well over 20 pounds, but most of all he was fast."

The Cow-Pasture Gobbler not only defeated Beam physically, but also became a memory that will last him forever. He's killed many turkeys since his frustrated encounter with the Cow-Pasture Gobbler. But a good turkey hunter loves to tell tales about the ones that got away, just as an angler does. No matter how many fish the angler catches, he always remembers that big bass he had right up beside the boat when it broke his line.

Another nemesis that wrote indelibly on Beam's memory was a turkey he hunted for two years.

"I'd tried everything I knew to kill this old turkey, but he'd always hang up just out of gun range. I knew he'd been shot at a time or two and probably been hit. He just wouldn't come into gun range, no matter what I did.

"One time I had him as close as 30 yards, but he was just over a little knoll. I couldn't see him, and he never would come on in where I was. He'd stand behind that knoll and gobble and gobble, but wouldn't come any farther. I thought about charging him and taking a quick shot when he tried to run off or when he went into the air. However, I decided he was probably quicker than I was—so I wouldn't get a shot and would only spook him.

"There was only one way to go to that turkey, because if I tried to circle him he'd be able to see me. But one morning he was roosting in a different hollow, not in his usual one. I moved in close to him and set up. I knew that day would be the time I'd get that old gobbler.

"I gave him a few tree calls. He fired right back with a series of gobbles. When he flew down and hit the ground, I called to him. But he moved away like he was going to leave me. I decided not to move on him, because I was so close. I felt he'd see me if I tried to move closer. He got on top of a ridge a few hundred yards away and started to gobble.

"I decided I'd wait him out—no matter how long the process took. I didn't call for about an hour. Finally the old boy gobbled at about 50 yards, just on the other side of some small cedars. I could hear him drumming and strutting and coming to me. I had my gun up. Within the next few minutes, the gobbler that had fooled me for so long would be standing right in front of the bead on my shotgun.

"Then I heard a noise behind me. Though I knew there was either a deer, another turkey, or another hunter back there, I tried not to notice. The old gobbler was closing ground on me now and gobbling. But the noise behind me was really playing on my nerves.

"Finally, I couldn't stand the suspense any longer. I eased my head around and saw two gobblers behind me. They spotted my movement and began to putt. When they did that, they spooked the gobbler in front of me. So all three turkeys left without my ever firing a shot. The two turkeys behind me were within 15 yards, but there was just no way for a shot."

The Carolinas have many great turkey hunters. Jim Beam is definitely one of them. When you listen to hunters like him talk, you'll notice their favorite tales are not about the fine birds with the long beards, big spurs, and heavy bodies. The turkeys they remember most are the ones that got away. And these birds are the ones that continue to lure them into the woods each spring.

Turkeys
in the Rain

by John E. Phillips

*T*he alarm clanged. I pulled my warm sleeping bag over my head. The opening morning of turkey season had arrived, but I didn't want to go hunting. The rain was coming down so hard on the tin roof that the sound reminded me of what Noah must have heard when he closed the ark door with all the animals inside. No, today was not a good day to turkey hunt.

"Come on, boy," Don Taylor, my hunting companion, said from the darkness. "Let's get up and at 'em. Those turkeys have to be somewhere today. All we've got to do to take one is find them."

I didn't share Don's optimism. In this driving rain, I figured the turkeys had two choices: They could keep their feet tightly secured to a limb to prevent being washed off, or they could try to become waterfowl.

But after rousing from the sleeping bags, we began to don our camo hunting gear and play the silent game of I'll-go-if-you'll-go, matching one another's insanity.

We'd driven 200 miles from our homes to greet this drenched dawn. For the past seven years, Don hadn't failed to bag a turkey or have a guest bag one on opening morning. And this year, he'd spent weeks scouting and learning the natures of the wily gobblers we were to hunt. The balance of skill between them and us should have tipped heavily in our favor. But Don had forgotten one important key in his planning—the weather.

The night we left home, the forecast was a 100 percent chance of rain. And now, as we prepared to leave the rustic cabin where we'd spent the night, there was no doubt that for once the weatherman had been absolutely correct.

The short dash from the cabin to the pickup truck thoroughly soaked our rainsuits. After we drove two miles to the base of the ridge Don had selected to call from, we sat in the truck, watched the pelting rain, and waited for the first dripping rays of sunlight.

"We took a turkey off this ridge last season," Don said. "And I saw turkeys working it all last week. But I don't believe we'll be able to hear one gobbling this morning. We'll just have to go in, sit down, call, do a lot of looking, and have plenty of luck. Maybe the rain will let up a little if we wait till just after daylight.''

I figured no smart turkey would open his mouth to gobble in this downpour, for fear of drowning. As the sun tried to peep through, the rain continued to fall in torrents. Finally Don looked at me, grinned, and said, ''Let's go, John. We're not going to kill any turkeys sitting here in the truck.''

Through the pouring rain, we worked our way to the top of a steep, heavily wooded ridge. We sat down next to a large red oak on the edge of a fire lane that went down both sides of the ridge. Once the camouflage nets were over our heads and the shotguns loaded, Don whispered: ''You look down the right side of the ridge, and I'll watch down the left. I'll do the calling. You do the shooting.''

I knew he was being extremely optimistic, as rain ran under my shirt collar and slid down my back. And after 20 minutes of calling, we'd seen no turkeys.

In a hushed voice, Don said, ''Let's get up and move down the ridge, and try to call from another spot.'' I eagerly agreed. As we stood up and started to move away from the tree, I looked down Don's side of the fire lane and quickly grabbed his arm.

''Don't move, Don! I see a turkey moving this way about 200 yards down the fire lane. When he steps off to the side, we can set up and try to take him.''

As soon as the big gobbler walked behind some bushes, I went to the front of the tree and sat down with my gun on my knee and ready to shoot. Don moved behind the tree and began to call.

The gobbler slowly waddled and fed up the fire lane. He was not the classic monarch of the spring woodlands with bronze feathers turning glints of sunlight into hues of green, blue, purple, black, and gold. This turkey looked like a hulk of drenched, nondescript feathers matted over the huge frame of an awkward bird. Luckily for me, however, he had heard Don's clucking and yelping and was headed straight toward us.

The hair was standing up on the back of my neck as I anticipated taking a shot. Then Don whispered, ''I'm afraid he's going to see the truck. I pulled a little too close this morning so we wouldn't have to walk far and could get back in the truck quickly once we'd tried calling. I really didn't think we had a chance of seeing a turkey. We could get lucky, but I bet the hunt will be over when that turkey gets even with the truck.''

When the turkey was 75 yards from us, he looked to his left and saw the mirrorlike reflection of the windshield. Slowly he turned at the bottom of the hill and started away from us. No amount of calling would bring him back.

Behind 1–0 in the turkey-versus-hunters contest, we decided to move on down the ridge 150 to 200 yards in front of him, walk over to the side of the ridge he was on, and change callers. Then maybe we could take him. But 20 more minutes of intensive calling proved fruitless. Now the score was turkey 2, hunters 0.

Giving up on that gobbler, we moved across the ridge and began calling for a different one. But nothing answered Don's mouth caller.

We stood up to walk toward the crest of the ridge again. Ten yards from our calling spot, however, we met with a rude surprise. The giant gobbler we'd worked all morning flushed 20 yards away from us, and flew back over the hill.

Apparently he'd heard us when we called. But he took longer than we'd anticipated to get to us. So when he arrived on one side of the ridge, we'd already crossed over and were calling on the other side. Anxious to meet his hen, the gobbler walked to the ridgetop, heard us calling on the other side, and continued to come until we flushed him.

The hunt was over. We'd had two opportunities to take a fine gobbler but made critical mistakes that cost us our trophy. Still, against all odds we had called, seen, and almost taken a turkey on a day when most sane hunters would have stayed at home. Final score: gobbler 3, hunters 0.

It was 9:00 A.M. Since we were already soaked, there was no point in giving up. Don said, "I've seen another flock of turkeys about a mile from here in a field. They usually show up about this time of day. If we're lucky, we may find a gobbler to work."

As we walked, the toes of our boots sank deeply into the soft earth. We forded a small, swollen branch and walked up a narrow tractor road, heading toward the field.

"I see a turkey on the road," Don said. He took out his binocular. "It's a hen. We've got to flush her before we get to the field, or she'll compete with us for any gobbler that may be there." We ran up the road directly at her until she leaped into the rain and flew far back into the woods.

As we approached the pasture, we came to a bottom with sparse hardwoods and no underbrush. From there we spotted a large flock of turkeys in the field about 150 yards in front of us. Apparently our approach had frightened them. They were frantically flying out of the field. We stopped and waited motionless.

"There are three turkeys still in the field," Don said. "I believe they're hens. But I'll check them out." He slowly retrieved his binocular from inside his camo rain slicker, and glassed them. "Two of them are hens. The third one I believe is a hen. No, wait a minute. It's a gobbler—a long-bearded gobbler!"

Don lowered the binocular gradually. "All we can do is wait him out. If we move at all, he's going to see us. If he walks out of the field, we may be able to get in close and call him back, and possibly take him. But if he doesn't move out, we don't have a chance."

We had no back cover, no front cover, and no side cover. We stood like trees in the forest for 30 minutes, waiting for the gobbler to walk out of the field. But he wouldn't leave his sanctuary in the open. "He's going to hang out there all day," Don said.

At this point, the gobbler seemed to have us in checkmate. There was no right move for us to make. But out of the unrelenting rain and our near hopeless situation, I got an idea.

"Don, would you agree we have absolutely no chance of taking that gobbler?"

"Yep."

"Then would you also agree that anything we do won't lessen our chances?"

"Probably."

"Well," I said, "I'm going to get down on my stomach and try to crawl to that big tree 30 yards in front of us. If I make it without spooking the turkey I'll sit down there, and you try to call him from here. If I don't make it, at least we'll have given it our best shot."

"I've got a better idea," Don said. "We'll both try to get to the beech tree. If I stand here in the open and call, he's going to see me for sure. If you'll get down and crawl, I'll watch the turkey. When his head is down feeding, I'll crawl behind you. When his head comes up, I'll tell you to stop. Getting to that beech tree is the only chance we've got to call him. But you've got to realize that once we get there, he still has the winning hand. He's got two hens with him, he's in an area where he normally likes to feed, and there's no reason for him to come into the woods to find another hen. But like you said, we've got nothing to lose. So let's try for him."

I slowly moved behind Don and used his body as a blind while I got down on the ground. There was 2 to 4 inches of rain water covering the woods floor. I felt icy wetness creep up my shirt sleeves, slither over my belt and down the front of my britches, and force its way into my leather boots.

Slowly and deliberately, we crawled. I moved my right arm forward, placed my shotgun on the ground, and watched as it disappeared under the water. Now I had another worry. Would my gun fire after being underwater for so long? But Don and I were committed—even though the chance of success was remote. The challenge that makes a hunt was before us.

"Whoa!" he said, watching the turkey and crawling behind me.

I hugged the ground. In a few minutes I heard "Okay," and crawled again. For 15 minutes I moved to the cadence of "Whoa," "Okay," "Whoa," "Okay." Finally, after what seemed an eternity, I dragged my soaking body to the dark trunk of a large tree. Don rose right behind me.

"I can see the turkeys," he whispered. "Can you?"

"Yeah."

"Another hen has come into the field. Now he's got three hens. I don't believe we have a prayer. But we've made it this far, so let's see the hunt to the end. Put your gun on your knee. Be ready to shoot. And I'll get out my call."

**The turkey looked as though he had been through a washing machine.
Well, judging from this photo, so did I.**

Instead of the clucks and yelps that most hunters start with, Taylor
did some rapid cutting and cackling. Next, he did the young gobbler's
squealing call, and then more cutting and cackling. He called much more
aggressively—longer and louder—than I ever would have.

He's blowing the hunt, I thought.

Yet I knew Don was a master turkey caller. And I had to rely as much
on his ability to call as he had to rely on my ability to shoot, if we were
going to take the gobbler. We were playing pairs poker. He was running
the bluff. My job was to sit stone-faced and watch the opponent.

Slowly the gobbler's head came up, and I saw him start to move cautiously in our direction. Then he stopped and began to feed again. Luckily, the hens stayed where they were, so the gobbler was isolated in the field.

After two or three minutes of waiting, Don started calling once more. His calls sounded like an irritated hen who couldn't believe the proud old gobbler wouldn't strut right out of that field and into the woods to meet her for a date. As a matter of fact, Don's calling sounded like a rebuke. And the big, wet gobbler, evidently feeling his manhood had been challenged, craned his neck skyward and once again walked toward the edge of the woods where we were hidden. He came proudly, as if to say, "How dare she talk to me like that!"

Finally, 60 yards from us at the edge of the field, the gobbler broke into a full strut. Wet as he was, he still put on a magnificent show of woods nobility. Tail fanned, wings dropped, and head curled in a neat question-mark, he displayed his finery for the hen he thought waited just beyond the field.

To break the turkey out of his strut, Don once again started to squeal and call, cut and cackle on his mouth yelper. My eyes burned with the sweat washed into them by the rain. My muscles ached and cramped from sitting so long wadded-up against the tree. Yet Don continued to call.

Finally he stopped and spoke under his breath. "He's coming, John. Can you see him?"

"No. There's three trees between him and me."

"That's okay. I'll tell you when he's in range."

I could see parts of a huge hulk darting in and out among the trees. But I could never see the whole turkey at once. The rain continued down.

"You can take him now," Don whispered.

But I didn't have a clear enough view to make the shot. The hunt had been too hard, and the stalk too long, to take a chance on wounding the turkey or missing him. I decided that unless I got a clear shot at close range, the turkey would go free. I wouldn't mar the most exciting hunt of my life by wounding him.

So I waited, cheek against the stock, one eye closed, the other looking right down the barrel. For two more minutes I watched his wet body and head snake in and out of the trees. Finally he stepped into a clearing and craned his neck. I fired. The hunt was over. The turkey had a nine-inch beard and weighed 19 pounds.

But the turkey itself was not the trophy. The hunt was the prize. The day would be one to remember forever—a day when fate had dealt us all the wrong cards. In a high-stakes poker game, we had played a pair of deuces, bluffed our way through, and won—against all odds.

The Origin of the Mouth Yelper

with Jim Radcliff, Jr.

*I*f my daddy hadn't been bitten by a mad dog, the mouth yelper might never have been invented. Daddy used to have some fine bird and turkey dogs. One day a rabid dog got in with Daddy's dogs and bit one of them. Then that one went mad and bit Daddy.

In those days, around 1920, there were only two places in the South to take the treatment for rabies—Atlanta and New Orleans. We were living in Mobile at the time. Since both places were too far to commute to, Daddy spent three weeks in New Orleans getting a shot in his stomach every day for 21 days.

Having a lot of time on his hands there, he visited the French Quarter, where he met a ventriloquist who made bird calls. After making friends with the man, Daddy asked him to make a turkey call.

"I've never heard a wild turkey call," the man said.

Being experienced at calling turkeys with a wing bone, a cedar box, a leaf, or anything else around, Daddy didn't take long to improvise something to imitate a turkey's yelp. The ventriloquist tried but couldn't imitate the sound.

"I can't do it," he said, "but I'll make you a bird call. Maybe you can use it to imitate a turkey."

So Daddy played with the bird call. The man taught him how to manipulate it, bring the diaphragm into play, and force the wind across it. Gradually, Daddy learned to make the right sound on the little caller.

All this took place before the spring turkey season that year. Daddy's business partner and turkey-hunting rival was Fred Stimpson. Normally the best of friends, they became great rivals when the dogwoods bloomed and the gobblers started to strut. That spring after Daddy came back with his mouth yelper, he really ripped Mr. Stimpson's britches, outscoring him left and right. Mr. Stimpson simply couldn't understand why Daddy was doing so well.

After turkey season was over, Daddy drove up to Jackson, Alabama, where Mr. Stimpson lived, to show him his secret. Mr. Stimpson had a

The late Jim Radcliff Sr., inventor of the mouth yelper, loved hunting and fishing. He is shown here in the mid-1950s. (Virginia Benton photo)

nice white house with a white picket fence, and with a long, high porch in front and several steps leading up to it. When Daddy drove up, Mr. and Mrs. Stimpson were sitting on the porch. Daddy had nothing on his mind except devilment.

Mr. Stimpson called out, "Well, get out, Jim. Come in and sit a spell."

Daddy's reply went something like this: *Cluck, yelp, yelp, yelp.*

Astounded, Mr. Stimpson asked, "What did you say?"

Yelp, yelp, yelp was Daddy's reply.

"The hell you say!" Mr. Stimpson yelled as he flew down off the porch. Knocking open the white picket gate, he got right in Daddy's face. "Open your mouth!"

"I ain't gonna do it," replied Daddy.

Without hesitating, Mr. Stimpson pulled one of the sticks off the picket fence. Rather than have his head knocked off, Daddy opened his mouth and showed him the mouth caller.

"I've got to have one of those things!" Mr. Stimpson growled.

Daddy went home and made his partner a mouth yelper—about two sizes too big. After choking and gagging from trying that oversized yelper for two months, Mr. Stimpson had such a sore mouth he couldn't enjoy a cup of coffee. Daddy finally felt the joke had gone far enough and made him a good one.

The mouth yelper stayed pretty much in south Alabama for many years after 1920, passing from friend to friend all over Mobile and Jackson. The secret was let out in 1953, when an article about the mouth yelper appeared in a major magazine. Now the mouth yelper is found in all parts of the country.

So when you're in the woods this spring, and you get that big gobbler to come in, be thankful that a mad dog bit my daddy.

The Greatest Turkey Fighter of Them All

by John E. Phillips

*E*very year when turkey season starts, I think of Henry Ott of Jackson, Alabama. Ott, a quiet fellow highly respected in his community, has never been known for flat-out lying. Like many hunters, though, I suspect he might embellish the facts a little to improve a story about turkeys. But there was one time when he didn't have to stray from it at all.

"John," he told me, "as sure as I'm standing here, the whole thing really happened."

Ott had decided to take his 13-year-old nephew, Tommy Deas, turkey hunting. Putting the boy between himself and the turkey, he began to call. "I figured the turkey would come to Tommy and he'd kill him, but it didn't work out that way. Instead the turkey came up on my end."

At about 40 steps Ott poured the lead to the bird. The gobbler lay on the ground flopping. Placing his right foot on the turkey's head and his left on the feet, Ott proceeded to take out his pocketknife.

"What are you doing?" questioned Tommy.

"The game's over, Tommy," Ott said. "I'm putting this old turkey out of his misery. There's no sense in letting him suffer."

With that explanation, he pushed the blade of his knife through the turkey's head. The old gobbler spread his wings, quivered, and expired. The two hunters then unloaded their guns and prepared to carry the turkey and their empty guns from the woods. But as they went back to pick up their prize, that "dead" turkey made one flop and was up on his feet running.

"I chased him through the woods for about 40 yards," Ott remembered later. "And as I dove for him on a run, I caught him by the tail feathers."

The mighty old bird suddenly lurched and nothing but the tail feathers were left in Henry's hand. Quickhanded Ott reached again, however, and grabbed the left wing. Once more the powerful turkey fought back, and this time left Ott with a handful of feathers, a lump on his head, and blood streaming down his face.

When you're pitting bare knuckles against hard spurs and crashing wings, Henry Ott of Jackson, Alabama, will go down as one of the legends.

"As I grabbed the right wing, the left wing hit me on the forehead, bloodied my face once more, and knocked me to the ground. The right foot came up next and spurred me in the top of the hand and in my palm. His left foot caught me in the leg and spurred me in three places."

By now Ott's arms were also suffering from the onslaught of those cutting spurs, but our Ott still fought back. He knew that if he failed, the gobbler would escape, die, and rot in the woods. This sportsman fought for his prize like a boxer in the last round, mustering all the strength he could to put his opponent away.

So Ott, nearly exhausted, began to give the battle his maximum effort. Finally securing both of the gobbler's feet in his hands, he stroked the air with that turkey and landed the final blow, flinging him into a pine tree.

When the battle was over, telling who had won was almost impossible. The turkey had no tail feathers, wing feathers, or breast feathers, and was covered with blood. Ott also was covered with blood—his own—and was nearly as battle-scarred as the old bird.

Many of the gentler sex may assume this is a barbaric demonstration of man's attempt to prove his superiority over lower critters. However, if we look more closely, we see that the turkey was mortally wounded and would have wandered off, died, and been totally wasted. But because of Henry's valiant efforts, the bird was preserved and made a fine meal for his family.

As legendary heroes of the past were immortalized through the singing and telling of their exploits, so the people of Jackson, Alabama, will sing and tell about the greatest turkey fighter of them all—Henry Ott—long after he has gone to that great roosting tree in the sky.

Part **8**

AFTER

YOU SCORE

Since a wet plucking is usually the easier, fill a large pot of water heated to boiling. Then either pour the boiling water over the turkey or dunk the bird into the pot. (Sara Bright photo)

Preparing and Cooking Wild Turkey

with Sylvia Bashline

The wild turkey is different from the turkey you buy in the grocery store. These suggestions should help you prepare and cook him properly.

In warm weather, which is common in spring hunting, gut your turkey in the field as soon as possible. In cooler weather, you may be able to wait until you get home to take the entrails out. When field dressing, be sure to reach deep into the cavity and remove all the lung material, which is red and spongy. This lung material will spoil very quickly.

Putting your turkey in the passenger compartment of a warm car can also hasten spoilage. Store it in the trunk of the car, or if the weather is cool, keep it outside the vehicle.

The turkey should be plucked when you arrive at home. If the bird is still warm, the feathers may pull out very easily. But if the bird is cool, I'd suggest a wet plucking.

There are all kinds of fancy ways to pluck a turkey, but the simplest and easiest is to fill a big pot or tub with water, put it on the stove, and bring the water to a boil. Then remove it from the stove and dunk your turkey into the steaming-hot water. Slosh the turkey up and down for about a minute to loosen the feathers. Begin to pluck it in the same direction that the feathers grow—from the neck toward the feet. You don't want to pluck the feathers by pulling them backwards, because this action may tear the skin. Next, singe your turkey to make sure you've removed all the pin-feathers. You may even need to use a pair of tweezers.

If the turkey is to be cooked in the next day or two, you can keep it in the refrigerator. Be sure to cover it with plastic wrap, and put it in the meat cooler if possible. If the meat cooler is too small, just store it on a shelf in the refrigerator.

If the turkey is to be frozen for later use, it should be triple wrapped. For the first layer I use Reynolds Wrap clear plastic. I eliminate all the air I can between the wrap and the turkey, since the more air that's trapped there, the greater the chances of freezer-burning the turkey. The next layer is foil. Again I wrap the turkey very tightly, trying to exclude all the air. The last layer is freezer paper. On the outside of the freezer paper, I write how much the turkey weighed and the date it was put into the freezer.

I've always found that cooking a turkey within two months of the kill is best, even if it's been in the freezer. But a turkey in the right freezer will often be good for as long as a year. The right kind of freezer is one that's not self-defrosting, because the fan in a self-defrosting freezer pulls the moisture out of food even when it's well-wrapped.

A big disappointment may come when you cook the turkey. Since the wild turkey is not bred for its breast, there's not a large amount of breast meat as there is on a commercial turkey. The wild turkey must survive and reproduce in the wild, and to do so he doesn't need a real heavy breast. The wild gobbler has to work for a living and isn't a welfare case like the tame turkey in a pen. So you shouldn't expect as much breast meat from him as you would from his barnyard cousin.

Pluck the feathers in the direction they grow—that is, from the neck toward the feet. (Sara Bright photo)

Also, the wild meat will be drier than the meat of the tame turkey. If the turkey is to be roasted, you should plan to do a great deal of basting to keep it moist and tasty. I recommend placing cheesecloth over the breast and keeping that cheesecloth moist with a buttery sauce. The recipe you use will determine the kind of basting sauce. However, one of my favorites for basting is made from ½ cup of orange juice, ½ cup of butter, and a small amount of grated orange peel for added flavor.

One problem is that if you cook the turkey until the legs are just right, then the breast will be a little dry. For that reason I often separate my turkey, using one recipe for the breast and another recipe for the legs and wings.

Listed below are some of my favorite wild turkey recipes from the *Bounty of the Earth Cookbook.* The first two recipes are actually my own.

ROAST TURKEY WITH PEANUTS

10- to 14-pound wild turkey	peanut dressing
1 cup butter	½ cup dry white wine
salt and pepper	½ cup chicken bouillon

Rub the turkey with butter, sprinkle with salt and pepper, and stuff with peanut dressing (recipe follows). Use skewers to close the body opening. Place the turkey in a roasting pan and cover completely with cheesecloth. Mix the rest of the butter with the wine and bouillon, and baste the turkey with this mixture every 25 minutes until you can baste with pan juices. Place the turkey in a 350-degree oven for the first hour, and then lower to 325 degrees for the remaining time. Roast for 20 to 25 minutes per pound.

PEANUT DRESSING

2 stalks celery, chopped	2 eggs, beaten
1 onion, finely chopped	1 cup chicken bouillon
3 teaspoons melted butter	½ cup white wine
3 cups roasted peanuts	½ teaspoon sage
4½ cups dry bread crumbs	pepper to taste

Sauté the celery and onion in the butter. Chop the peanuts coarsely and mix all ingredients together. The dressing should be quite moist to keep the turkey from drying. This should be enough dressing for a 12-pound wild turkey.

ROAST WILD TURKEY

10- to 14-pound turkey	butter
salt and pepper	1½ quarts dry bread crumbs
1 pound pork sausage	1 teaspoon salt
1 onion, chopped	¼ teaspoon pepper
2 apples, peeled, cored,	4 tablespoons parsley, minced
and chopped	chicken bouillon

Sprinkle dressed turkey with salt and pepper. In a frying pan, cook the sausage and onion for 10 minutes. Add the apples, bread crumbs, salt, pepper, and parsley. Mix well. Add enough bouillon to make a moist dressing. Stuff the turkey. Place in a roasting pan and cover with a double thickness of cheesecloth soaked well in butter. Roast in a 325-degree oven for 20 minutes per pound. Keep basting with butter and then with pan juices. A 10-pound turkey will serve five to six people.

The next recipe is from Shirley Grenoble, who was a director of the National Wild Turkey Federation and a vice-president of the Pennsylvania chapter, besides being an avid turkey hunter.

ROAST TURKEY WITH BREAD DRESSING

1 wild turkey	turkey giblets, diced
1 cup diced onion	1 cup melted butter or margarine
1 cup finely chopped celery	15 cups stale bread cubes
salt and pepper to taste	

Sauté onion, celery, and giblets in butter. When almost tender, reduce heat to very low, add bread cubes, salt, and pepper, and cover. Let the mixture steam, turning occasionally until bread cubes are moist. Makes enough dressing for a 15-pound turkey.

For a variation, ½ cup of chopped apples, raisins, or almonds may be added to the dressing.

Stuff the turkey with dressing, skewer, and truss. Place in roaster, add 3 cups hot water, and cover. Roast at 250 degrees for approximately 20 minutes per pound.

The late Roger Latham, outdoor editor of the *Pittsburgh Press* and author of the *Complete Book of Wild Turkey*, took his share of wild turkeys and experimented with many ways of cooking them. "One delightful variation," he said, "in case you get tired of roast wild turkey all the time, is to quick-fry the breast meat. When the turkey is still uncooked, remove the meat from each side of the breast in one large fillet. Then lay each piece of white meat on a table or board, skin side down. Carefully cut thin steaks about a third of an inch thick.

"Salt the pieces. Let them stand for a few minutes in a pile, and when good and moist, dust each with flour. Shake off the excess and drop in a sizzling frying pan of hot butter or margarine. Brown quickly on one side, flop over and brown the other side. This should only take a very few minutes, and the meat should not be overcooked. Fry it fast like you would a good steak, and it will almost melt in your mouth. The meat will be juicy and delicious, and bear little resemblance to the same meat when roasted."

This last recipe comes from Rob Keck of the National Wild Turkey Federation.

SHAKE 'N BAKE TURKEY
WITH RUNNING-GEAR GRAVY

The turkey should be skinned rather than plucked. White breast meat is filleted from the bone. Remove the one main tendon from the breast. Skinning and cut-up time is approximately 15 minutes. All appendages are disjointed. Cold-water soaking may be necessary if excessive blood appears.

Cut the breast fillets across the grain into pieces about ¼ inch thick, 3 inches long, and 1½ inches wide (about the size of a large oyster). When feeding a crowd, cut thinner and smaller pieces.

Mix 2 cups of milk and 3 beaten eggs in a mixing bowl (more of each ingredient if needed). Into a second bowl pour ½ pound of bread crumbs (these have proven superior to most other types of breading for this treat).

With a meat fork immerse the breast pieces in the eggs and milk; then place them in the bread crumbs. Repeat the process; the double breading seals out excess grease from the meat.

A deep fryer or iron skillet may be used. Heat the oil to 365 degrees. Drop the breaded pieces into the heated oil and turn them one time in the required 10 minutes. (When you drop the cold meat into hot oil it cools the oil; so make sure the oil remains hot enough to set the breading. In the deep fryer, use 3 gallons of oil so there is no significant cooling.)

Remove the fried meat from the skillet or fryer, and place it in a lined pan with paper towels to soak up the excess grease. Then put the pan in a warm oven until all the turkey breast is fried.

Make a thick gravy from the neck, back, giblets, and legs. The leg meat, which gives it the name "running-gear gravy," should be cooked, browned, seasoned, cut up, and added to the thickened both. This gravy is delicious on the fried meat as well as on potatoes or rice.

Prepared with this recipe, a 15-pound turkey easily feeds eight.

An electric smoker allows you to smoke hickory chips, while the water pan steams the turkey with seasonings. (Sara Bright photo)

Denise Phillips'
Turkey Cookery

by John E. Phillips

Throughout American history, the wild turkey has been a preferred food of both city and rural dwellers. During the late 1800s and early 1900s, many woodsmen earned a living by taking wild turkeys for the tables of the townfolk and the meat of the wild turkey is still highly prized and praised. Try some of these recipes from the kitchen of my wife, Denise, and you'll understand why.

SMOKED WILD TURKEY

1 to 2 cups cooking sherry
2 lemons, sliced
one 10- to 20-pound turkey
seasoned salt

thyme
poultry seasoning
butter, melted

If you use an electric smoker like our Brinkmann Sportsman's Smoker, cooking wild turkey couldn't be easier. Simply put soaked hickory chips in the proper place in the smoker and fill the water pan partially, adding cooking sherry and sliced lemons to the water.

Cover the turkey generously all over with seasoned salt. Then add thyme and poultry seasoning to taste. With a large syringe you may inject melted butter, additional seasoned salt, thyme, and poultry seasoning into the carcass. This really adds to the flavor and makes the meat very moist. Place the turkey on the rack and seal the smoker.

If your smoker isn't electric, use the chart below and fill the bottom of the smoker with charcoal. Light the entire amount of charcoal, and let it stop flaming. Then place hickory chips on top of it. Put the pan of water above the charcoal, according to the chart. Then follow the same directions given for the electric smoker, to prepare and cook the meat.

Wt. of Turkey	Charcoal	Water	Smoking Time
8–12 lbs.	10 lbs.	6 qts.	8–10 hrs.
13–16 lbs.	12 lbs.	7 qts.	10–12 hrs.
17–20 lbs.	15 lbs.	8 qts.	12–14 hrs.

HOT TURKEY CASSEROLE

2 cups cooked, chopped turkey
½ cup chopped almonds
2 tablespoons chopped pimento
¼ teaspoon pepper
2 tablespoons lemon juice
2 cups chopped celery

1 cup shredded Swiss or
  Cheddar cheese
⅓ cup chopped green pepper
1 teaspoon salt
½ cup mayonnaise
1 cup crushed potato chips

Combine all ingredients except potato chips. Spoon into a greased, two-quart casserole dish. Bake at 350 degrees for 30 minutes. Remove from oven, and place potato chips on top of the casserole. Return to oven briefly, to brown.

TURKEY FRITTATA

½ cup finely chopped onions
1 tablespoon butter
8 eggs
½ cup milk
1 teaspoon salt
1 teaspoon Worcestershire sauce
4 to 5 drops hot-pepper sauce

2 cups cooked rice
1 can (4 oz.) chopped
  green chilies, undrained
1 medium tomato, chopped
½ cup shredded Cheddar cheese
2 cups cooked, chopped turkey

Cook onions in butter in a 10-inch skillet over medium heat until tender. Beat egg yolks with milk and seasonings. Beat egg whites until fluffy, but not dry. Stir rice, chilies, tomato, and turkey into the egg yolk-milk-seasonings mixture.

Mix in beaten egg whites. Pour into pan. Reduce heat to medium low. Cover and cook until top is almost set, 12 to 15 minutes. Sprinkle with cheese, cover, and remove from heat. Let stand for 10 minutes. (Or after mixture is poured in pan, place in oven and cook at 350 degrees for 30 minutes.)

Joel Davis (left) guided Denise Phillips to her first wild gobbler some years ago. Not many both take turkeys and cook them too.

BRAISED WILD TURKEY

1 turkey
salt and pepper
1 lb. salt pork, sliced
1 carrot, sliced
2 to 3 sprigs parsley

1 quart consommé
1 onion, sliced
1 large stalk celery, chopped
bay leaf
pinch of thyme

Wash and drain turkey. Pat dry. Season cavity with salt and pepper. Stuff with half the salt-pork slices, and cover with the rest. It may be necessary to secure the slices with toothpicks. Brown in oven at 400 degrees for one hour.

Combine consommé, onion, carrot, parsley, celery, bay leaf, and thyme. Remove salt pork and discard. Add consommé mixture to turkey and cover tightly. Bake in 300-degree oven for two to three hours or until tender. Baste frequently with consommé mixture.

SPAGHETTI/TURKEY CASSEROLE

1 cup chopped celery
¼ cup chopped onion
3 tablespoons chopped green pepper
3 tablespoons butter
1½ cups turkey gravy
1 cup chicken broth or any combination of the gravy and broth
½ cup cream
1 teaspoon salt
dash of pepper
1½ cups chopped, cooked turkey
1 package (8 oz.) spaghetti
½ cup buttered soft bread crumbs

Sauté celery, onion, and green pepper in the butter. Add the 2½ cups gravy and broth, cream, salt, pepper, and turkey. Cook spaghetti per directions on package. Combine spaghetti and sauce. Pour into two-quart baking dish. Sprinkle with crumbs. Bake at 350 degrees for 30 minutes.

Turkey

Taxidermy

by John E. Phillips

*T*he turkey stands at 20 yards, head erect and in the ideal position for the hunter to take him. The shotgun has been patterned on the range, the hunter has been patient, the aim is deadly, and all that's left is the squeezing of the trigger. BANG! The shotgun blasts, and the turkey tumbles.

Once you have arrived at the scene of the kill and are quite sure you have the gobbler in hand, you need to decide whether you'll eat him or mount him. If a turkey dinner is more important than a lovely gobbler for your wall, then field-dress him immediately.

However, if a mounted trophy displaying all the beautiful colors of the wild is what you want, then forget the field dressing. Instead, get the turkey immediately to the taxidermist or into the freezer. Don't drag the turkey all over town, leave him in the trunk of a hot car for a day or two, or wait until your brother-in-law gets off the night shift to show the turkey to him. Even if you decide not to mount the turkey, there are still several trophies you can make from him besides a turkey dinner.

If mounting the turkey is one of your reasons for hunting him, let's look at the options a skilled taxidermist offers you. And I choose the word "skilled" very carefully. There are many men and women who hang out shingles bearing the title of taxidermist. However, this does not mean they're skilled in taking a pile of feathers and a dead head and making a lifelike re-creation of the wild turkey you hunted. So if you want a good mount, my advice is to look at a finished product by the taxidermist before you trust him with your turkey.

The best time to select a taxidermist is prior to the season when you have plenty of time to look at the work of several and choose the best. Once you know the taxidermist you'll be taking the turkey to, you have several options as to the way the turkey's head, the most colorful and noticeable part of the mount, is prepared.

I've been a taxidermist since the mid-60s, besides being an outdoors

A mount of the actual head may crack behind the eye and across the top. This results from the drying of very thick skin. (Sara Bright photo)

This is a latex head, which lacks much of the detail of the real turkey's head and appears very artificial. Since the technology in latex forms has been improving, the appearance of latex turkey heads should continue to improve. (Sara Bright photo)

A freeze-dried turkey's head looks realistic and doesn't crack like air-dried heads. (Sara Bright photo)

writer, so I've observed the evolution of various ways of dealing with the head. At first the only option open to the taxidermist was to skin the head and neck, remove the meat, preserve the wattles and skin as best he could, and pray that once the new head was finished the skin wouldn't crack for at least two or three years. The taxidermist knew that the head was going to crack eventually. He just hoped that before it did the customer would forget who'd mounted the turkey.

Next came the polyurethane and latex-rubber heads. These heads could easily and unnoticeably be attached to the body, and when skillfully painted could often fool even the keenest-eyed hunter into believing the head he saw was the head he'd shot. Although many of these heads looked artificial, they were widely used because they did prevent the cracking that happened with the natural heads.

The third and what I consider the best choice is freeze drying. Here, the gobbler's neck and head are removed from the body, posed in a lifelike position, and placed in a freeze-dry machine, which removes all the moisture from the head without shrinking it. The head stays intact, is preserved, and won't crack.

The color of the head must always be restored by painting, since there's little color remaining in it once the turkey is killed. The number-one complaint of hunters is that the head, when painted by the taxidermist, is not the same color it was when the turkey was bagged. But there's a very good reason for this alteration. The color of a turkey's head changes according to his emotional state, his sexual state, the time of the year he's killed and the environment where he's found. I've seen turkeys' heads in the woods that were solid white, solid blue, solid red, an off-shade of violet, and all these colors in various mixtures.

Most often when a hunter sees a turkey, the bird's head will be relatively white on top, blue or violet around the eyes, and either red or white on the wattles. But this is not an absolute description of every turkey's head that a hunter might see. To get the mount's head the color you want, make sure you and your taxidermist have a clear understanding in the matter, or else depend on his judgment.

The next decision is what posture the turkey will be mounted in and where it will be displayed. Actually, this decision-making process should be in the reverse order. Where the mount is to be displayed dictates the posture it should have.

For instance, the wall of a small house trailer generally is not a good place to hang a large, flying turkey. That's not to say a turkey cannot be hung on the wall of a house trailer. But what the trailer resident should realize is that more than likely the tip of one wing will touch the ceiling, while the tip of the other wing will touch the carpet. Every dog, cat, child, and inquisitive adult who walks into the trailer will ruffle the turkey's feathers, pull feathers out, break the head and wings, or fall into the turkey and smash it completely. If a turkey is mounted in a flying position, which I believe is the way to show off the most turkey, display it on a large wall and out of reach of exploring hands.

If you have a smaller place where you want to display your trophy, then a walking, sneaking, or strutting mount may be better suited. Measure the area where you will stand the mount or hang it. Then check the measurements with your taxidermist to be certain your trophy can be displayed in the place you've chosen.

Remember also that quality taxidermy is much like good pudding. The instant stuff doesn't taste as good and doesn't please you nearly as much as the pudding that's cooked long and slow with the love and care that reflect the skill and concern of the one who prepared it. Allow the taxidermist plenty of time to practice his ancient art.

If a whole mounted turkey is not what you desire, a skin mounted on barn wood can make a beautiful and interesting display. This mount does not require an artificial body and does not use the turkey's head and feet.

To make this type of mount, start by skinning the turkey along the stomach as you would for a normal mount. Remove the head just above the beard, split the underside of the wings, and remove the meat from between the bones. Using Instant Mounting Fluid (available from Touchstone Taxidermy Supply, Rt. 1, Box 5294, Boisser City, LA 71111), inject

Left: **You can conserve space by mounting your turkey in flight. But first consider the length of the wingspread (Sara Bright photo).** *Right:* **Or you may prefer to mount your gobbler standing, or even strutting.**

the tail butt and the tips of the wings where a small amount of meat may remain. With a knife, razor blade, or scissors, remove all excess meat and fat from the turkey's skin. Now rub powdered borax into the skin and into the cavity in each wing where the meat was removed.

Next, stretch the skin out, so the fleshy side is down and the feather side is up. Place a nail in the skin on either side of the back. From this base nail, run string to other nails around the edge of the wings so the string forces the feathers to lie down flat on the wings. Also place nails between each of the tail feathers that have been spread. Run a length of cord from one nail to the next, making a loop around each, to hold the tail feathers down and in place.

Once the wings and tail are secured, allow the skin to dry in a warm, dry place for three to four weeks. While the skin is drying, search the countryside for an old barn door or siding to mount it on. Once the skin is dried, nail it to the wood. Use the feathers to hide the nail heads. You can easily fashion a loop hanger with a length of clothesline so your skin mount can be suspended from the wall. This mount makes an attractive hanging for a den or office.

Even if a hunter doesn't have his gobbler mounted, he'll save the feet, beard, and tail most of the time. The tail is usually spread, and then the tail, beard, and feet are allowed to dry. After a few years, these trophies are often relegated to the garage or the back of some closet or drawer, and eventually may rot. But a hunter can mount the parts of his turkey trophy instead, in an attractive display.

The tail and feet must be preserved to ensure that decay and insects won't destroy them. Get a large hypodermic syringe from a drugstore or from a feed store that carries veterinary supplies. Fill it with a preservative solution like the Instant Mounting Fluid. Inject this into the fleshy part of the tail. Next, spread the tail on a large piece of cardboard or wood and use either pins or nails to hold it in place. Store the tail in a warm, dry area so it will dry in the proper position.

Inject fluid into the feet along the tendon on the back of the leg, the palm of the foot, and each toe. Lay the feet on their sides, curling the toes

THE BARNWOOD SKIN MOUNT

To mount a turkey's skin on barnwood, skin the turkey along the stomach like you would to have the bird mounted. Remove the head just above the beard, split the underside of the wings, and remove the meat from the bones. After injecting Instant Mounting Fluid into the tailbutt and wing tips, remove the excess meat. Rub powdered Borax into the skin and the cavity in each wing.

together the way your hand looks when it's cupped and all the fingers are touching. Let the feet dry until they become rigid. Rub borax into the meat attached to the beard, and put it in the same place to dry.

Once the specimens are dry, make a covering for the butt of the tail using velvet. An ideal velvet covering, a skullcap, can be purchased from the San Angelo Company, Inc., P. O. Box 984, San Angelo, TX 76902.

If you are blessed with woodworking skills and can create your own panels on which to attach the tail, feet, and beard, do so by all means. If not, choose a panel offered by any of the taxidermy supply houses across the country. These panels come already finished. All you do is add a hanger to the back.

To attach the turkey's tail to the panel, use nails and hot glue. A hot-glue gun can be obtained from a hardware store or most taxidermy supply houses. Place the tail in the center and a little high on the panel, with the velvet covering over the butt. Then attach the feet on either side of the mounted tail, using one of the strong instant glues available at most hardware and discount stores. Mount the beard just below the tail. Small pieces of rawhide may be glued over the butts of the legs and the meat of the beard to make a more attractive mount.

Another option is to add the wings to the tail-foot-beard combination.

Below left: After stretching the skin out skin-side down and feather-side up, place a nail in the skin on each side of the back. Here the taxidermist is running string to nails around the edge of the wing. The string helps hold feathers down while the skin dries. *Below right:* Here the cord runs from one nail to the next. Allow the skin to dry in a warm, dry place for three to four weeks. Then drive the nails through the skin to attach it to barnwood and to hide the nail heads under the feathers.

To preserve each wing, make an incision on the underside and pull the skin back, exposing the muscle and bone. Remove the muscle from the bone, leaving the skin intact. Sprinkle borax into the incision, then rub it into the skin and along the bone below the incision. Next, use cotton to replace the tissue that was removed, and sew up the incision with braided nylon casting line or with quilting thread.

Thoroughly inject fluid into the rest of the wing, from the incision to the tip. Stretch the wing out and allow it to dry. Use the same procedure on the other wing.

Once the wings are dry, dust them off. Before placing the tail on the mounting panel, attach the wings by running wires from the back side of the panel over and around them and back through the panel. Twist the wires firmly so the wings remain secure. Next, mount the tail in the center of the panel and slightly high, overlapping part of the wings. Flank the tail with the preserved feet. You also can make a small incision in the velvet covering for the tail, and glue in the turkey's beard.

Since the real trophies from an old gobbler are his beard and spurs, another possibility is to mount only the beard and feet. Inject the feet with the fluid, then put the toes together and curve the feet into the desired position. Apply borax to the meat on the beard.

When the feet and beard are dry, use a piece of rawhide or deerskin to cover the ends of the legs and the meat on the beard. Shellac the feet to make them shine, if you wish, or leave them natural. Purchase or make a small panel. Then use either hot glue or instant glue to attach the feet on either side of it. In the center of the panel, glue the beard above the feet. Then attach a brass nameplate engraved with your name, the date you took the gobbler, how much he weighed, and where he was killed. You can do this for each of your gobblers and keep up with them in this way.

Still another way to preserve the spurs is to saw them off the legs. Glue a jeweler's clasp to the butt of each spur, then attach earring wires to the clasps to fashion a pair of spur earrings for your favorite female. Coat the spurs with shellac or clear gloss to make them shiny. Or, use the spurs as tips for bolo ties, tie tacks, cuff links, or centerpieces for belt buckles or necklaces.

And since the wild turkey is one of the most beautiful of creatures, with iridescent feathers that change color as light of varying intensity strikes them, why not make feathered jewelry? A bit of glue, a few beads, some wires, and rawhide are all that's required for the project.

Check with your local craft store to obtain surgical posts for earrings, loops for necklaces, rawhide for headbands, and other materials that make beautiful jewelry with the addition of a feather.

The wild turkey offers many trophies besides a tasty dinner for the table. And because this wary bird is so highly prized by all who hunt him, there should be more than one way to preserve the memory of the hunt.

Part **9**

TURKEY
MANAGEMENT

A poult is most susceptible to predators during its first two weeks of life. (Leonard Lee Rue III photo)

How to Have
More Turkeys

with Dr. Dan Speake

*T*o have plenty of turkeys to hunt, we've learned through our research that the turkey must have a good dispersion of its seasonal habitat needs. In other words, in good turkey range there should be certain habitat for nesting, another type of habitat for the rearing of the young, and different habitats for fall and winter. If you don't have all these kinds of habitat on a particular piece of property, then that property will not be able to maintain as large a number of turkeys as land that does meet these requirements.

To have more turkeys to hunt, you must have good habitat for the hens. During the spring of the year you need quality nesting habitat close to a clover field, for instance, which would be a good food source. And by providing the habitat requirements for the hen, the gobblers will go where the hens are.

If that nesting area and clover region are close to good brood range, then you have an ideal condition for producing plenty of turkeys during the spring. And when you provide good habitat like this for the hens, you're not only participating in good management for future turkey production, but also concentrating the gobblers in a very small area. So if the hunter provides habitat for the hens, he'll have many gobblers to hunt.

Each of the different types of habitat is important. Good nesting habitat may be a broomsedge field with some briar thickets. Nesting habitat needs to be the kind of place where the hen can make her nest on the ground and feel relatively safe and secure. Ideally, nesting areas will feature low, herbaceous vegetation with scattered brush. And a field of clover next to this nesting region will yield excellent food for the turkeys and for the young poults.

We've learned through our research that the first two weeks of the poults' lives is when they are most susceptible to predators. Therefore, to ensure future generations of turkeys, there should be a good brood site close to the nesting area and the clover patch. This brood site should contain grasses and shrubs that are about knee-high. Then the poults can move

This is quality turkey nesting and brood-rearing habitat for spring and summer. Shrubs and grasses about knee-high allow the poults to move through the grass, shielded from the view of predators. (Dan Speake photo)

Young poults feed on insects, in this case gypsy moths. However they still can't fly and must rely heavily on camouflage to survive. (Leonard Lee Rue III photo)

through the low grass unprotected, invisible to predators, and the hen can stick her neck up and look over the grass for predators. If the hen has this type of habitat to raise her poults in, she will raise a much higher percentage of them than if she has to expose them in an open pasture or field.

Yet another limiting factor to good turkey range is the presence of predators. By removing a good number of the predators of the wild turkey, you can increase the survival rate of the poults and of the developed birds.

One of the worst predators on the small poults is free-ranging dogs, which destroy turkey nests and can greatly impact a turkey population. Through our research we've determined that the free-ranging dog in many regions is the number-one predator of turkeys. By removing these dogs, we can increase the numbers of turkeys that survive each year. And free-ranging dogs in turkey range have another disadvantage, because, as any hunter knows, when dogs start barking toms quit gobbling.

The raccoon is another predator that destroys many turkey nests and kills young poults. Not only will raccoons wreak havoc on the turkey population, but raccoons are also a menace for the hunters who plant chufa (a grass that produces a nutlike root) for turkeys. Raccoons will get in, dig up a chufa patch, and eat the chufa that was intended for turkeys.

Chufa is important to turkeys, because it can be utilized during the fall and winter for turkey food when other sources of food may be scarce. If the raccoons get into the chufa patches, they can quickly deplete the supply of winter food that the hunter has planted for the turkey. So one of the best methods to increase the number of turkeys on a piece of property is to reduce the number of predators that are depleting the turkey population.

After providing good habitat and food for the hens and young poults and removing predators, hunters can further increase the number of turkeys on their hunting lands by controlled burning. If you control-burn during the winter in a pine forest, the burning releases the nutrients in the soil and will create a generous green-up in the spring. Gobblers like to hang around a pine woods that has been burned, and feed on those young, green shoots. But just setting the pine woods on fire in the wintertime is not an effective way to control-burn. Hunters should work with their departments of conservation and forestry commissions to know when, where, and how to burn for the best effect.

To determine just how important good habitat is, at our Research Unit we've studied turkeys in mountainous areas and along coastal plains to try to determine home range. We've learned that in mountainous regions, a turkey home range of 5,000 acres is not uncommon, whereas in the coastal plains where the habitat is better, a turkey's home range may only be 1,000 acres.

In the places we studied in the mountains, we were looking primarily at hardwood forests which provided excellent fall and winter habitat but little or no habitat for nesting and the rearing of young. However, in the

Affixing radio transmitters to the backs of turkey poults, scientists can continually track their movements. (Dan Speake photo)

A young bird with radio transmitter mounted on its back is here being released. Biologists have learned that in mountainous regions, where food is less plentiful, a turkey's home range may be as large as 5,000 acres. Whereas in coastal plains, where food is abundant, a turkey's home range may only be 1,000 acres. (Dan Speake photo)

Good fall and winter habitat is often in the area where a hunter finds mast-producing trees. Dr. Speake looks for mature hardwoods, especially along stream bottoms. (Dan Speake photos)

coastal plains the habitat was broken between hardwood forests and agricultural fields, which was better year-round habitat for the turkeys. The turkeys didn't have to travel as far for their seasonal habitat needs. From this study we learned that a big hardwood forest is not as conducive to producing and holding turkeys as a forest that's broken with fields and agriculture.

Openings in the woods are very important to the wild turkey. From this information we soon realized that a hunter could look at an aerial photo of a given piece of property and tell where turkeys should be during certain times of the year.

Personally, I would look for mature hardwoods, especially along a stream bottom, interspersed with long meandering fields or pastures. I wouldn't mind if there were several clear-cuts in this region, but preferably these clear-cuts wouldn't be more than a year or two old. The first two or three years after an area has been clear-cut, it provides excellent habitat for the poults in the spring.

If you are going to have good turkey hunting year after year, then you must provide suitable habitat with openings in the woods. Also, you must do controlled burning, plant clover for the turkeys' spring food and chufa for their fall food, and remove as many predators as possible. These measures will increase the poults' survival, and therefore increase the numbers of turkeys that you have to hunt.

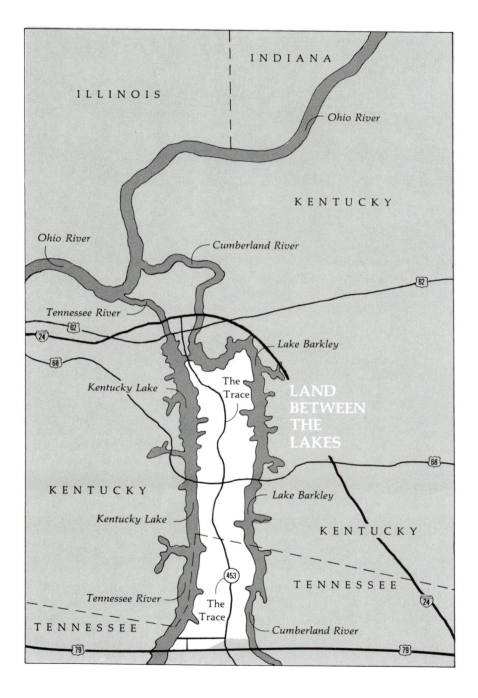

The Flock that Baffled Biologists

by John E. Phillips

*T*he turkeys at the Land Between the Lakes (LBL) on the Tennessee-Kentucky border broke all the rules. They mystified hunters, and they baffled biologists. And if a change hadn't taken place, the flock might have gotten in deep trouble.

Today, however, Land Between the Lakes is one of the best turkey-hunting areas in the nation. LBL, which is owned by the Tennessee Valley Authority, is a 170,000-acre peninsula that lies between Kentucky Lake and Lake Barkley. There are an estimated 3,500 turkeys on the peninsula, and each year new records in harvest are being set.

But during the 1970s, in spite of intensive management, protection from hunting, and close attention to the recommendations of biologists, the turkey population at LBL did not expand. Let's look at the history of these mysterious LBL turkeys.

The first turkey hunt in 41 years was held on LBL in 1960, before the TVA took over management of the land. Twelve turkeys were harvested for 375 hunter days expended. The first LBL hunt managed by TVA came in 1965, and six turkeys were harvested. In 1966, 19 were taken, while 27 were killed in 1967. Hunts from 1960 until 1975 were held only on the Kentucky portion of LBL, because there were no turkeys in the Tennessee portion when the hunting began.

The harvest records stayed fairly low indicating little growth in the flock.

YEAR	HARVESTED
1968	13
1969	4
1970	6
1971	8
1972	12
1973	12
1974	10
1975	13

"Everyone we talked to told us we were doing everything we should to increase our turkey population," says Dennis Sharp, the wildlife biologist for the turkey program at LBL. "We couldn't figure out what we were doing wrong. The turkey population at LBL kept fluctuating in the late '60s until the early '70s.

"About 1965, we opened up water holes and did spring planting for the turkeys. We mowed parts of the woods where turkeys would have good places to dust and eat bugs in the spring. We opened up spots in the woods where new vegetation could grow and provide more food. We did everything we knew to improve the habitat and increase our turkey population."

Rick Lowe, the supervisor of wildlife management at LBL, explains further: "We expended quite a bit of money and manpower to build up LBL's turkey flock during this period. But utilizing all the knowledge and resources available to us, we were still unable to expand the flock to the area's potential. The turkeys on LBL became a mystery not only to us but also to other biologists."

For years the rule of good turkey management had been to improve the habitat, increase the amount of food, and protect the flock. The turkey population was then supposed to grow. Although the rule was followed, the mysterious turkeys at LBL continued to be in short supply.

So, according to Sharp, "We began to look in another direction. The man who's now in charge of the state turkey biologists for Kentucky, George Wright, was still a student at Auburn University in the early '70s. George came to LBL to do his master's thesis. His objective was to solve the mystery of the turkey flock that would not expand. George used radio transmitters on the LBL turkeys. He did some recaptures, he studied nesting habits, and he evaluated predation on the turkeys and their nests."

From this intensive study, Wright drew conclusions about three factors that radically affected the turkeys at LBL. Recognizing these factors helped solve the mystery:

• The native turkeys at LBL had a lower percentage of first-year hens nesting or attempting to nest than other strains of turkeys found in other places.

• The renesting efforts of the LBL turkeys were much lower than in other turkey flocks, when the nests were destroyed by a flood or predator or when the hen was scared off the nest by a human.

• There was considerable nest predation, primarily by raccoons, skunks, and opossums.

Then the biologists at LBL began a study of the turkey-management programs of Tennessee and Kentucky, to determine if the two states were doing anything that might help solve the mystery of the LBL gobblers.

"Each state had been involved in turkey restoration," Sharp explains. "Although Kentucky did not have a large nucleus flock to use for restocking, Tennessee did. So Kentucky had to acquire turkeys from other regions for

A cannon net is fired over a flock of turkeys to capture them. (Gulf States Paper Company photograph)

Turkeys entangled in a net can be safely removed and restocked to another area. (Tennessee Valley Authority photo)

restocking. The LBL biologists studied the progress both states were making.

"Throughout the 1950s and early '60s, the state of Kentucky had been taking turkeys from the Kentucky woodlands portion of LBL and stocking them on Kentucky's wildlife-management areas. So the biologists compared the flocks resulting from the LBL releases with the turkey flocks that had been released from other states. The turkeys from places other than LBL were much more successful in repopulating. Also, the turkey flocks grew much quicker in the areas where the LBL turkeys had not been released.

"From the results of this research, we began to theorize that when the turkey population on LBL got as low as history records it did and when the gene pool got that small, then many characteristics became genetically locked into the turkeys at LBL. And one of the undesirable traits that we believe became locked in was the poor nesting characteristics of the LBL hens."

George Wright's study found that one of the critical factors in the low numbers of turkey on LBL was that the hens would not renest if their nests had been disturbed. And predators were not the only nest disturbers these LBL hens have disliked. Even if a person walked by and frightened a hen off of the nest, she might not return to the nest to hatch eggs she'd laid. And she wouldn't renest in the same season as other turkeys in other areas might. Later in a graduate study done by Larry Pharris and conducted in the late 1970s, researchers discovered that 80 percent of the turkey nests at LBL were being predatorized.

From these studies it was evident why the turkeys on LBL were in such low numbers and that there was need to introduce a new strain of birds that would renest after their nests had been disturbed.

Says Sharpe, "Once we determined we had a problem with reproductive vigor, we decided to bring in turkeys from other areas and add them to our flock, to diversify the gene pool and improve the reproduction of the LBL turkeys. In 1973 we brought in turkeys from Missouri and released them in the Tennessee portion of LBL. We traded striped bass for Missouri turkeys, to help Missouri's striped bass programs and improve our LBL turkeys.

"We allowed no turkey hunting in this new release area, and we watched the turkeys carefully. We began to see more turkeys and more broods. We believed that the Missouri turkeys were in fact raising the population on this particular portion of LBL.

"Then in 1976 we had our first turkey hunt on the Tennessee part of LBL where these turkeys were released. Twelve gobblers were harvested that year. Then 20 were harvested in 1977, 11 in 1978, 21 in 1979, 43 in 1980, and 63 in 1981.

"When we saw these results on the Tennessee part of LBL, we decided to go ahead and take other Missouri birds and introduce them into the Kentucky portion, to improve the gene pool there.

"So we traded Missouri more fish for 50 turkeys. These birds were released in February 1981. As a result of this stocking, we feel that we have more turkeys now on LBL than there have been before. And we have the statistics to prove it, starting in 1976 with turkey hunts in all parts of LBL—both Kentucky and Tennessee:

YEAR	HARVESTED
1976	38
1977	46
1978	23
1979	33
1980	50
1981	84
1982	104
1983	179
1984	213
1985	291
1986	463
1987	518

"The turkeys have spread out to virtually every watershed on the place. And LBL now has turkeys where traditionally there have been none. All of them seem to be doing real well."

Another factor that helped to restore the LBL gobblers was the liberalization of the raccoon harvest.

"Wright finished his research in the early '70s," Sharp says, "but a follow-up study conducted by Murray State University in 1978 actually identified the nest predators. The biologists constructed some dummy turkey nests and armed them with Instamatic cameras that were triggered by switches and took pictures of whatever predators came to the nest.

"Forty-nine percent of the turkey nests were destroyed by raccoons. At that time LBL had a very high raccoon population. Although we permitted hunting of raccoons, we had a restrictive bag limit."

Rick Lowe explains, "To reduce the coon population and decrease turkey nest predation, we permitted the outdoorsmen to hunt more nights on LBL and take more coons per night than had been previously permitted."

And these less restrictive coon-hunting regulations on LBL have not been to the detriment of the coon population. As a matter of fact, several national coonhound field trials are held annually on LBL.

The mystery of the LBL gobblers has provided new information for turkey researchers. No longer can anyone assume that improvement of habitat and protection of turkeys are all that is required to improve turkey poplulations.

Dennis Sharp emphasizes that "each area of land must be looked at individually and analyzed to determine the present condition of the turkey flock. Some factor or factors including mortality, reproduction, and food

Since the coon is a natural predator of turkeys and turkey nests, removal of this predator through hunting can benefit the turkeys.

habits may be limiting turkey flocks. And some flocks may be at their potential. Restocking is not a cure-all. Each region is different.''

The riddle of the LBL gobblers has been solved for the time being. Now the outdoorsmen who hunt LBL have plenty of turkeys to try to fool, and more turkeys are being harvested than ever before. Through the research conducted at Land Between the Lakes, biologists and hunters in other areas can more effectively evaluate their land's turkey potential, and through good management provide more turkeys to hunt.

The
Masters

Sylvia Bashline, of Spruce Creek, Pennsylvania, is food editor of *Field & Stream* magazine. She has for many years been telling people how to handle the wild harvest from field to table. For example, a wild turkey shouldn't simply be cooked like a full-breasted store-bought turkey. Ms. Bashline's several excellent books include *The Bounty of the Earth Cookbook, Cleaning and Cooking Fish,* and *Savory Game Cookbook.*

Jim Bashline photo

Jim Beam, a nationally recognized competitive turkey caller, has won numerous contests. From the vantage of his many years of turkey hunting, he can speak volumes on the subject. The turkeys that Jim remembers most vividly are not the ones that have fallen to his 12 gauge, but the old gobblers that have gotten away. He lives in Cherryville, North Carolina, and hunts in several states.

Hugh Blackburn, of Gulf Breeze, Florida, is a member of the Archery Hall of Fame. He has often been the Florida state archery champion, has also won the Southeastern Archery Championship, and has placed in national competition sponsored by the National Field Archer's Association. Marksmanship aside, Blackburn has found that specialized gear and techniques are needed for turkeys. Workaday, he is a regional sales manager for the Bear Archery Company.

Jay Brown, of Monroe, Louisiana, may be one of his state's most knowledgeable turkey hunters, as well as one of the nation's best turkey callers. Jay has won the Louisiana and Arkansas state turkey-calling championships several times, besides the Southwest Open Friction, and has placed as runner-up in national contests.

Paul Butski, of Niagara Falls, New York, was a winner of the Levi Garrett All-American Turkey Calling Championship, and has been the winner of state, regional, and other national turkey-calling contests. A veteran woodsman, Butski is also owner and creator of Butski's Game Calls. He hunts turkeys in Alabama in the early spring and then catches the season in New York State.

Tom Fegely photo

Nathan Connell is a wildlife biologist who for 10 years guided hunters to turkeys at the Westervelt Lodge in Aliceville, Alabama, and presently does some wildlife and hunting consulting. Connell feels that the success of a hunt in swamp country often depends less on calling ability and hunting tactics than on how much water is in the swamps and how deep the hunter is willing to wade.

Kelly Cooper, of Picture Rocks, Pennsylvania, is a professional turkey caller and owner of Kelly Kallers. He has been a winner of the Eastern Open, the Pennsylvania State, and the Masters' turkey calling contests.

Charles W. Burchfield photo

Charles Elliott, of Covington, Georgia, is one of the deans of outdoor journalism. He is a retired field editor of *Outdoor Life* magazine and the author of numerous outdoors books, including *Turkey Hunting with Charlie Elliott*. He has also served as director of Georgia's state parks and of the Georgia Game & Fish Commission.

Ray Eye, of Dittmar, Missouri, has won many regional and state turkey calling and owling contests. He has also been a runnerup in national contests. Eye considers owl hooting to be the most important and most misunderstood call in turkey hunting.

Charles Farmer is an outdoors writer-photographer and radio personality. Among his books are *The Official Hunter Safety Manual; Creative Fishing; Backpack Fishing; Digest Book of Canoes, Kayaks, and Rafts;* and *Family Book of Camping Lists.*

J. Wayne Fears, of Heflin, Alabama, is one of the most widely published outdoor writers. He has also outfitted hunting expeditions throughout North America. As a turkey guide since 1974, he's averaged 50 days a year hunting the eastern wild turkey. His many books include *Complete Book of Outdoor Survival, Successful Turkey Hunting, The Wild Turkey Book,* and *The Complete Book of Canoe Camping.*

David Hale, of Cadiz, Kentucky, is considered by many top turkey hunters to be as good at hunting without a caller as he is with one, although he is co-owner of Knight and Hale Game Calls. In recent decades, Hale has taken over 50 gobblers and has called very little to any of them. To become a master turkey hunter, Hale believes a hunter must first learn to hunt turkeys and then learn to call them.

Dave Harbour is a contributing editor of *Sports Afield* magazine and has hunted the wild turkey for over 50 years. He's written two books on turkeys: *Hunting the American Wild Turkey* and *Turkey Hunting and World Records.*

Doug Harbour, an outdoor writer, is the son of well-known turkey authority Dave Harbour and has been guiding for and hunting Merriam turkeys since 1970. Each season, in Colorado, he guides 18 to 20 hunters to Merriam gobblers. His hunter-success rate has averaged 80 percent.

Bill Harper, president of Lohman's Calls in Neosho, Missouri, has called turkeys in every situation imaginable because he often has to find and call turkeys for his customers to take. He's also challenged by many hunters to try to bag old boss gobblers that nobody else can. Using his firing-'em-up method, Harper takes many gobblers that other hunters give up on.

Brent Harrell, of Monroe, Louisiana, has won several state turkey-calling championships. When just 19 years old, he was one of Louisiana's most successful turkey hunters. His biggest turkey to date, which he killed in Oklahoma, weighed 22 pounds and had a 10½-inch beard and 1-inch spurs.

Seab Hicks, of Coffeeville, Alabama, is one of the nation's leading contenders in turkey-calling contests and is a representative for Ben Lee Calls. Hicks guides turkey hunters each season and acknowledges that if certain turkeys aren't taken, they can drive hunters insane.

Rob Keck is the executive vice-president of the National Wild Turkey Federation, in Edgefield, South Carolina. Keck has hunted turkeys since 1959, in 28 different states and is considered a master caller and hunter.

Tom Kelley, of Spanish Fort, Alabama, has written for many major outdoor magazines and is also the chief instructor for the Westervelt Lodge Turkey Hunting School at Aliceville. He's a vivid storyteller, as evidenced by his books, *The Tenth Legion* and *Dealer's Choice*. Kelley is a man who can describe his half-century of hunting compellingly.

Harold Knight, of Cadiz, Kentucky, is a professional caller as well as a call manufacturer. He holds the world record for the best overall typical eastern turkey, which scored 80⅜ points, based on a formula that credits beard, spurs, and weight (in this case 26 pounds, a big wild turkey!). Knight enjoys introducing new hunters to the sport.

Ben Rodgers Lee has probably taught more people how to call turkeys than any other man alive. His teaching vehicles include seminars, lectures, store promotions, demonstration tapes, and award-winning performances in calling contests. Lee is based in Coffeeville, Alabama, but hunts turkeys across the United States.

Billy Maccoy, of Lineville, Alabama, is one of the nation's top turkey callers, having won the National Turkey Calling Contest. Maccoy travels around the country to hunt and call with hunters who utilize many different techniques. At home, he hunts a nearby national forest—a difficult proposition because there's usually a great deal of competition for a good gobbling bird.

Walter Parrott, Doe Run, Missouri, has won turkey-calling contests in Missouri and throughout the Midwest. He also has a win in the World Contest in the friction calls division. Parrott believes that in certain cases the gobble is often the only call that can sucker an old tom into gun range.

Aaron Pass, of Marietta, Georgia, is an editor for Game and Fish Publications and has written many articles about turkey hunting. He's served as a judge in numerous regional and national turkey-calling contests. A keen observer, Pass looks more deeply and sees more broadly than most who look at the same scene or subject.

John E. Phillips, author of this book, has been hunting and fishing since early childhood. Phillips writes for five newspapers and has sold over 1000 magazine articles. His books include *Taxidermy for Fun and Profit, Alabama Outdoor Cookbook, Bass Fishing Skeeter Pros,* and *50 Ways to Make More Money in Taxidermy.* Of all the game he as hunted, Phillips deems the wild turkey the most challenging.

Wilbur Primos, of Jackson, Mississippi, has been hunting turkeys since 1964 and has taken more than 100 gobblers. He has even raised wild turkeys in order to study them. Primos also manufactures turkey calls and counts as his trophies "great days in the woods spent talking to gobblers."

Jim Radcliff Jr., of Andalusia, Alabama, comes from one of the South's most noted turkey-hunting families. His father, the late Jim Radcliff Sr., originated the mouth yelper in the 1920s. Jim Jr., like his dad did, enjoys hunting all types of game.

Terry Rohm, of Blain, Pennsylvania, has been turkey hunting since 1965 and is a representative for Ben Lee Calls. Rohm is an avid participant in turkey-calling contests, and has won the Pennsylvania State contest, the Pennsylvania State Friction, the U.S. Open, and the National Turkey Calling Championship.

Dan Speake has a Ph.D. in wildlife management and has studied the wild turkey for the Alabama Cooperative Fish and Wildlife Research Unit since 1965. When asked if he liked to hunt turkeys, he replies, "Does a hog like slop or a turkey like chufas? If I could eliminate work during March and April and get by on four or five hours sleep, I would not require much else to be happy."

Sara Bright photo

Gary Stilwell, of Hedgesville, West Virginia, has won every major turkey-calling contest in West Virginia, and has won the Mid-Atlantic Turkey Calling Contest often. He's also an avid turkey hunter. Most hunters try to get gobblers excited to pull them in, but Stillwell believes you can get a gobbler too excited to call him into range.

Lewis Stowe, of Gastonia, North Carolina, has been a World Turkey Calling Champion, as well as the winner of state and regional turkey-calling contests. Stowe says little but thinks a lot. Many outdoorsmen are convinced that Stowe knows what a turkey is thinking almost before the turkey does.

Glenn Terry, Of Martinsville, Indiana, has won the Indiana State and the Ohio Open turkey-calling contests, and has placed in regional and national contests, including the Levi Garrett All-American Turkey Calling championship. Terry, who hunts newly released turkey flocks in Indiana, also hunts old established flocks in other states each spring.

Lovett Williams has a Ph.D. in wildlife ecology and was a wildlife biologist with the Florida Game and Fish Commission from 1962 until 1985. He has spent many years studying the wild turkey and has written two books on the subject—*The Wild Turkey* and *The Voice and Vocabulary of the Wild Turkey*. He is also the producer and narrator of an audiocassette series called "Real Turkeys," featuring the voices of wild turkeys. Williams' books and cassettes are available by mail: 2201 SE 41st Ave., Gainsville, FL 32601.

Jim Zumbo of Cody, Wyoming, is an editor-at-large for *Outdoor Life* magazine. Each season he hunts five western states for all the major game, including both the Merriam and the Rio Grande turkeys. Zumbo hunts turkeys as western tradition dictates—with a rifle.

Affliction (turkey affliction), 13
Alabama (Turkey Calling Contest) State
    Open Non-Resident Division, 149
Ammunition, 50, 51
    handgun, 82
    muzzleloader, 78
    rifle, 208
    shotgun, 77, 204, 208, 255
    See also Bullets
Army Artillery School (distance estimat-
    ing tests), 82
Arrows
    heads, 217, 219
    stoppers, 216

Bashline, Sylvia, 275
Beam, Jim, 259
Beard, 13
Bent Creek Hunting Lodge (Alabama),
    242
Blackburn, Hugh, 219
Blinds, 220, 223
Blue Ridge Mountains (Georgia), 64
Bounty of the Earth Cookbook (Bashline),
    277
Bowhunting
    with decoys, 223
    equipment for, 216–17, 219, 223
    shot timing and placement, 220, 224
    techniques, 217, 219–20, 223
    turkeys vs. big game, 215, 221
    vs. shotgun hunting, 224
Bows, 217
Broad River Management Area (South
    Carolina), 259

Brood sites, 295
Brown, J. C., 177, 180
Bullets handgun, jacketed hollow-point
    vs. solid nose, 82
Butski, Paul, 135

Cackling, 15, 110–11
Calling, 59
    contests, 69, 98, 149, 193, 257
    defined, 15
    devices
        box callers, 15, 100, 139, 147, 181,
            183
        diaphragm callers, 18, 24, 69, 139,
            159, 183, 204, 234
        friction callers, 16, 22, 25, 26, 27,
            29, 139, 147, 151, 157, 159, 204,
            234
        hen-turkey wing, 106
        Lohman's crow call, 99
        manufacturers, 241, 243
        mouth yelpers, 151, 204
            origin of, 269–70
        Noble whistle, 54
        tube callers, 28, 30–31, 100, 151
        wing-bone callers, 32
    learning, 49
    movement, 206,
    position, 121
    techniques, 18, 23, 24, 25, 69, 105–12,
        117–20, 121, 128, 134, 135, 136,
        137, 139, 150, 151, 152, 157, 162,
        168, 169, 174, 181, 200, 206, 234,
        254
        afternoon, 103

bad-weather, 194, 197
double calling, 20, 228–29
fall and winter, 51–52, 147–48
gobbling, 113–16
for Merriam turkeys, 207, 212
morning, 99–101
for pasture and field turkeys,
    191–92
for Rio Grande turkeys, 203–04,
    205–06
spring, 54–55
for trophy turkeys, 189
vs. hunting, 95–98
See also Calls
Caller types, 15
Calls
gobbler, 109–10
hen, 105, 107, 110–12
scouting, 133
timing of, 105–06
See also Calling
Camouflage, 51, 58, 86–88, 189–90
for hunting Merriam turkeys, 207,
    209–10
western vs. eastern, 204
Camp, Doug, 61
Chufa, 17, 299
Clothing and equipment, 51, 58, 73,
    85–90
See also Ammunition, Camouflage,
    Guns
Clucking, 17, 108
Colburn, Mike, 231
Compasses, 127
Complete Book of Wild Turkey (Latham),
    278
Connell, Nathan, 199
Controlled burning, *See* Management
Cooper, Kelly, 223
Crow call, 18
Cutting, 18, 69, 111–12, 228
double, 229–30

Darty, Fred, 187
Decoys, 18
bowhunting with, 217, 223
regulations state, and, 223
Dewell, Cliff, 217
Diaphragm caller, 18

Displaying. *See* Strutting
Distance, judging, 82–83
Dogs as predators, 21
Dominant gobbler, 20
Dorsett, Charles, 247
Dorsett, Glenn, 247
Dorsett, Toxey, 247
Double calling, 20
Droppings, 20
Drumming, 21, 109–10

Eastern wild turkey (*Meleagris gallopavo
    silvestris*)
range, 36, 37
vs. Merriam, 209, 210, 211
Earl, 21
Eastman, Robert, 217
Elliott, Charles, 61
Eye, Ray, 121

Farmer, Charles, 215
Fears, J. Wayne, 73, 77, 99
Feather characteristics, 14
Field-dressing, 275
Fields, Danny, 146
Florida turkey (*Meleagris gallopavo
    osceola*)
coloration, 37
range, 37
Fly-up/Fly-down cackle, 21
Footgear, 85, 87
Friction call, 22

Gobble, 22
Gobbler, 22
Gobbling, 109
Gould turkey (*Meleagris gallopavo mexi-
    cana*)
range, 37
Gulvas, Denny, 193
Gulvas, Ed, 193
Guns, 50, 51, 73
for beginners, 241
choosing, 78
for hunting Merriam turkeys, 208
requirements of, for turkey hunting,
    80
See also Handguns, Muzzleloaders,
    Rifles, Shotguns

Hale, David, 163, 241
Handguns, 81
    ammunition for, 82
    scopes for, 81
Harbour, Dave, 203
Harbour, Doug, 209
Harrell, Brent, 153
Harper, Bill, 117, 125
Head color (turkey), 41
Hicks, Seab, 191
Hunters, master, characteristics of,
        43–44
Hunting
    locations, 138, 143, 149–50, 161, 166,
        174, 179
    regulations, 80
    rifle, 207–08
    seasons, 40
    skills, developing, 45–50, 55, 75
    strategy, 71
    strut zones, 125–32
    techniques, 16, 57–60, 62, 69, 70, 71,
        100–01, 103, 126, 128, 137,
        150–51, 152, 157, 159, 164, 166,
        181, 253, 254
        bad-weather, 196, 263
        double-circle, 153
        hen-country, 167–68
        for Merriam turkeys, 207
        swamps, 199
        team-hunting, 235, 237, 239, 249
        for trophy turkeys, 188, 189
        for walking birds, 169–70
    vs. calling, 95–98
    See also Bowhunting

Infection (turkey infection), 23
Insect repellent, 89
Instant Mounting Fluid, 288
Intergrade, 23

Jake, 23
Jenkins, Allen, 180

Kee-kee run (call), 108–09
Keck, Rob, 173
Kelley, Tom, 141
Kentucky Lake, 301
Knight and Hale Game Calls, 241
Knight, Harold, 43, 57, 95, 137, 166, 241

Lake Barkley (Kentucky–Tennessee), 301
Lake of the Ozarks, 130
Land Between the Lakes (Kentucky–
        Tennessee), 137, 163, 301
    map, 300
Latham, Roger, 278
Lee, Ben Rodgers, 51, 69, 146, 169, 217
Levi Garrett/All American Turkey Call-
        ing Championship, 193
Longbeard, 24
Lost call, 26, 106
Lowe, Rick, 302

Maccoy, Billy, 227, 231
Management, 31, 259, 301
    controlled burning, 17, 297
    foods favored, 295–297
    poult susceptibility to predators,
        295–297
    programs, study of, 302
    restoration efforts, 301
    studies, 302, 305
Map use, 133, 160
Masters' Turkey Calling Championship,
        193
Mauch, Dick, 216
Meleagris gallopavo. See Turkeys, wild
Meleagris gallopavo gallopavo. See Mexican
        turkey
Meleagris gallopavo intermedia. See Rio
        Grande turkey
Meleagris gallopavo merriami. See Merriam
        turkey
Meleagris gallopavo mexicana. See Gould
        turkey
Meleagris gallopavo osceola. See Florida
        turkey
Meleagris gallopavo silvestris. See Eastern
        wild turkey
Merriam turkey *(Meleagris gallopavo mer-
        riami),* 207–12
    behavior, 207, 208, 209, 210, 211
    breeding difficulties, 207
    calls for, 207, 212
    clothing, camouflage, for, 207, 208,
        209–10
    coloration, 37
    habitat, 209
    hunting
        techniques for, 207

time of day for, 211
locating, 210
range, 27, 207
vs. eastern, 209, 211
Mexican turkey *(Meleagris gallopavo gallo-
pavo)*, 36
range, 37
Moorer, Robert, 252
Moorer, Roy, 145, 147, 251
Mouth yelper, 24
Murray State University, 305
Muzzleloaders, 78

National Open Turkey Calling
Championship, 149
National Wild Turkey Federation, 55
Noble whistle, 24

Ocoee National Forest (Tennessee), 65
Ott, Henry, 271
Owl hooter, 24
Owl-hooting, 121
Owling, 25
Ozark Mountains, 121

Parrott, Walter, 113
Pass, Aaron, 67
Pattern board, 25
Pecking order, 25
Peg, 25
Phillips, John E., Jr., 241
Phillips, Terry, 149
Population (turkey), 38
Poult, 25
Predators, 21, 26, 41, 297, 305
Primos, Wilbur, 105
Purring, 26, 112
Push-button call, 26
Putting, 26, 108

Raccoon as predator, 297, 305
Radcliff, Jim, Jr., 269
Radiotelemetry, use of, in research
studies, 143
Rangefinder, 82–83
Recipes, 277–84
Research studies, 143
Rifles, 80
where to aim with, 80
for Merriam turkeys, 208

Rio Grande turkey *(Meleagris gallopavo
intermedia)*, 203–06
coloration, 37
range, 37
Rohm, Terry, 57, 133
Roost, 26

Salter, Eddie, 257
Scopes, 81
Scouting, 27, 137, 161, 167, 203
calls, 133
car-, 135
Set-up, 27
Sharp, Dennis, 302, 305
Shock gobble, 27
Shooting,
learning, 49–50
positions, 58
techniques, 233
Shot, copper-plated vs. lead, 77
Shotguns
hunting with, vs. bowhunting, 224
for Merriam turkeys, 208
patterning, 25, 30, 73, 82
for Rio Grande turkeys, 204
short-barrel, 80
sights, bead, 83
slings, 83
See also Shot
Sign, 31, 47
hen vs. gobbler, 52
learning to read, 47–48
places to look for, 53
Slate call, 27
Slings, shotgun, 83
Snood (or Snoot), 27
Snuff box, 28
Southern Sportsman's Lodge (Alabama),
231
Southwest Open Turkey Calling Cham-
pionship, 149
Speake, Dan, 143, 295
Spur, 28
Stand, selecting a, 232
Stilwell, Gary, 157
Stowe, Lewis, 167
Striker box, 29
String Tracker, 216

Strutting, 29, 126, 165
    and aiming, 211
Strut zones, 29
    characteristics of, 126
    locating, 126–27

Taxidermy
    field care, 285
    head-color restoration, 287–88
    jewelry, 292
    methods, 287
    mounting, 288–90
    pose, choosing the, 288
    preserving, 290–92
    taxidermist, choosing a, 285
Taylor, Don, 263
Tennesee Valley Authority, 301
Terry, Glenn, 161
Terminology, 13–32
Tombigbee River, 245
Tombigbee swamps (Alabama), 199
Topographical maps, 133, 134, 161
    use of, in locating strut zones, 127
Topperwein, Adolph, 252
Treading note, 30
Tree call, 30
Turkeys, wild (*Meleagris gallopavo*)
    behavior
        drumming, 21
        eastern turkeys, 209–211
        when frightened, 41
        hen, 112
        knowledge of, 45-47
        Merriam turkeys, 207, 208, 209, 210
        reproductive, factors affecting, 304
        roosting, 199
        seasonal, 146
        social, 20, 25, 29, 136, 141, 142, 146, 147, 167, 180, 184, 197
        strutting, 20, 29, 125, 126, 165
        study of, 143
        vocal, 129, 135, 197
    breeding range and sites, characteristics of, 295
    coloration, 36, 37
        head, 41, 42, 288
    decline of
        habitat destruction and, 38
        hunting and, 38, 40
    diet, 17, 41, 52, 146, 200–01, 242, 297, 299
    habitat, 179, 299
        fall and winter, 297
        nesting, characteristics, of, 295
    name, derivation of, 36
    physical characteristics, 13, 27, 28, 32, 41
    populations, 38, 301, 302, 304
        factors affecting, 295
    predators, 21, 26, 41, 297
        effect of, 305
        poults' susceptibility to, 295
    ranges, 36, 37
        home, 297
        past vs. present, 38, 40
    restoration efforts, 38–40
    subspecies, 36–37
    vocalizations, 15, 17, 18, 21, 22, 23, 26, 27, 30, 32, 105–12
    See also Eastern wild turkey, Florida turkey, Gould turkey, Merriam turkey, Mexican turkey, Rio Grande turkey
Tree call, 105–06
Trophies, scoring, 30
Tube caller, 30
Turkey dog, 31

U.S. Open Turkey Calling Championship, 193

Wattles, 32
Wavy call, 112
Williams, Lovett, 45, 143
Wing-bone caller, 32
World Turkey Calling Contest, 257
Wright, George, 302

Yelping, 32, 106–07

Zumbo, Jim, 207